James A. Bellanca • Robin J. Fogarty • Brian M. Pete

How to Teach
Thinking
Skills

Second Edition

7 Key Student Proficiencies for
College and Career Readiness

Solution Tree | Press *a division of*
Solution Tree

555 North Morton Street
Bloomington, IN 47404
800.733.6786 (toll free) / 812.336.7700
FAX: 812.336.7790

email: info@SolutionTree.com
SolutionTree.com

Visit **go.SolutionTree.com/instruction** to download the free reproducibles in this book.

Printed in the United States of America

Library of Congress Cataloging-in-Publication Data

Names: Bellanca, James A., 1937- author. | Fogarty, Robin, author. | Pete, Brian M., author.
Title: How to teach thinking skills : seven key student proficiencies for college and career readiness / authors, James A. Bellanca, Robin J. Fogarty, and Brian M. Pete.
Description: Second Edition. | Bloomington, Indiana : Solution Tree Press, [2019] | Previous edition: 2012. | Includes bibliographical references and index.
Identifiers: LCCN 2019010246 | ISBN 9781947604896 (perfect bound)
Subjects: LCSH: Thought and thinking--Study and teaching.
Classification: LCC LB1590.3 .B45 2019 | DDC 370.15/2--dc23 LC record available at https://lccn.loc.gov/2019010246

Solution Tree
Jeffrey C. Jones, CEO
Edmund M. Ackerman, President

Solution Tree Press
President and Publisher: Douglas M. Rife
Associate Publisher: Sarah Payne-Mills
Art Director: Rian Anderson
Managing Production Editor: Kendra Slayton
Production Editor: Alissa Voss
Content Development Specialist: Amy Rubenstein
Copy Editor: Jessi Finn
Text and Cover Designer: Rian Anderson
Editorial Assistant: Sarah Ludwig

To our friend and colleague from
Down Under, Elaine Brownlow—
Champion of thoughtful schools
for over thirty years.

Acknowledgments

In this second edition of *How to Teach Thinking Skills: Seven Key Student Proficiencies for College and Career Readiness* (previously *How to Teach Thinking Skills Within the Common Core*), our primary goal remains the same as in the first edition: we want to help teachers come to terms with the emerging and increasingly accepted role of "teachers as teachers of teachers." Several new paradigms and trends in the arena of education have guided and informed the thinking and learning behind this book.

First, the push toward collaboration among educational professionals—a natural extension of the advent and institutionalization of professional learning communities—has become the new norm. The spirit and structures of faculty teams working together to ensure student success dictate a different learning philosophy. This philosophy needs to drive the transfer and transformation of learning (Coyle, 2009; Ericsson and Pool, 2017; Fogarty & Bellanca, 1993; Hirsch, 2017; Perkins & Salomon, 1998; Schmoker, 2018; Willingham, 2017) so it meets instructional best practice.

Another group of educational professionals made concerted efforts to include clear and far-reaching emphasis on teaching and learning as thoughtful, mindful experiences. Their respect for 21st century skills of collaboration, communication, critical and creative thinking in next-generation K–12 classrooms is changing the face of schooling as we know it. This book was born on the back of such change, and we wish to acknowledge those molders of educational thought, those innovative and adaptable educators who are consistently striving for new ways of achieving student success in an ever-changing world.

Roger and David Johnson's cooperative learning research (1989, 2005)—and their understanding of cooperative learning as a bed for critical thinking, conflict resolution, and problem solving—provided us with a substantive foundation for creating the classroom environment that supports this book's ideas. Additionally, the thinking cadre of Reuven Feuerstein, Ya'acov Rand, and E. John Rynders (1988), Edward de Bono (1995), Howard Gardner (1984), Arthur Costa and Bena Kallick (2009), Ron Ritchhart and David Perkins (2008), Robert J. Marzano (1998), John Barell (2007), Jay McTighe and Grant Wiggins (2013), and Fogarty & Bellanca (1993) inspired our focus on research about transfer theory, especially regarding thinking skills and problem solving.

Equally important, we want to acknowledge the model that easily transfers and applies the thinking skills to classroom practice. In essence, we see this book as a funnel for best practice in improving achievement and advancing students' 21st century skills of sound decision making, productive problem solving and creative ideation for the college and career choices of our future citizens.

In addition, we wish to acknowledge our publication team at Solution Tree—Jeff Jones, CEO extraordinaire; and especially Douglas Rife, president and publisher of Solution Tree Press, who encouraged a second edition of this best-selling book. Finally, but never forgotten, our thanks to the professional team that passionately supports this work, as this team transformed the drafts of our manuscript into a final, polished publication.

Jim, Robin, and Brian
2019

Solution Tree Press would like to thank the following reviewers:

Kris Blair
Director of Curriculum
Massillon City Schools
Massillon, Ohio

Brad Cawn
Solution Tree Associate
Chicago, Illinois

Brian Dean
Solution Tree Associate
Trinity, Florida

Patty Paxton
Integrated Technology K–5 Teacher
Krause Elementary
Armada, Michigan

Lindi Wilson
Curriculum Instructor
Barrett Elementary School
Birmingham, Alabama

Gwendolyn Zimmermann
Assistant Principal
Adlai E. Stevenson High School
Lincolnshire, Illinois

Visit **go.SolutionTree.com/instruction** to download the free reproducibles in this book.

Table of Contents

Reproducible pages are in italics.

1 Critical Thinking   17

2 Creative Thinking   45

5 Collaborative Thinking   129

About the Authors

James A. Bellanca is nationally recognized as a practical innovator who provides teachers and administrators with the how-to knowledge to make abstract ideas concrete and ready to go on the next school day. He is a senior fellow with the Partnership for 21st Century Learning and editor of its innovative online publication *P21 Blogazine.* He is the 2013 recipient of the Malcolm Knowles Award for lifetime contribution to the field of self-directed learning from the International Society for Self-Directed Learning and an advisor to the GEMS Education 21st Century Competencies group.

With his extensive experience as a classroom English and language arts teacher, alternative school director, professional developer, intermediate service center director, business owner, and not-for-profit executive, Jim has developed expertise for transforming mandates, such as the Common Core State Standards, into practical classroom tools that enrich instruction and engage students.

He is president of the Illinois Consortium for 21st Century Schools and lead trainer for MindQuest: Project-Based Learning in the 21st Century Classroom, which helps schools with large English learner populations and students of color and poverty adopt the project-based learning model of instruction. Jim has worked with educational leaders in the United States, Australia, New Zealand, Norway, and Israel. His specialty is the application of group investigation and inquiry models of learning as the primary methods for helping school leaders and teachers adopt 21st century models of instruction. His aim is to help school districts design, implement, and assess programs that promote 21st century skills to increase academic performance among all students, including high-risk populations.

Jim works closely with Solution Tree Press to identify emerging authors who address the themes and practices that define and describe 21st century learning. He has authored or coauthored multiple Solution Tree Press how-to books about thinking in the Common Core, enriched learning projects, and leadership for the Common Core. He coedited the *Leading Edge* series title *21st Century Skills: Rethinking How Students Learn* with Ron Brandt and edited *Deeper Learning: Beyond 21st Century Skills* and *Connecting the Dots: Teacher Effectiveness and Deeper Professional Learning.* Currently, he posts on a learning blog for the Illinois Consortium for 21st Century Schools (available at https://ilc21.org/blog) and is completing manuscripts on blueprints for personalized learning and pathways to deeper learning outcomes.

Robin J. Fogarty, PhD, is president of Robin Fogarty & Associates as a leading educational consultant. She works with educators throughout the world in curriculum, instruction, and assessment strategies. Working as an author and consultant, she works with students at all levels, from kindergarten to college. Her roles include school administrator, and consultant with state departments and ministries of education in the United States, Puerto Rico, Russia, Canada, Australia, New Zealand, Germany, Great Britain, Singapore, Korea, and the Netherlands.

Robin has written articles for *Educational Leadership, Phi Delta Kappan,* and the *Journal of Staff Development.* She is author of *Brain-Compatible Classrooms, 10 Things New Teachers Need to Succeed,* and *Literacy Matters: Strategies Every Teacher Can Use.* She is coauthor of *How to Integrate the Curricula, The Adult Learner: Some Things We Know, A Look at Transfer: Seven Strategies That Work, Close the Achievement Gap: Simple Strategies That Work, Twelve Brain Principles That Make the Difference, Nine Best Practices That Make the Difference, Informative Assessment: When It's Not About a Grade, Supporting Differentiated Instruction: A Professional Learning Communities Approach, Invite, Excite, Ignite: 13 Strategies for Teaching and Learning,* and *The Right to Be Literate: 6 Essential Literacy Skills.* Her work also includes a leadership series titled *From Staff Room to Classroom: The One-Minute Professional Development Planner* and *School Leader's Guide to the Common Core.* Most recent works include *Unlocking Student Talent: The New Science of Developing Expertise, Metacognition: The Neglected Skill Set for Empowering Students,* and *Thinking About Thinking in IB Schools: How We Know What We Know.*

Robin earned a doctorate in curriculum and human resource development from Loyola University Chicago, a master's in instructional strategies from National Louis University, and a BA in early childhood education from the State University of New York at Potsdam.

To learn more about Robin's work, visit www.robinfogarty.com or follow @robinfogarty or @RFATeachPD on Twitter, Instagram, or Facebook.

Brian M. Pete is co-founder and CEO of Robin Fogarty & Associates. He has followed a long line of educators—college professors, school superintendents, teachers, and teachers of teachers—into a career in education. He has a rich background in professional development and has worked with adult learners in districts and educational agencies throughout the United States, Europe, Asia, Australia, and New Zealand.

Brian has an eye for the teachable moment and the words to describe skillful teaching. He delivers dynamic, humor-filled sessions that energize the audiences of school leaders, teachers, and teacher leaders with engaging strategies that transfer into immediate and practical on-site applications.

Brian is coauthor of *How to Teach Thinking Skills Within the Common Core, From Staff Room to Classroom: A Guide for Planning and Coaching Professional Development, From Staff Room to Classroom II: The One-Minute Professional Development Planner, Twelve Brain Principles That Make the Difference, Supporting Differentiated Instruction: A Professional Learning Communities Approach, The Adult Learner: Some Things We Know, A Look at Transfer: Seven Strategies That Work, School Leader's Guide to the Common Core, Everyday Problem-Based Learning: Quick Projects to Build Problem-Solving Fluency, Unlocking Student Talent, Metacognition: The Neglected Skill Set for Empowering Students,* and *The Right to Be Literate: 6 Essential Literacy Skills.*

Brian earned a bachelor of science from DePaul University in Chicago and is pursuing his master's in fiction writing from Columbia College in Chicago. To learn more about Brian's work, visit www.robinfogarty.com, or follow @brianpete or @RFAteachPD on Twitter, LinkedIn, Instagram, or Facebook.

To book James A. Bellanca, Robin J. Fogarty, or Brian M. Pete for professional development, contact pd@SolutionTree.com.

Introduction

Upon its publication, *How to Teach Thinking Skills Within the Common Core: Seven Key Student Proficiencies of the New National Standards* (Bellanca, Fogarty, & Pete, 2012) became a well-thumbed K–12 resource for tens of thousands of educators worldwide. It modeled how to teach rich, domain-specific content, grounded in the rigor of the Common Core State Standards (CCSS) and supported by the lifelong relevance of higher-order, complex thinking skills.

The original version of the book was intended to be a user-friendly, practical guide that teachers could easily reference by scanning lessons for a particular thinking skill. We planned that teachers would systematically address the thinking skills by either grade levels or departments, in a synchronized effort within their building or professional learning community. In that way teachers could infuse the explicit teaching of thinking skills in their everyday lessons. Designed to clarify the mass of information—both obvious and obscure—embedded in the national standards and, at the same time, delineate an adaptable, practical approach to teaching complex thinking, that first edition became a quick-win resource for staff.

In this revised second edition, we have modified the title to accommodate the dramatic move of many state departments of education away from the initial version of the CCSS as they chose instead to adopt their own versions of state standards. When states signed on to the CCSS, they accepted all the provided standards verbatim. However, according to the National Governors Association Center for Best Practices and Council of Chief State School Officers (NGA & CCSSO, 2010b), states were "allowed to add an additional 15 percent on top of the core."

That 15 percent rule gave way to the customization of standards to accommodate state, regional, and community concerns. For example, New York State (New York State Education Department, 2015) added standards primarily under the umbrella of Reading: Literature standards. Indiana and Massachusetts added standards (Indiana Department of Education, 2011; Massachusetts Department of Elementary and Secondary Education, n.d.), including handwriting standards, to their Writing and Language anchor standards. Minnesota added an additional Speaking and Listening anchor standard on viewing, listening, and media literacy (Minnesota Department of Education, 2016).

Other states declined to participate in the Common Core. Virginia, for example, stated that the "Standards of Learning (SOL) for Virginia Public Schools establish minimum expectations for what students should know and be able to do" (Virginia Department of Education, 2011). Likewise, Texas's standards, the Texas Essential Knowledge and Skills (TEKS), remain that state's focus for student proficiency expectations (Texas Education Agency, n.d.a).

In addition to the CCSS and individual state standards, teachers may subscribe to other research-based or discipline-specific learning standards. These tangential standards, likewise rich, relevant, and rigorous in their demands, include the College, Career, and Civic Life (C3) Framework for Social Studies State Standards (National Council for the Social Studies, 2013); social-emotional learning (SEL) standards; the Next Generation Science Standards (NGSS Lead States, 2013); the International Society for Technology in Education (ISTE; www.iste.org/standards) standards; and the National Council of Teachers of Mathematics (NCTM; www.nctm.org /standards) standards.

Yet, at the end of the day, "The various state-redesigned learning standards are really quite similar in a lot of ways" (McGee, 2014). In fact, most 21st century standards tend to emphasize what people call *college and career readiness* (CCR)—providing students with the skills and talents they need to not just survive but thrive in a 21st century world of study and work. In a review of changes to state standards since the Common Core, Achieve.org (2017) found that the majority of the twenty-four states reviewed included the essential elements of college and career readiness in their ELA and mathematics curricula, and the majority of states displayed a "strong" rating—the highest available—for clearly and fully addressing each CCR element within their amended state standards. This reflects an ongoing commitment among the states to preparing students to meet a range of postsecondary literacy and mathematical demands.

Thus, this second edition, under the new title *How to Teach Thinking Skills: Seven Key Student Proficiencies for College and Career Readiness*, aims to better serve the plethora of student learning standards that many states crafted separately and to accommodate their emphasis on the 21st century skills essential for student success in the classroom, in college, and in the workforce. While examples of the original CCSS are sprinkled throughout the new text, the focus in this edition is on the explicit teaching of thinking skills, and how such teaching can be embedded in lessons now tailored to helping students achieve college and career readiness.

Additionally, this second edition specifically includes examples of teaching thinking skills within technology-enhanced lessons. After all, using technology, students must now (1) process information, (2) produce evidence of learning, and (3) present the results in compelling, media-savvy ways. More specifically, current expectations are for students to access data and information through search and research skills on the World Wide Web; to create and produce curricular-relevant products using digital construction techniques; and to develop visual, graphic, and animated presentations to communicate their work to others. Further expectations focus on the complexity of student thinking and the expert execution of technological tools to enhance, enrich, and engage learning with more rigorous, robust, and real-world understandings. The new technological additions to this book serve to accommodate these major changes that have occurred in classrooms as digital-rich tools augment almost every aspect of schooling.

The inclusion of technology-based lessons in this text is also to provide readers with examples of lessons that incorporate technology with the appropriate amount of rigor necessary for college and career readiness. Technological applications in the classroom on their own do not automatically raise the level of student thinking or help students to become career and college ready. For example, in pre-technology times, a student, while studying the American Revolution, might copy a passage from the Encyclopedia Britannia and stick it on poster paper along with a drawing of George Washington crossing the Delaware. Such a presentation would not be judged as an authentic demonstration of learning. Likewise, if today a student cuts and pastes the same quote from a website, downloads a picture, and includes both in a PowerPoint presentation that they then upload to the class website, the student is clearly demonstrating that they are adept at using technology but the level of thinking is still very low. The student is using technology tools to consume, construct, and communicate, but without much rigor.

Rather, rigorous application of thinking skills can be enhanced with technology to extend and elaborate on the topic under study. The goal of the technology integration lessons included in this book and available at **go.SolutionTree.com/instruction** is to show how technology can enhance and enrich the teaching of higher-order thinking skills in the classroom and, at the same time, demonstrate that the career- and college-ready skills of the 21st century do indeed thrive in a technology-rich environment.

In sum, we have based this effort on the rationale that, despite the different state standards that educators may work with, the goal of all standards-based learning is to prepare students to be college and career ready. Consequently, our mission in writing this edition remains the same. The second edition aims to ensure teachers frame

K–12 classroom instruction with rich subject-matter content, mindful rigor in the standards, and enduring digital relevance for lifelong learning.

It is our hope that this book will again prepare teachers and teaching staffs to teach thinking skills within their state-mandated standards from their designated source, and to continue to help their students apply their ever-strengthening thinking skills across the curriculum. In the end, we believe this will have enduring results, in that these skills will serve students through their high school and college years and on through their chosen and often-changing careers. It all begins with a strong educational foundation framed by sound learning standards, critical thinking skills, and relevant content knowledge that will pique student interest and excellence.

Twenty-One Thinking Skills for the 21st Century

If the goal of learning standards is to help today's schools prepare all students to have college and career readiness with rich and rigorous 21st century skills, teachers clearly need to answer the question, How can schools best take advantage of their state standards in improving classroom instruction and curriculum aligned to next generation demands? The answer to this challenge cannot be more of the same, with content regurgitation serving as best practice. Teachers worldwide often repeat the refrain, "We need to teach our students how to *think*. They don't stop and think; all they want is to finish and answer right." This book's goal is to help educators alleviate this concern by facilitating systematic, deliberate instruction of 21st century thinking skills. If students are to become productive problem solvers, sound decision makers, and creative innovators, educators must emphasize and explicitly teach complex thinking skills within their content areas.

In response to this need, *How to Teach Thinking Skills* identifies twenty-one complex cognitive skills that are most prominent in K–12 instruction. It groups these twenty-one skills within seven overarching cognitive proficiencies, or thinking skill sets, that encompass the most desired student skills for deeper learning: (1) critical thinking, (2) creative thinking, (3) complex thinking, (4) comprehensive thinking, (5) collaborative thinking, (6) communicative thinking, and (7) cognitive transfer. The book generalizes these rigorous skills so they are approachable and applicable to every student, no matter what grade level or subject—and without loading extra busywork onto teachers, who already have more than enough planning to do. In this light, the book builds on teachers' prior knowledge so each teacher can focus on the specific standards that impact his or her classroom and select the thinking skills most likely to help students master those standards through higher-order processing.

Most of the thinking skills featured in this book were chosen because they are the most frequently occurring typical and traditional curricular verbs that appear in the

CCSS (see table I.1 for a depiction of the frequency of each term used in CCSS ELA and mathematics standards). With confidence from our experiences in the classroom, and following an analysis of the frequency of the same terms within ten U.S. states' standards (see table I.2, page 6), we believe the same terms are typical of K–12 curricular learning tasks across many states' adapted curricular scope and sequence charts. These do, in our judgment, form the quintessential thinking skill compendium used in most complex texts, and thus we have specifically included these in the twenty-one thinking skills necessary for college and career readiness. Please note the following synonyms for these seven skills that do appear on the list: *produce* and *create* (generate); *relationships* and *sequence* (associate); *ask/answer* (hypothesize); *justify* and *demonstrate* (reason); *relationships* (connect); *create* and *produce* (synthesize); and *comprehend* and *describe* (generalize). One last note—a number of the previously listed skills are embedded in the creative production and presentation of performances that the exemplars and performance tasks require. Thus, it seems prudent to address the part that creativity plays in student achievement.

Table I.1: High-Frequency Words Within the State Standards

Grades K–5				Grades 6–12			
ELA		**Mathematics**		**ELA**		**Mathematics**	
Understanding	33	Represent	47	Analyze	73	Solve	66
Read	28	Understand	40	Determine	50	Understand	54
Write	22	Solve	36	Develop	41	Interpret	47
Demonstrate	19	Recognize	27	Research	33	Relationships	45
Clarify	18	Interpret	22	Clarify	32	Find	43
Develop	18	Find	21	Write	31	Graph	39
Produce	17	Explain	20	Relationships	30	Represent	38
Relationships	16	Compare	19	Demonstrate	28	Apply	34
Describe	14	Describe	18	Understanding	27	Describe	24
Compare/contrast	13	Write	14	Create	26	Explain	23
Explain	13	Identify	12	Read	26	Prove	21
Answer	13	Understanding	11	Evaluate	22	Write	19
Introduce	10	Divide	9	Reflection	20	Compare/contrast	17
Sequence	10	Determine	9	Read/comprehend	20	Recognize	17
Determine	8	Graph	9	Introduce	17	Evaluate	13
Accurate	8	Apply	9	Produce	17	Determine	13
Read/comprehend	8	Sequence	7	Organize	17	Identify	11
Point of view	8	Read	5	Point of view	15	Compute	10
Apply	7	Answer	5	Apply	14	Develop	9

continued →

Grades K–5				Grades 6–12			
ELA		Mathematics		ELA		Mathematics	
Research/projects	6	Create	5	Compare/contrast	12	Produce	8
Create	6	Justify	4	Explain	11	Inferences	8
Decode	6	Analyze	4	Inferences	10	Analyze	7
Reflect	5	Develop	3	Sequence	9	Sequence	7
Retell	4	Compute	2	Identify	8	Divide	7
Recall	4	Relationships	2	Solve	8	Calculate	7
Sequences	4	Define	2	Projects	8	Decide	7
Inferences	4	Evaluate	1	Answer	8	Define	6
Identify	4	Produce	1	Sequences	7	Answer	5
Collaborate	3	Calculate	1	Accurately	7	Create	4
Organize	3	Sequences	1	Interpret	6	Verify	3
Ask/answer	3	Organize	1	Collaborate	3	Sequences	3
Short research	3			Reflect	3	Justify	2
Interpret	3					Read	2
Know and use	3					Understanding	1
Analyze	2					Reflection	1
Solve	1						

Table I.2: A Comparison of Frequency of Thinking Skills Terms Within the Common Core and Ten U.S. States

CCSS or State Standard	ELA Grade 4 Thinking Skill: Determine	Math Grade 4 Thinking Skill: Represent
Common Core	6	10
Arizona	8	7
California	5	10
Colorado	6	10
Georgia	5	10
Indiana	6	7
Maryland	11	12
Minnesota	6	9
New York	4	7
Pennsylvania	3	5
Washington	6	10

Source: Arizona Department of Education, 2019; California State Board of Education, n.d.; Colorado Department of Education, n.d.; Georgia Department of Education, n.d.; Indiana Department of Education, 2011; Minnesota Department of Education, 2016; New York State Education Department, 2015; Pennsylvania Department of Education, n.d.; School Improvement in Maryland, n.d.; Washington Office of Superintendent of Public Instruction, n.d.

As is indicated by the frequency analysis in table I.2, specific thinking skills and traditional content rarely need substantive changes, so the twenty-one thinking skills that were the focus of the first edition remain the same in this book. However, we must advise readers that, in addition to the usual content tinkering by local, regional, state, and national educational publishing developers, a deluge of curriculum material continuously flows into the standard framework of the disciplines, as they well know. These ongoing developments, discoveries, innovations, and general housekeeping measures keep teaching and learning in the classroom focused on the most important and the most urgent matters in a changing world.

A Practical and Explicit Exposition

This practical handbook is divided into seven student proficiencies: (1) critical thinking, (2) creative thinking, (3) complex thinking, (4) comprehensive thinking, (5) collaborative thinking, (6) communicative thinking, and (7) cognitive transfer. Tabs along the side of the book provide quick access to each proficiency. Each proficiency then identifies three essential thinking skills—one per chapter—for explicit teaching, providing a manageable synthesis of the new standards. *Explicit* means that the skill is clearly and compactly defined so that a student has an unequivocal understanding of the term, with nothing left to suggestion. In the explicit approach, teachers illuminate the targeted skill and teach a formal lesson about it. All attributes are identified, so there is no room for confusion or doubt about how to use the skill appropriately.

This book dissects each skill for explicit teaching across elementary, middle, and secondary levels. The lessons target *process* as content. In this way, instead of merely plucking an exemplar from the standards for test prep, teachers work through a process to unpack the complex thinking skills inherent in the core standards. Feature boxes throughout the text provide "Examples From the State Standards" that refer to the highlighted thinking skill. These example standards, taken directly from the national and various state standards, serve to give readers the skills they need to dissect their own state standards and align their teaching of thinking skills with similar standards in their own state documents. In the end, by strengthening students' complex thinking and problem-solving skills, teachers will enable students to deepen their comprehension of the text lesson modeled, as well as adapt similar performance tasks to fit their specific needs.

Although some school teams may decide to create a schedule to address all twenty-one thinking skills over a designated period of time, with a scope and sequence approach, we do not expect that every teacher will study or implement every one of the twenty-one skills. Teachers' selections may be driven by their own grade-level and subject-area standards and the particular needs of their students. Often, for implementation with fidelity, less is more. Thus, some schools may prefer to have each teacher focus on the two or three key skills that he or she can develop with the deepest student competence and confidence over the month, quarter, semester, or entire school year.

The Three-Phase Teaching Model

Each chapter follows a three-phase model for unpacking a skill. These three phases provide the road map for each explicit lesson. The three-phase model, an application of Lev Vygotsky's zone of proximal development theory, calls for the gradual release of responsibility to the learners, empowering the learners to *own* their learning (Vygotsky, 1978). It is a scaffolding approach that prepares the student for a highly personalized and independent path to mastery performance and strong transfer of learning. As Douglas Fisher and Nancy Frey (2008) explain, the gradual release of responsibility follows this path: "I do, we do, you do together, you do alone." The teacher teaches the skill explicitly, demonstrating and vocalizing the learning; the teacher and student try it together, with the teacher monitoring and providing guidance; and finally, the student performs the skill on his or her own with confidence.

Using this well-respected learning process, we have translated Vygotsky's gradual release model to one of our own, ranging from *teacher in charge* to *student in charge*.

1. Teacher in charge: The Talk-Through (participation modeled and monitored verbally)

2. Teacher and student together: The Walk-Through (guided student participation)

3. Student in charge: The Drive-Through (student participates on their own)

Phase I: The Talk-Through—Explicit Teaching Lesson

In phase I, the Talk-Through, the teacher explicitly presents the thinking skill in a formal lesson. This lesson focuses on a key idea, well-developed scaffolding, strategic integration, and adequate time for reflection and review. The goal is knowledge of the targeted skill—for instance, "What does it mean to analyze?"

The Talk-Through has five components.

1. Motivational mindset (the hook)

2. Order of operations (the menu of steps)

3. Instructional strategy (an interactive, collaborative experience)

4. Assessment (the appraisal and judgment)

5. Metacognitive reflection (the time to look back, look over, and look ahead)

In this first phase, teachers engage students with a *motivational mindset*. This is a hook or advance organizer (Ausubel, 1960; Marzano, 1991), an activity that arouses interest and curiosity about the learning, stirs up prior knowledge, and preferably provides an engaging hands-on experience that illuminates the skill in action. Next, the teacher delineates the thinking skill with an acronym called the *order of operations*. This represents the cognitive procedures used for executing the thinking skill. Each chosen acronym helps both teachers and students remember the steps involved. After this introduction to the process, teachers present the user-friendly, high-energy *instructional strategy* that requires students to work together to address the thinking skill, explicitly noting its parts and procedures and determining how the skill can be used across content areas and grade levels. Next, teachers ensure student understanding of the skill and its potential applications with the model's *assessment* suggestion. Finally, to bring closure to the explicit lesson, teachers offer a *metacognitive reflection* that acts as a deliberate look back on the practiced skill and how it may affect students' lives. Reproducible versions of activities from the instructional strategy section can be found in appendix A (page 213).

Phase II: The Walk-Through—Classroom Content Lesson

In phase II, the Walk-Through, the teacher guides the practice of the thinking skill within a content-based lesson, providing directed, collaborative support to ensure the students' appropriate application of the skill. This phase includes tailored content lesson examples for elementary, middle, and secondary levels. To assist teachers with content and grade-appropriate lesson selections for this guided practice, each chapter provides strategies adaptable for all three levels.

Phase III: The Drive-Through—CCR Performance Task Lesson

In phase III, the Drive-Through, the teacher helps individual students transfer their understanding of the thinking skill to authentic applications using performance tasks identified in their state standards. In the ELA and mathematics standards, the performance tasks may be in the state document in a specified section, or they might be embedded in the standards themselves. This phase includes state CCR performance tasks for elementary, middle, and secondary levels.

With performance tasks, the opportunity for students to work on the tasks first in groups and then individually may strengthen the gradual release of responsibility as practical and possible. These joint tasks allow students to collaborate in making direct connections between the selected thinking skill, the new standards, and the rich application to rigorous texts before the final accountability step in which each student must show his or her understanding.

To guide the gradual release of responsibility, teachers create effective formative assessments that include the thinking skill. Prior to the final Drive-Through phase, the teachers may create a balanced rubric for formative assessments. This rubric will provide guiding criteria for both elements of the standard: the thinking process and the content. With minimal teacher guidance in this third phase, students should be able to identify the targeted thinking skill, construct the response as directed in the performance task, and self-assess and reflect on their work as guided by the rubric. When needed, teachers will provide additional performance tasks, coach, or make other interventions based on the progress students are making. As the quarter or semester continues, the teacher may add increasingly difficult tasks to the mix so that students are able to develop their standards-based thinking skills with more and more challenging content. In this way, the standards move from being a checklist to being a developmental guide that reveals the advances students make over the course of a quarter, a semester, or a year as they move to the final summative assessment of the grade-level standard.

The Teacher's Role in the Three Phases

When teachers intentionally release responsibility for learning tasks to the students, their instructional roles change. In phase I, the teacher models, explains, explicates, and enunciates instruction about the targeted skill. The teacher asks many productive questions, displays visuals, and listens to and clarifies student responses while building students' clear understanding of the skill's meaning. The teacher defines, gives examples, checks for understanding, and assesses the students' knowledge of the skill. During this "teacher teaches student" phase, teachers may occasionally structure a cooperative learning task such as a think-pair-share but always with the purpose of helping all students gain a more exact grasp of the targeted skill's key attributes and best uses.

In this phase, two basic "I do, we do" models of instruction are helpful. Some teachers may be more comfortable relying on a traditional direct instruction model. With the thinking skill as the content, these teachers will direct the class through phase I—hook, exposition and modeling of the operation, check for understanding— until they can assess their students' grasp of the skill's definition and readiness for guided practice.

A second group of teachers will prefer to use inquiry-based instruction with more emphasis on the "we do" as the means of defining the key term. Their hook might be an essential question they pose to the class (for example, "What does it mean to analyze?"). Often with students in their collaborative groups, these teachers will engage students in an exploratory activity that introduces the students to the thinking skill by doing it (for example, a mini-analysis of a familiar object) before they ask students, usually in teams, to identify key attributes of the cognitive experience (for example, "When you analyzed this story, what did you do? What steps did you take? What was helpful?"). The teacher will then continue the more interactive "I do, we do" instruction with other collaborative strategies to illuminate the attributes identified and to help students form a final all-class answer to the essential question. With the answers synthesized by the teacher, the students are ready to take greater responsibility for their learning and practice embedding the skill in their course content.

In phase II, teachers take one step back from their direction of the class. The mix of "I do, we do" gives way to "we do, but alone." In this phase, the teachers increase the students' control of the learning activity. This is best done in collaborative groups that the teacher has prepped to learn cooperatively (Johnson & Johnson, 1981).

In this phase, it is important that the teacher's facilitation skills come to the fore and replace the telling and questioning models that dominated in the first phase. Teachers' attention moves from individuals in the whole class to individuals in the small groups. The teacher works beside the groups, moving from one to another—observing, checking for understanding, taking notes, coaching, cuing and questioning, mediating students' thinking, and providing students with multiple opportunities to reflect on how successfully they are developing their thinking and are applying the new skills to the called-for curriculum content. And teachers do this without providing answers or quick solutions. Facilitation serves as the heart of the purposeful guidance the teacher provides in this phase while observing progress or lack of progress, responding to a question, providing feedback based on observation data, and moving students to higher levels of challenge with pertinent questions about their use of the assignment's skill.

The line between what teachers do to facilitate practice in phase II and what they do to facilitate transfer in phase III is a matter of how they complete the work. In phase II, teachers have set up the situation so the student teams practice embedding the targeted skill in a specified lesson with team members helping each other. Novice teams may work in pairs to provide a buddy to share the task with and to build confidence to work alone next time.

More experienced teams may collaborate in groups of three or five. The teacher is not the sole helper because phase II teams help each other with the trial runs of the task. When teams get stuck, the teacher intervenes, first encouraging the students to figure out the problem. Only when they cannot does the teacher step in to mediate their thinking.

After the teacher determines that the teams have had sufficient practice to warrant independent application, he or she moves to phase III performance tasks. In these tasks, individuals take on the responsibility of completing the assignments. These tasks are cases of "You do alone." In a sense, these tasks can be lightly guided pretest work. They show each student's ability to fulfill the standard at the level the teacher expects. Using a rubric, the teacher can ask students to complete one or more standards-aligned performance tasks, showing how well they can address the thinking challenge with the assigned material. Ultimately, the teacher decides how many transfer tasks the student needs in order to reach the desired level of competence before a final assessment.

Among the three phases, there is no magic moment that indicates when the teacher's role changes. As teachers become more experienced with the nuances of the roles in each phase, they will develop a sense of what works best and when to move forward with the student or students.

A Road Map

Road maps (or GPS maps, in this age of technology) help travelers make long trips through unfamiliar territory to a wished-for destination. This book's road map (figure I.1) displays the journey that teachers will take from the beginning of a state standards–aligned lesson or project to its end. The road map traces the learning progression for an entire explicit lesson about a targeted thinking skill through the three phases. The display is designed so teachers can reproduce the list and write commentary to guide the skill's instruction through the three phases.

In addition to the three-phase model, each chapter contains road signs that help mark the way. Each chapter begins with an introduction to the thinking skill, including a vignette that places the skill in a real-world setting, a definition of the skill, and examples of what the skill looks and sounds like in the classroom. At the end of each chapter, reflection questions help readers further personalize the chapter's information and learn from their own doing.

Technology Integration for a Digital Generation

In terms of changes in the classroom landscape, it has become quite clear that 21st century thinkers not only are immersed in technology but thrive with the pace of technology immersion in schools and in their lives. For this reason, we have listened to our first-edition readers, who have encouraged us to provide more instruction about how they might thoughtfully infuse technology to enrich the teaching of thinking skills. In response, we have looked to our own experience and the experience of classroom teachers with whom we work and provided instruction on incorporating

Talk-Through: Explicit Teaching Lesson

Motivational Mindset: Hook, motivational curiosity builder, advance organizer
Order of Operations: Step-by-step delineation of the skill
Instructional Strategy: "Process as content" for classrooms
Assessment: Thinking skills, formative assessment, check for understanding
Metacognitive Reflection: Reflection on the learning, application of it to one's life

Walk-Through: Classroom Content Lesson

▶ Elementary Level
▶▶ Middle Level
▶▶▶ Secondary Level

Drive-Through: CCR Performance Task Lesson

▶ Elementary Level
▶▶ Middle Level
▶▶▶ Secondary Level

Reflection Questions

Figure I.1: The explicit instruction road map.

technology into featured lessons. (Additional lessons integrating technology can be found online at **go.SolutionTree.com/instruction**.) Our technology integration for thinking skills introduces alternate ways that K–12 teachers can enrich a thinking skill lesson as they develop students' digital skills. We encourage educators to take their students from intuitive, entertainment-focused technology users (playing games, sending text messages, and watching videos) to conscientious and competent learners. Educators can do this by helping students develop their digital skills as part of more mindful interactions within their world of living and learning.

Integrating digital tools into classroom lessons is remarkably helpful in developing student thinking, as indicated by a wealth of newly emerging technology standards within the states' curricular frameworks. Let us be clear that we are *not* looking to ready every student for a career in computer technology. Such an outcome is beyond the scope of K–12 teachers' work, and truth be told, classroom teachers often find themselves having to catch up to their tech-savvy students. Rather, this book intends to help teachers teach thinking to every student, including students learning English as a second language and students with special needs in regular classrooms. Students competently and confidently adopt digital tools that enhance and entertain in their *leisure* time. We aim to create proficient technology users who can enhance and advance technological skills during their *learning* time.

Thus, in this edition, we include not just lists of tools (see appendix B, page 225) but also descriptive applications of how teachers can integrate specific digital tools into the model lessons to develop students' digital learning skills. (Appendix C [page 233] lists the websites and tools that we mention in chapters throughout the book.) While we have referenced up-to-date resources, please be aware that the fast-paced nature of digital change may leave some of these tools by the wayside as other up-and-coming tools take their place. Some ways in which teachers can stay current on technology innovations are through traditional courses, workshops, or team trainings; or by designating a go-to technology leader within the school, department, grade, or district. Schools may even choose to adopt more creative methods, such as holding an informal after-school meeting known as *Appy Hour*, in which attendees come armed with an innovative app to share, or by setting aside time in the school's opening workshops in which teachers in grade-level or department teams share apps they have discovered over the summer that would enhance classroom instructional time (in one school, this method is known as *Savvy Appy Demo Day*). We encourage schools to adopt such methods in their efforts to extend the lessons of this book to the ever-changing digital resources available to them.

Notably, our approach to technology integration asks the teacher to add collaboration to the mix. In real-world work situations, the majority of companies link teams with digital networks that have sharing capability. From medical facilities to military deployment areas, banks, road construction job sites, restaurants, insurance companies, travel centers, weather stations, and urban fire departments, shared technology is the norm. We rely on cooperative learning as evidence-based best practice (Marzano, 1991). Thus, most technology integration examples in this book ask educators to promote pairs and trios—and, at times, groups of up to five students—working together with a single digital tool. This increases engagement as students develop their digital skills and advances collaboration as an essential deeper-learning strategy. A hallmark of cooperative learning is its practicality in focusing all team members on their individual responsibilities to achieve their sought outcomes. A well-made cooperative rubric will hold each student accountable for a job on the team and ensure collaboration toward the final outcome. Energized by rotating their roles, team members learn how to share in the development of their collaborative skills and contribute to the accomplishment of a team goal while also learning the content individually.

In the new sections highlighting technology integration, this book provides two ways for readers to incorporate technology into the lessons. First, the Digital Integration Task section provides basic suggestions that help teachers integrate technology into that lesson. These digital tool suggestions will allow educators and their students to build early confidence and competence in using technology as a support to thinking skills. Then, readers will encounter grade-level digital variations and more advanced tools that help teachers address the talents and needs of their specific students.

For special needs or English learners in classrooms, we suggest that educators facilitate cooperative learning teams that provide *learning buddies*. This basic strategy will ensure these students successfully learn. As a guideline, be sure to create heterogeneous teams that distribute special needs and English learners, so their peers can provide skill coaching within the team. It should not concern teachers that the more able students take on additional duties, as the best way to learn anything deeply is to teach it.

A Note to the Reader

This book highlights the most crucial thinking skills students are now expected to acquire and use with accuracy and finesse, not just to pass the test, but rather to prepare for life, learning, and work after high school. Teaching students how to think mindfully and purposefully, infusing digital-rich tools into our curriculum, and following Vygotsky's gradual release of responsibility model is complex, demanding work that increases the challenges of teaching and learning.

Therefore, it may seem daunting to follow the three-phase model with twenty-one skills in seven student proficiencies. But it doesn't have to be. Start by paying attention to one skill. Since it is as unlikely that you will have to teach every skill as it is that you will have to teach every standard, focus on a few chapters that best align with your students' needs and your curriculum. Less is more. Additionally, the close examination of a high-frequency thinking skill serves to illustrate how students can use these microskills more efficiently. In truth, students actually will use a number of thinking skills simultaneously when actually making decisions or solving problems. This book presents a part-to-whole technique that models the selected twenty-one skills individually for ultimate integrated use as students continue to accumulate skillfulness in complex thinking in more holistic ways.

To make your first skill choice, start with your grade's ELA or mathematics standards. If you teach in another subject area, simply go to the ELA Informational Text standards. Select a standard that makes you think, "Oh, yes, this is important for my students," or "Yep, this one gives my students lots of trouble." Identify the key word in that standard, and then review this book's corresponding chapter with that standard in hand. Plan what you are going to do using the road map template, implement it, and assess the results. Once you have conquered this first skill, move on to the next and expand your repertoire.

How to Teach Thinking Skills: Seven Key Student Proficiencies for College and Career Readiness should become a well-thumbed resource for you and your colleagues as you balance teaching domain-specific content with the targeted, explicitly stated cognitive operations in the standards. The book is intended to be a user-friendly, practical guide that you can reference easily, whether scanning for the specific skill that needs attention or systematically addressing the skills through a synchronized effort by a professional learning community. It is designed to clarify the mass of information, both obvious and obscure, in your state's CCR standards and to delineate an adaptable, practical approach to teaching the complex kinds of thinking represented in and supported by your state's standards. Above all, it is meant to simplify the adoption of your state standards as a useful guide for daily instruction.

As a reminder, one of the biggest questions about the standards—any standards—relates to their appropriate role in education. Are standards merely an extension of the factory model of learning that was favored in the 20th century? Are the standards just a tool to fix up and improve an overly scientific approach to teaching and learning that may be based on faulty theory and bad practice? What other alternative does our society have for ensuring that all students are prepared with the knowledge and skills that will give them the best chance to live, learn, and succeed in the coming decades?

The list of twenty-one skills is not the be-all and end-all of student proficiencies. Changes to the standards will undoubtedly come in the future as they did in the past. This is our next-generation iteration of our first book on thinking in the standards-based classroom. It is our hope that new iterations will continue to improve their worth to classroom teachers and improve the quality of the standards themselves.

Critical Thinking

Critical thinking was central to great teaching in the days of the Greek philosophers Plato and Aristotle. Aristotle set the course of Western education when he defined the educated mind and established a standard of action by telling us that no idea should go unchallenged. The English essayist Francis Bacon (1625) introduced the how-to for challenging ideas when he wrote, "Read not to contradict and confute; nor to believe and take for granted; nor to find talk and discourse; but to weigh and consider." More recently, Jean Piaget (as quoted in Duckworth, 1964, p. 499) brought his prodigious mind to the subject when he said:

> The principal goal of education in the schools should be creating men who are capable of doing new things, not simply of repeating what other generations have done—men who are creative, inventive, and discoverers. The second goal of education is to form minds which can be critical, can verify, and not accept everything they are offered.

None of these philosophies seem to advocate for more memorization, more drills, or more reduction of the curriculum to facts and procedures to be tested so teachers can find the one correct answer regurgitated on a standardized test. Instead, they hold high expectations for the development of students' minds by challenging ideas; weighing and considering; creating, inventing, and discovering; and being critical. For this to happen, they know that teachers need the resources to engage their students in thinking about important, relevant issues, never to "accept everything they are offered."

For those who hope to advance their education into college or to compete for a significant job in the new global economy, the ability to think critically is a well-recognized imperative and an essential part of the next generation of state standards.

Critical thinking is the bricks and mortar of problem solving and decision making. In this student proficiency, three skills spring forward: (1) analyzing, (2) evaluating, and (3) problem solving. First, the quintessential critical thinking skill of *analyzing* initiates the study of left-brain or inside-the-box thinking skills that saturate the CCR standards. They also call for students to spend a large amount of time *evaluating* and *problem solving*, attributes that have been selected as the other two skills explored in this set of critical thinking skills.

The example performance tasks for the English language arts standards make apparent the interdependent nature of these key critical thinking skills. In the example performance tasks related to stories, dramas, and poetry, students complete the assessment with the most significant results when skilled in how to analyze, evaluate, and solve problems. Mathematics and other content areas also require students to think critically. They explicitly ask students to analyze for nuance; to evaluate point of view, evidence, and perspective or bias; and to solve problems, some of which are tight and well defined and others of which are loose or open-ended.

When students develop their proficiency with these three intertwined skills through explicit instruction that deepens their understanding of the standards' content, teachers can return to the high expectations of Socrates, who said, "I cannot teach anybody anything. I can only teach them to think."

Chapter 1: Analyze

*No way of thinking or doing, however ancient, can
be trusted without proof.*

—Henry David Thoreau

Marybelle wasn't too sure. The last time Sammy had invited her out, they had
ended up at a party she knew would infuriate her mother. Most of the kids there
had been seniors. There had been no parents present, and this time, she thought
she smelled marijuana. Sammy told her not to worry. Marybelle's best friend said
the same thing and added that her parents would never find out and that she
should stop worrying and just have some fun. The more her friends talked, the
more alarmed Marybelle became. Marybelle's mother had told her, more than
once, "When smoke smells funny, there's more than fire. Just figure it out and
get out." This sounded like one of those times that her mother had talked about.

Critical thinking begins with the ability to *analyze*, the most prevalent thinking
skill in the survey of high-frequency thinking skills (see table I.1, page 13). Analysis
involves the tedious task of taking ideas and objects apart, looking carefully at the
various components, and then reorganizing the ideas by the similarities and differences found. Analyzing is, in fact, the opposite of synthesizing, the act of putting
ideas together.

Analysis spills into many other thinking skills that require the parceling of information for the sake of clarity and understanding. This cognitive skill is inextricably linked
to exercises in which similarities and differences are identified. For example, analysis
is embedded in comparing and contrasting, classifying and sorting, discerning point

of view and nuance, and prioritizing, sequencing, and delineating. Table 1.1 provides examples of what this thinking skill looks and sounds like in the classroom.

Table 1.1: Analyze Look-Fors and Sound Bites

Looks Like	Sounds Like
Students with their heads together, discussing a character's strengths and weaknesses	"This is one characteristic." "Here is an example of each quality." "This item belongs in another group." "There are forty units for each of the eight groups." "Let's take this apart, piece by piece." "Analyzing is a puzzle to find each separate piece."
Students highlighting parts of speech in the text or on the screen by underlining or using colors	
Students sorting songs into musical genres with labeled piles	
Students using caps or boldface to accentuate text	

Analysis may be the most valuable left-brain critical thinking skill for K–12 students. As Marybelle's story suggests, analysis is also a big deal when it comes to figuring out what's up with friends outside the school walls. Inside or outside of school, analysis—the ability to figure out situations, make sense of schoolwork, understand how little clues can solve big problems or ease big decisions—is a premier survival skill for today's young people.

Throughout their school experiences, students will be asked to perform rigorous analyses. In mathematics, they will analyze data; in literature, they will analyze setting, theme, character, motivation, and relationships to plot; in chemistry, they will analyze soil; and in the visual arts, they will analyze a painter's style. As they move out into the job world, they will analyze a financial statement, a political candidate's position, or a complex health care statement.

Analysis is one of the basics in the thinking process. Unless students do it well, what follows as new learning will be flawed. In this sense, then, analysis is like the start of a race. The better the runner is able to get ready and get set, the better he or she will start.

Examples From the State Standards: Analyze

Phonics and Word Recognition: RF.4.3. Know and apply grade-level phonics and word analysis skills in decoding words.

Key Ideas and Details: RL.8.1. Cite the textual evidence that most strongly supports an analysis of what the text says explicitly as well as inferences drawn from the text.

Source for standard: Michigan Department of Education, n.d.b.

Explicit Teaching Lesson

In the Talk-Through, phase I, the educator teaches the thinking skill explicitly. There are several elements to aid the teacher in this phase: motivational mindset, order of operations, instructional strategy, assessment, and metacognitive reflection.

To *analyze* is to separate any material or abstract entity into its constituent elements. Related terms include *diagnose, examine, classify, differentiate,* and *distinguish.*

Motivational Mindset

To begin the lesson on the skill *analyze,* teachers might hook learners by staging a taste test between two brands—for example, Coke and Pepsi (or two kinds of gum, cough drop, or toothpaste). This is a learner-friendly, high-energy exercise that will engage students in a hands-on way and encourage them to begin to think about analysis.

Order of Operations

When analyzing anything—whether it is a complex character in a novel, the chemicals that compose a compound, or the causes of a global event—the steps are the same. PART is an acronym used to help students learn this process.

Preview the whole situation.

Assess similarities and differences.

Reorganize by these similarities and differences.

Turn the analysis into a summary or synthesis.

First, analysis calls for a preview of the whole, a global look at the entire situation or circumstance, taking in as much information as possible. For example, if students are analyzing the elements of a culture in world history, they will preview the related chapter in the textbook. The next step is to assess the obvious parts, elements, or components. Students will find the attributes of a culture, such as how it is ruled, what the people do, how they survive, and so on. Next, students reorganize the information by labeling the parts: government, aesthetics, regional resources, and so forth. Finally, they turn the analysis of the parts into a succinct summary of facts. In effect, the analysis of how things are alike and different, the actual separation of parts, results in a synthesis.

Instructional Strategy

An effective strategy to explicitly teach the skill of analyzing is the *fishbone diagram*. W. Edwards Deming (1982) references this tool as part of formal brainstorming; management could use this tool to analyze components that are needed in attaining goals. The fishbone is a graphic that allows participants to sort the parts of a bigger idea into headings, subheadings, and details. Figure 1.1 is a completed fishbone diagram on an English literature theme: the American Dream.

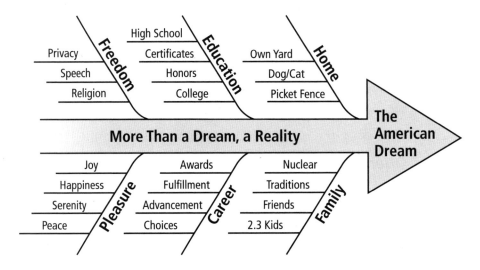

Figure 1.1: Fishbone diagram example.

Visit **go.SolutionTree.com/instruction** *for a free reproducible version of this figure.*

Select a topic or concept that is appropriate for your subject area, and guide the students through the process of analyzing the key parts, subheads, and details using the fishbone diagram (see appendix A on page 214, or visit **go.SolutionTree.com /instruction** for a free reproducible version of this figure). These elements are called the *head of the fish* (target idea), the *spine* (underlying theme), the *ribs* (subheads), and the *riblets* (details).

Assessment

To check for students' understanding of how to use the skill, ask them to complete one of the following three assessments.

1. What data did you use from the text to show the *relationships or key parts* you diagrammed?

2. Explain why the big-idea themes that thread the content of the current study unit are important to the unit.

3. Analyze your own health and wellness using a fishbone diagram.

Metacognitive Reflection

To promote students' thinking about analysis, divide the students into teams, and ask them to discuss how often they use the skill of analyzing and whether PART needs to be tweaked for clarity.

Classroom Content Lesson

In the Walk-Through, phase II, teachers practice the thinking skill within content-based lessons, providing guidance to ensure the proper application of the skill. ELA standard 10 recommends literature and instructional texts that are available for coupling with grade-level lessons (available at www.corestandards.org/ELA-Literacy/standard-10-range -quality-complexity/).

▶ Elementary Level

Read aloud a grade-level story from the elementary list recommended by ELA standard 10 (available at https://bit.ly/2m12DmL). Ask the students to brainstorm the events of the story. Pick ten to fifteen events from the list, and invite groups to each sketch a fishbone on an 8 × 10 newsprint sheet or overhead slide. Ask one group to come forward and tape its sketch on the board for all to see, or use a SMART Board to project the slide. Have a group discussion about the display. Teachers might ask about key details ("Describe three details of your favorite character"), craft and structure ("Give one clue from the text that the story was fictional"), knowledge and ideas ("Name one thing you already knew, and one thing you learned"), or text complexity.

▶▶ Middle Level

Present a fishbone diagram to the class. Using a current event, walk the students through filling out the diagram to show the causes of the event.

Assign students to organize themselves into cooperative groups of three. Give each group markers and a large sheet of newsprint on which to create a fishbone diagram. Help them find magazines or newspapers with stories they can analyze for cause and effect. At the end, allow a carousel hunt around the room so all can see. In a carousel hunt, teams post their completed posters on the classroom walls. With one team member staying by the poster to answer questions, the others take a walk around the classroom, moving from poster to poster at your signal. They can ask questions, give constructive feedback, or discuss the poster's content.

▶▶▶ Secondary Level

Ask students to participate in a think-pair-share to determine what strategies are most important when making a proof for an isosceles triangle. Have the students discuss and narrow the list to three, such as (1) review theorems and postulates; (2) review the properties of lines, angles, and triangles; and (3) establish the logical progressions. Assign a common problem for the pairs to solve with the three strategies. Ask matched pairs to review others' ideas and to generate a discussion for the whole class.

CCR Performance Task Lesson

During the Drive-Through, phase III, the thinking skill is transferred to authentic applications using selected performance tasks from the state CCR standards, allowing educators to make a direct connection between the selected thinking skill and the new version of the standards. While Michigan's state standard is presented as the example in this chapter (see "Examples From the State Standards: Analyze," page 20), the Common Core State Standards' *Appendix B: Text Exemplars and Sample Performance Tasks* (NGA & CCSSO, 2010b) is applied as a resource to the performance tasks in this section. There are almost always similarities among the state standards, and readers can consider the teaching of thinking skills within this example as they would their own state standards. The key is that the task requires a performance that demonstrates evidence of learning in concrete, meaningful, and real-world applications.

To deepen students' confidence with this skill, the teacher facilitates the student work, moving the students closer and closer to independent practice. Once the students are able to employ the skill independently, they are ready to transfer it across the curriculum. (For additional performance tasks, browse the state standards that appear in the References and Resources section, page 241.)

▶ Elementary Level

The following sample performance task illustrates the application of the ELA standard RL.4.5 (Reading: Literature, grade 4, standard 5):

> Students refer to the structural elements (e.g., verse, rhythm, meter) of Ernest Lawrence Thayer's "Casey at the Bat" when analyzing the poem and contrasting the impact and differences of those elements to a prose summary of the poem. (NGA & CCSSO, 2010b, p. 70)

▶▶ Middle Level

The following sample performance task illustrates the application of the ELA standard RI.6.3 (Reading: Informational Text, grade 6, standard 3):

> Students analyze in detail how the early years of Harriet Tubman (as related by author Ann Petry) contributed to her later becoming a conductor on the Underground Railroad, attending to how the author introduces, illustrates, and elaborates upon the events in Tubman's life. (NGA & CCSSO, 2010b, p. 93)

▶▶▶ Secondary Level

The following sample performance task illustrates the application of the ELA standard RST.9–10.1 (Science and Technical Subjects, grades 9–10, standard 1):

> Students cite specific textual evidence from Annie J. Cannon's "Classifying the Stars" to support their analysis of the scientific importance of the discovery that light is composed of many colors. Students include in their analysis precise details from the text (such as Cannon's repeated use of the image of the rainbow) to buttress their explanation. (NGA & CCSSO, 2010b, p. 138)

 ## Technology Integration

> **Featured technology:** SMART Board, Google Share, ClassTools (www.classtools.net), Diamond 9 model (www.classtools .net/education-games-php/diamond9), Microsoft Word, Google Docs (https://docs.google.com) essay template, digital portfolio

The following tasks provide guidance on incorporating technology into lessons using this chapter's instructional strategy.

Digital Integration Task

First, display a blank fishbone diagram (see appendix A, page XX) on the SMART Board. Share it on student computers so that every student or group of students has the fishbone diagram displayed on a computer screen. During this skill's instructional strategy, select a topic for the fishbone, and facilitate a whole-class conversation to generate the key words for the major headings, or ribs, on the fishbone. (For specific topic ideas appropriate for different grade levels, see the following section on Grade-Level Digital Variations.)

Next, assign one heading to each group of students, who then fill in the supporting information (the riblets) on their computers. When it is time to share, have each group upload its contribution to the fishbone diagram on the SMART Board so the whole class can see the connections their fellow students made.

While the class discusses the connections, ask driving questions that prompt students to think more deeply than simply identifying what connections they see. You may consider the following questions.

- "Why did you (or your group) make that connection?"
- "How does _____ connect as a part to the whole?"
- "What other ideas in this lesson ask you to connect specific details or evidence (the parts) to the main idea (the whole)?"
- "How do you think the fishbone might help you analyze other ideas in other classes?"

Make adjustments to the fishbone based on this discussion. Finish with a metacognitive task in the Talk-Through phase (page 21).

Grade-Level Digital Variations

The following sections provide grade-level variations for incorporating technology into lessons.

▶ Elementary Level

Go to the Class Tools website (www.classtools.net), and explore its online tools. Use a tool such as QR Treasure Hunt Generator to create a series of questions and answers that will lead students to an important object. During your next science lesson, have students search with all five senses and follow the QR codes to find the object. What do they see, hear, touch, smell, or taste? Use this to introduce the lesson, and have the five senses serve as the five headings on the fishbone diagram.

▶▶ Middle Level

Divide the class into collaborative teams. Take the six American Dream ribs from the fishbone exercise (home, education, freedom, family, career, and pleasure), and randomly assign each team one of these topics to now serve as the head for a team fishbone diagram. Invite each team to brainstorm a new set of ribs for the topic it has received. Let the teams complete their team fishbone, and then use their work to construct a giant American Dream fishbone on the SMART Board. Discuss the connections that were made. For example, the team assigned "freedom" may have identified "freedom of religion," "freedom of speech," and "freedom to learn" as three of its ribs. On the "religion" rib, they added "pick my church," "burned churches," and "no prayer in school," among others. Encourage students to ask questions such as "What do you mean by _____?" and "What's the connection to the American Dream?"

▶▶▶ Secondary Level

Set up your class's collaborative teams with roles, guidelines, a driving question, and a rubric. Collaborative teams consist of three to five members who agree on a common goal or a single answer to a driving question (a higher-order thinking question such as "What chances do you think you have for accomplishing your American Dream?" or "How well are you living the American Dream?"). Each team member will have a role with responsibilities—for example, coach (leads the team, keeps the team on schedule, keeps all members included), recorder-reporter (keeps notes of decisions, makes report to class), and materials manager (collects and stores materials and equipment). The teams may create and name the roles themselves. For multiday tasks, teams may elect to revolve roles. In addition, the class will agree to follow and assess guidelines for collaboration—the norms for working on a team. Examples may include "Listen to each other," "Encourage all to participate," "Do your job in the team," "Seek consensus," and "Help each other." Turn the norms into criteria in a rubric so that you and the students can each assess how each person is improving in use of collaborative skills. If you want to assess digital skills developed in the team, add criteria for assessment of members' ability to use the digital equipment.

Find the Diamond 9 model online (available at www.classtools.net/education -games-php/diamond9), and display it on your SMART Board. Study the instructions provided online for engaging students, and adapt them to your students. Model how students can use this tool to analyze the American Dream or the next big idea in your curriculum's scope and sequence. Set teams to work with their analysis. After you have checked their completed teamwork, assign each student to write an essay responding to the driving question you gave (see examples on page 26) by using Google Docs or Microsoft Word. Invite teammates to proofread and give feedback on each other's essays. After feedback changes, invite each student to place his or her essay into a digital portfolio (such as the one available at https://sites.google.com/site /resourcecenterportfolio/how-to-use-google-sites; Eportfolio Resource Center, n.d.) for you to read and give feedback and grade if you choose. Complete the lesson with the metacognitive reflection given in the Talk-Through phase (page 21).

Reflection Questions

These questions are designed to enrich your learning from doing. Such reflection enables you to deepen your understanding of the lessons you have just provided. You might also consider modifying these questions to further guide your students' reflection on this thinking skill.

1. How does the skill of analyzing connect to something you already do in your classroom?

2. How might you integrate this skill more explicitly in your lessons?

3. What is the most helpful takeaway concerning this critical thinking skill?

4. What will you do to help students become better with this skill? Be specific.

5. How might you take apart or analyze the state standards? Where would you start? What questions and criteria would you have to consider before attempting the task?

6. How do you think technology enhanced this lesson on *analysis*?

Chapter 2: Evaluate

*It is the mark of an educated mind to be able to
entertain a thought without accepting it.*

—Aristotle

"Mom," Jaime started. "I've got a question for you. Why does that man on the news keep saying that Mexico is a bad place?"

"Just because he says something like that doesn't mean he is right. You have to evaluate what he is saying."

"And how do I do that? I don't know what *evaluating* means."

"It means you must require that he show you proof for what he is saying. What are his facts? Then you balance those facts against facts from the other side. When you look at both sides and think about the facts, you are evaluating. So what facts do you know about Mexico that would give a different side?"

Evaluation is the complex mental act of placing a value on the nature, character, or quality of a person, object, event, concept, theory, or practice. It is a judgment, a weighing of the value. Evaluating is critiquing an essay, scoring a mathematics test, judging a contest, appraising a project, assigning a grade, or determining worth.

It sounds so simple and straightforward, yet evaluation is a complicated process that, at best, involves making an assessment against a set of given criteria and assigning a value based on how well the object or action measures up. Evaluation is the significant final step in the critical thinking process, although it may also be necessary throughout the process.

Table 2.1 provides examples of what this thinking skill looks and sounds like in the classroom.

Table 2.1: Evaluate Look-Fors and Sound Bites

Looks Like	Sounds Like
Students peer editing a partner's written work	"The unique vocabulary was great for the reader."
Students critiquing a presentation with a checklist	"A flawless paper! Nothing to edit."
Students holding scores up, using a scale of 1 to 10	"I like the precision of the work."
Teachers facilitating a class's "Applause Meter"	"That was my absolute best."
	"Judging the winner was difficult."

Evaluation is a thought process that students and adults are required to exercise over and over on a daily basis. How skillfully they employ the process determines how well they solve problems. In this information-laden world, every citizen is faced with the challenge of hearing diverse ideas, theories, and opinions and making sound judgments regarding whether the information he or she is receiving is valid and reliable. Are the facts straight? Is there bias hidden in the writer's or newscaster's point of view? How trustworthy are the sources?

The strongest rationale for building the skill of evaluation may be its value outside the classroom, when students must assess misinformation that can bring harm. However, that position would unfairly limit the value of evaluation in schoolwork, family life, and careers. Every time a problem arises in an individual's life, that person must use evaluation skills to solve the problem. Some decisions in the real world are light and easily managed: "What's the best choice for dinner tonight?" "What shirt and tie look best together?" "What form of transportation is fastest?" Other evaluations help resolve more serious problems: "Should I look for a new position more in line with my skills and preferences?" "When should I pop the question?" "Which college makes the most sense for me?"

In school settings, both simple and complex problems require evaluation and judgment. Simple problems involve finding the conflict in a novel or replicating an experiment in the lab. More complexity is involved when selecting the best strategy for evaluating a persuasive speech. In all instances, however, evaluation is a prime skill to master in pursuing critical thinking and in responding to many state standards.

Examples From the State Standards: Evaluate

Integration of Knowledge and Ideas: 6.RI.8. Trace and evaluate the argument and specific claims in a text, distinguishing claims that are supported by reasons and evidence from claims that are not.

Comprehension and Collaboration SL.3 CCR Anchor Standard: Evaluate a speaker's point of view, reasoning, and use of evidence and rhetoric.

Source for standards: Maryland State Department of Education, 2014a, 2014b.

Explicit Teaching Lesson

In the Talk-Through, phase I, the educator teaches the thinking skill explicitly. There are several elements to aid the teacher in this phase: motivational mindset, order of operations, instructional strategy, assessment, and metacognitive reflection.

To *evaluate* is to determine or set a value or worth of an object or action. Related terms include *judge, calculate, compute, measure, audit, appraise, examine, inspect,* and *review.*

Motivational Mindset

To begin the lesson on the skill *evaluate,* teachers might hook the students by asking them to evaluate a recently completed activity (for example, an essay, an art project, or a lab experiment) using a scale of 1 to 10. They can use three criteria of their choosing. Provide options for them to consider, such as content, presentation, effectiveness, clarity, application, relevance, length, and examples. Students are to complete the evaluation and turn it in at the designated time. All submissions are anonymous.

Order of Operations

An evaluation begins with the essential criteria students will consider. Then the students weigh the evidence against the criteria and make a judgment about how well the evidence meets the criteria. Finally, the students calculate the total value and give a final judgment. This process is represented by the acronym JUDGE.

Justify essential criteria.

Use evidence to weigh against the criteria.

Decide how well the evidence meets the criteria.

Gather the sum total.

Express a final judgment.

For example, a grade 9 teacher assigns a persuasive essay using criteria developed with student input. The three critical criteria agreed on are (1) organization of logical argument, (2) evidence of persuasive language, and (3) reaction of reader or audience. When students finish reading their completed essays, both the student and the teacher assign a score of 1 to 5 on the student's essay for each of the three criteria. The students calculate their final totals, and the teacher conducts a discussion about the importance of the criteria in making the assessments.

Instructional Strategy

An effective strategy for developing students' evaluation skills is to use a *plus/minus chart* (see figure 2.1 for an example) with a think-pair-share collaborative follow-up. After distributing the chart, allow time for the students to fill it in and individually think about the appropriate evaluation of the statements. Then ask the students to share their answers with a partner and note any opinions that don't match. Have the students discuss these discrepancies and try to come to a common opinion. In a whole-class discussion, invite pairs to share some examples and their thought processes as they came to a consensus.

Instructions: Evaluate statements by marking a (+) for those you agree with, a (–) for those you disagree with, and a (?) for those you are unsure of.			
Statement	**+**	**–**	**?**
1. The federal government has too many regulations.			
2. Banks need more freedom when deciding on credit card charges.			
3. Regulations protect consumers.			
4. When it comes to banking fees, it is best for the buyer to protect himself or herself.			
5. Big business needs more control for the good of the consumer.			
6. Consumer protection is a primary responsibility of the state governments.			
7. If the government had been on the ball, there would never have been a collapse on Wall Street.			

Figure 2.1: Plus/minus chart.

Assessment

After hearing the different responses about the statements, invite the students to repeat a think-pair-share sequence to discuss the benefits of a plus/minus chart for evaluating a controversial topic. Have students justify their choice.

Metacognitive Reflection

Close the discussion by asking students to reflect on what they have learned about making judgments from this lesson. What is a takeaway they can share with peers?

Classroom Content Lesson

In the Walk-Through, phase II, teachers practice the thinking skill within content-based lessons, providing guidance to ensure the proper application of the skill. ELA standard 10 recommends literature and instructional texts that are available for coupling with grade-level lessons (available at www.corestandards.org/ELA-Literacy/standard-10-range -quality-complexity/).

▶ Elementary Level

Select three poems appropriate for your students. Project the titles on a SMART Board or screen, and read the poems. Ask all student pairs to choose the poem they like best and write down the reasons for their evaluation. Provide the pairs with a copy of a ranking ladder (see appendix A, page 215), and ask them to rank their top three reasons. Select two to four pairs at random to display and discuss their ranking ladders. Give feedback to refine their thinking.

▶▶ Middle Level

For this lesson, use cooperative groups of three to review JUDGE before setting up the criteria for what defines acceptable and unacceptable text messages with friends. After students have defined the criteria, ask them to use these criteria to evaluate specific texting behaviors and place each criterion on the appropriate side of a scale. To conclude, ask each group to come up with a single text message about what the group learned about evaluating text messages.

▶▶▶ Secondary Level

In this example lesson, invite the class to brainstorm with a web or concept map how to evaluate the accuracy of data used by an author. After students read a selected nonfiction book, have them use the criteria to judge the author's data use. Ask students in cooperative groups of five to examine assigned chapters, especially noting the author's use of language and facts. Allow each group to present its findings prior to a final assessment of the book's accurate or inaccurate data use. Conclude with a review of the essential criteria for making literary judgments.

CCR Performance Task Lesson

During the Drive-Through, phase III, the thinking skill is transferred to authentic applications using selected state CCR performance tasks, allowing educators to make a direct connection between the selected thinking skill and the new version of the standards. Again, while Maryland's state standard is presented as the example in this chapter (see "Examples From the State Standards: Evaluate," page 31), the Common Core State Standards' *Appendix B: Text Exemplars and Sample Performance Tasks* (NGA & CCSSO, 2010b) is applied as a resource to the performance tasks in this section. There are almost always similarities among the state standards, and readers can consider the teaching of thinking skills within this example as they would their own state standards. The key is that the task requires a performance that demonstrates evidence of learning in concrete, meaningful, and real-world applications.

To deepen students' confidence with this skill, the teacher facilitates the student work, moving the students closer and closer to independent practice. Once the students are able to employ the skill independently, they are ready to transfer it across the curriculum. (For additional performance tasks, browse the state standards that appear in the References and Resources section, page 241.)

▶ Elementary Level

The following sample performance task illustrates the application of the ELA standard RI.3.5 (Reading: Informational Text, grade 3, standard 5):

> Students use text features, such as the table of contents and headers, found in Aliki's text *Ah, Music!*, to identify relevant sections and locate information relevant to a given topic (e.g., rhythm, instruments, harmony) quickly and efficiently. (NGA & CCSSO, 2010b, p. 62)

▶▶ Middle Level

The following sample performance task illustrates the application of the ELA standard RH.6–8.6 (History/Social Studies, grades 6–8, standard 6):

> Students evaluate Jim Murphy's *The Great Fire* to identify which aspects of the text (e.g., loaded language and the inclusion of particular facts) reveal his purpose; presenting Chicago as a city that was "ready to burn." (NGA & CCSSO, 2010b, p. 100)

▶▶▶ **Secondary Level**

The following sample performance task illustrates the application of the ELA standard RH.11–12.8 (History/Social Studies, grades 11–12, standard 8):

> Students evaluate the premises of James M. McPherson's argument regarding why Northern soldiers fought in the Civil War by corroborating the evidence provided from the letters and diaries of these soldiers with other primary and secondary sources and challenging McPherson's claims where appropriate. (NGA & CCSSO, 2010b, p. 183)

Reflection Questions

These questions are designed to enrich your learning from doing. Such reflection enables you to deepen your understanding of the lessons you have just provided. You might also consider modifying these questions to further guide your students' reflection on this thinking skill.

1. What judgment did you make today that had little impact on your day?

2. What judgment did you make today that was very important?

3. Use a plus/minus chart to evaluate your performance on a specific challenging task you completed recently (tax preparation, vacation planning, family budgeting), using three criteria of your choosing. How effective were your criteria, and how might you improve them?

4. When evaluating your own teaching effectiveness, what evidence do you consider to be the most accurate data: summative (test scores) or qualitative (student behavior, peer reviews, parent comments)?

Chapter 3: Problem Solve

It's not that I'm so smart, it's just that I stay with problems longer.

—Albert Einstein

"Mosquitoes," the doctor said to the village council. "Mosquitoes."

"But how can a mosquito make a whole village sick? This week, four children in our village died," one council member said.

The council president said, "You live next to a swamp. The water is bad. That is a big challenge. We must find a way to safeguard the people."

"Yes, I understand the urgency," the council member replied. "But is it the mosquitoes or the bad water? Don't we have to attack both problems at once?"

"Both solutions are too costly for us. We have to find a simpler solution."

In Africa, mosquitoes are a major health threat. There is no money for fancy sprays or poisons as used in the Western world. This large, complex problem has befuddled the world health community. Finally, an affordable solution has been found. Simple cotton netting put over beds at night protects the villagers when they are most vulnerable.

Problem solving requires the thinker to employ several thinking skills, including critical thinking skills such as analysis and evaluation, as part of the process. Problem solvers may also rely on the other side of the cognitive coin, calling on creative thinking skills to arrive at an answer or create innovative solutions that meet a seemingly overwhelming challenge.

Problems come in two versions: (1) messy and (2) clean. *Messy*, or ill-defined, problems are authentic, real-world, multidimensional issues that can have many different valid solutions. They present challenges that are difficult to define. *Clean*, or well-defined, problems are those that can follow a set formula or a sequence of exact procedures to reach a solution. Following is an example of each.

- **Messy problem:** Mary's American History paper and presentation are due tomorrow in her 8:00 a.m. class. "OMG!" she texts her friend Kay. "What am I going to do? I've got my paper and presentation in history class tomorrow morning, and I forgot that Mom has me scheduled for my dental checkup at the same time. She wants to go directly to the dentist, and then she's going to drop me at school. I will miss the entire class. Help! This is such a mess."

- **Clean problem:** Two trains are speeding at each other with given speeds of 78 miles per hour on the same track. They are 12 miles apart at 12:00 p.m. At what time will they collide?

Table 3.1 provides examples of what problem solving looks and sounds like in the classroom.

Table 3.1: Problem Solve Look-Fors and Sound Bites

Looks Like	Sounds Like
Students huddled in groups	"What is the problem?"
Students using measurement tools	"How do we define this problem?"
Students creating a large graphic organizer	"What other ideas do you have?"
Students arguing	"What do you think the real problem is?"
Students recording ideas on the board	"Are the data sufficient? Reliable?"

Life is filled with challenges and problems. As students grow older, they rely less on others to solve their problems. Gradually, they become independent problem solvers who can get dressed, get to school, finish homework, and do their chores. Their problems become more complex, and they become aware of more and more challenges and problems that are out of their control—for example, water pollution, poverty, and territorial conflicts in many lands.

When problems get to a grand scale, another pair of terms—*wicked* and *tame*, used by John J. Kao (2007)—makes a distinction based on complexity rather than cleanliness or messiness. Wicked problems are the larger and more complex of the messy problems. These are complex national or global issues, such as water conservation, health care, population migration, drug wars, and national security, that have no easy solutions. Tame problems, on the other hand, often refer to home or school problems that need attention and some ideas to sort them out. Both require a similar set of problem-solving skills even though the tame problem is on a much smaller scale. Both situations need participants to gather facts, brainstorm ideas, and select the most plausible solution from a set of generated alternatives.

Learning to solve different types of problems will contribute to students' success in different domains. Messy problems are usually associated with the arts, literature, and social sciences such as psychology and anthropology. They are also the most prevalent problems students face in their everyday lives dealing with people and situations outside the classroom. Clean problems are often found at home, or maybe in science and mathematics where the parameters are more defined. Sometimes a situation involves both clean and messy problems. For example, when a fire inspector is trying to find the cause of a fire, clean problems (mathematical formulas) may be part of a larger strategy to solve messy and wicked problems.

Students benefit most when learning about the problem-solving process enhances their dispositions about problem solving. Included among the characteristics needed for productive problem solving are risk taking, questioning assumptions, openness to ideas, willingness to connect divergent ideas, respect for data, and attention to precision and accuracy.

Examples From the State Standards: Problem Solve

Approaching the Task as a Researcher: 11–12. Conduct research to answer a question (including a self-generated question) or solve a problem; narrow or broaden the inquiry when appropriate; gather multiple relevant, credible sources, print and digital; integrate information using a standard citation system.

Number Sense and Operations: Apply and extend previous understandings of multiplication and division to divide fractions by fractions.

6.NS.A. Compute and interpret quotients of positive fractions.

a. Solve problems involving division of fractions by fractions.

Source for standards: Missouri Department of Elementary and Secondary Education, 2016a, 2016b.

Explicit Teaching Lesson

In the Talk-Through, phase I, the educator teaches the thinking skill explicitly. There are several elements to aid the teacher in this phase: motivational mindset, order of operations, instructional strategy, assessment, and metacognitive reflection.

Problem solving is one of the skills that today's employers most desire (American Management Association, 2010). To *problem solve* is to use cognitive processing to find a solution to a difficult question or situation. Related terms include *challenge, prove, analyze,* and *synthesize.*

Motivational Mindset

To create an effective hook for the explicit lesson about problem solving, give the students an interesting problem to solve. In this scenario, each pair of students takes a single piece of yarn and ties the ends to their right wrists. They repeat this with a second piece for the left wrists so that the yarn overlaps and creates an X between the two of them. The challenge is to separate from each other by escaping the yarn entanglements without untying the yarn.

Have the pairs list the steps they took to try to solve the problem. Do not provide a "right way" as you guide the closing dialogue. Instead, ask the students to focus on what they have learned about problem solving.

Order of Operations

The goal of this lesson is to learn how to solve any problem—clean or messy—with a reliable yet adaptable approach. While many kinds of specific problem-solving strategies exist—including the scientific method, particular methods for specific types of mathematics problems, and resolution finding in literature and history—certain components are embedded in all of them, as represented by the mnemonic SOLVE.

Select the problem.

Opt for a strategy.

Look for information.

Verify facts and data needed.

Express alternatives and selected solutions.

An example problem to apply SOLVE focuses on seventh-grade students' tardiness to class. To determine how serious the problem is in their own class, the students choose to take a survey. Using SurveyMonkey (www.surveymonkey.com), the students provide information on how frequently they were late for class and how late they were. They ask the teacher to verify the data and then brainstorm strategies to diminish the tardiness.

Instructional Strategy

Work with the students to apply SOLVE to the following clean (table 3.2) and messy (table 3.3) problems.

Once the students have completed these five steps, review the acronym's letters and key words. Encourage the students to store SOLVE in their journals or to make a poster to help remind them of the process.

Table 3.2: Clean Problem

Middle-Level Mathematics: Clean Problem
Select the problem. If the day before the day before yesterday was Monday, what is the day after the day after tomorrow?
Opt for a strategy. **Strategy 1:** Draw a calendar to represent one week. **Strategy 2:** Divide the problem into two parts, befores and afters.
Look for information. **Strategy 1:** The day before the day before yesterday was Monday; mark the calendar, like a number line. **Strategy 2:** Plot the befores, and solve for the afters.
Verify facts and data needed. **Strategy 1:** Check the logic with a partner by talking through the problem. **Strategy 2:** Check the facts for each part with another team. Show the team your work.
Express alternatives and selected solutions. **Strategy 1:** Best answer; asks only for the correct answer. (Choose one solution.) **Strategy 2:** Solve the problem and express the answer obtained. (Rank the alternatives.)

Table 3.3: Messy Problem

Elementary-Level Social Studies: Messy Problem
A recent locker search of all sixth graders has fueled a controversy about students' individual rights to privacy as guaranteed by the Constitution. The teacher uses this local incident to address the social studies lesson on the Bill of Rights.
Select the problem. In groups of three, read the Bill of Rights, and apply your understanding to the recent locker searches. Were individual rights to privacy infringed upon? Why or why not? What is the evidence?
Opt for a strategy. Use one of three options. 1. Create a graphic organizer depicting the gathered information and judgment. 2. Develop a script for a play depicting an application of the Bill of Rights to the situation. 3. Present a persuasive speech advocating your point of view on this situation.
Look for information. Show evidence from at least three resources, such as an article, blog, editorial, podcast, YouTube video, or interview.
Verify facts and data needed. Cite all sources with publication title, author, and date. Have a peer review the material and give you or your team feedback for needed revisions or blanket approval.
Express alternatives and selected solutions. Present your findings and judgment with all necessary justification for your stand.

1

After this activity is finished, again return to SOLVE. Ask students to determine how helpful the mnemonic was as they went about solving the problem. Check for understanding and recall.

Assessment

Ask students to apply SOLVE to a real-world, ill-defined or messy problem. As a group, brainstorm a list of ill-defined problems. Have the students divide into collaborative groups of three and select one problem from the list. Make clear that they will use SOLVE as their guide for solving the problem and for determining how well they did. As each group presents its SOLVE example to the entire class, the listening students use a SOLVE rubric you create to assess the performances. The rubric should include (1) identifying the problem, (2) getting facts and dates, and (3) making sense of the data retrieved.

Metacognitive Reflection

Ask students to first share a *highlight* (knowledge or information) about problem solving and then share an *insight* (reflection or thought) about problem solving. For example, a knowledge highlight about problem solving is that you can learn a series of steps to follow that applies to any problem. An insight is that the steps do not necessarily go in the same order with each problem scenario.

Classroom Content Lesson

In the Walk-Through, phase II, teachers practice the thinking skill within content-based lessons, providing guidance to ensure the proper application of the skill. ELA standard 10 recommends literature and instructional texts that are available for coupling with grade-level lessons (available at www.corestandards.org/ELA-Literacy/standard-10 -range-quality-complexity/).

▶ Elementary Level

Select three clean problems from your curriculum. For example, use one-part or two-part mathematics problems or science questions about magnets, buoyancy, or living things. Guide the students through the SOLVE process with the first problem. Have them work with partners for the second selected problem. Ask several to share their thinking, and probe for clarity and reasons that the acronym is helpful. Use the third problem to check for understanding and determine what formative feedback might help.

▶▶ Middle Level

Provide the students with a messy problem relevant to the grade—for example, "Some friends are cyberbullying your best friend, and you feel caught in the middle," or "You hate the sport that your dad most wants you to play, and it's time for tryouts." Model and label each step of SOLVE before dividing students into pairs. Encourage them to use and label SOLVE. Invite several pairs to share their ideas, and probe the responses for clarity by asking students to provide facts or examples before giving each individual a messy problem to solve for homework.

▶▶▶ Secondary Level

Present a mixed clean and messy problem to students, or invite students to create their own—for example, "You have gotten a ticket for texting while driving that has a $100 fine that, if not paid, will cause you to lose your license. Texting while driving is verboten in your family. It is also a family policy that any driving fines are entirely the responsibility of the guilty party. You are the designated driver to the prom, and you have promised a ride to your younger brother, who doesn't have a license." Divide students into pairs so they can collaborate on this problem using SOLVE before sharing their solutions with another pair.

CCR Performance Task Lesson

During the Drive-Through, phase III, the thinking skill is transferred to authentic applications using selected performance tasks from the state CCR standards, allowing educators to make a direct connection between the selected thinking skill and the new version of the standards. While Missouri's state standard is presented as the example in this chapter (see "Examples From the State Standards: Problem Solve," page 39), the Common Core State Standards' *Appendix B: Text Exemplars and Sample Performance Tasks* (NGA & CCSSO, 2010b) is applied as a resource to the performance tasks in this section. There are almost always similarities among the state standards, and readers can consider the teaching of thinking skills within this example as they would their own state standards. The key is that the task requires a performance that demonstrates evidence of learning in concrete, meaningful, and real-world applications.

To deepen students' confidence with this skill, the teacher facilitates the student work, moving the students closer and closer to independent practice. Once the students are able to employ the skill independently, they are ready to transfer it across the curriculum. (For additional performance tasks, browse the state standards that appear in the References and Resources section, page 241.)

▶ Elementary Level

The following sample performance task illustrates the application of the mathematics standard 2.MD.8 (Measurement and Data, grade 2, standard 8):

> Solve word problems involving dollar bills, quarters, dimes, nickels, and pennies, using $ and ¢ symbols appropriately. Example: If you have 2 dimes and 3 pennies, how many cents do you have? (NGA & CCSSO, 2010c, p. 20)

▶▶ Middle Level

The following sample performance task illustrates the application of the mathematics standard 6.NS.8 (Number System, grade 6, standard 8):

> Solve real-world and mathematical problems by graphing points in all four quadrants of the coordinate plane. Include use of coordinates and absolute value to find distances between points with the same first coordinate or the same second coordinate. (NGA & CCSSO, 2010c, p. 43)

▶▶▶ Secondary Level

The following sample performance task illustrates the application of the ELA standard RH.11–12.7 (History/Social Studies, grades 11–12, standard 7):

> Students *integrate* the *information* provided by Mary C. Daly, vice president at the Federal Reserve Bank of San Francisco, with the data presented *visually* in the *FedViews* report. In their analysis of these *sources of information presented in diverse formats*, students frame and *address a question or solve a problem* raised by their *evaluation* of the evidence. (NGA & CCSSO, 2010b, p. 183)

Reflection Questions

These questions are designed to enrich your learning from doing. Such reflection enables you to deepen your understanding of the lessons you have just provided. You might also consider modifying these questions to further guide your students' reflection on this thinking skill.

1. Why would you introduce the skill of problem solving and the SOLVE process to students? How does this work with what you use now? Is it helpful? Why or why not?

2. How will you explicitly teach this skill? What topic can you use? Be as specific as possible.

3. What is your primary method for solving problems that arise in your own life?

Creative Thinking

Embedded in each state's new student standards are the big ideas of creativity and innovation. The three associated thinking skills provide students with ways to demonstrate authentic evidence of what they have learned in any of the disciplines in highly creative ways. Creativity taps into a number of higher-order thinking skills including imagination, wonderment, and connection making. It is often the magic link in problem solving and decision making because it brings to mind unusual, novel, and unique ideas. Creative thinking can be clever, wise, out-of-the-box thinking. It sometimes yields thoughts that seem outlandish, as the mind makes strange connections between ideas considered quite alien.

Innovation and creativity are inextricably linked. It has been said that innovation is imagination realized, and that only when the creative thought is put into action does innovation occur. In the broadest sense, imagination, invention, and innovation are of the same ilk. They signal original, fluent, flexible, and elaborative thoughts (Torrance, 1974), and they are the cornerstones of productive, generative thinking in the rich, rigorous, and relevant curriculum espoused in the state standards. They are also necessary for effective problem solving, shrewd decision making, and productive ideation in the future world of our young citizens.

With that in mind, the skill set of creative thinking has been dissected into three skills that call for explicit instruction with students across grade levels and content areas: (1) *generating* ideas, (2) *associating* and connecting, and (3) *hypothesizing* and validating.

Chapter 4: Generate

The way to get good ideas is to get lots of ideas and throw the bad ones away.

—Linus Pauling

Emily, a first grader, epitomized the youngster who is especially good at generating ideas. Every day, as the first graders entered the classroom, the teacher expected them to go to the little table where she was seated and tell her their "word of the day." It was the students' responsibility—in fact, their homework each night—to generate a word that they wanted to learn and work with the next day. Some students were very slow to generate their words, but not Emily. Her fluency, flexibility, and originality were like ever-ready batteries. After all, she thought like a scientist—an entomologist, to be specific, for she loved insects, bugs, and creepy-crawlies of all sorts and sizes. In the mornings, her words just flew from her: *caterpillar, butterfly, worm, garden snake, ladybug, jar, mosquito, microscope, meadow, net, tarantula*, and so on. Once she had her word written on the card, she went off to "study" her word in paint, sand, clay, or some other medium on the choice board. Then the elaboration began as she wrote her daily sentences (story) around her pivot word.

Generating ideas is often the first step in producing a product or performing a presentation, both of which are considered evidence of learning. For example, the innovative production of a toy dragon using all six simple machines or the culminating statement that clearly persuades in a lively debate provides real evidence of understanding by the students involved. In both situations, the students need to generate many ideas to bring it all to fruition. This kind of creative and innovative thinking requires rigorous classroom scaffolding for students to become effective users of the skill. Table 4.1 provides examples of what generating ideas looks and sounds like in the classroom.

Table 4.1: Generate Look-Fors and Sound Bites

Looks Like	Sounds Like
Students creating a web, map, or T-chart	"How about this . . . ?"
Students brainstorming a list of words	"Here's another crazy idea."
Students collaboratively writing lyrics	"Does this work?"
Students drawing lines to connect words	"Great idea! Where did that come from?"
Students developing an ABC graffiti chart	"Piggybacking on Joe's comment . . ."

Without skillfulness in readily generating a string of ideas, in all kinds of situations, students will lack an essential component in problem solving, decision making, and creative ideation. Brainstorming or generating ideas is a skill that can be explicitly learned with practice, rehearsal, and repetition. It is worth the effort, as it is at the heart and soul of creative endeavors, big or small.

Examples From the State Standards: Generate

Research to Build and Present Knowledge: W.7. Conduct short research projects to answer a question.

    a. Draw on several sources.

    b. Generate additional related, focused questions for further research and investigation.

Measurement and Data: 3.MD.4. Generate measurement data by measuring lengths using rulers marked with halves and fourths of an inch.

Source for standards: North Dakota Department of Public Instruction, 2017a, 2017b.

Explicit Teaching Lesson

In the Talk-Through, phase I, the educator teaches the thinking skill explicitly. There are several elements to aid the teacher in this phase: motivational mindset, order of operations, instructional strategy, assessment, and metacognitive reflection.

Generate means to bring into existence. Related terms include *brainstorm*, *produce*, *develop*, *form*, *list*, and *create*.

Motivational Mindset

To grab students' interest, teachers might orchestrate a brief relay race. Post a timely topic related to your area of focus on the board. Possible generic topics are government, scientific discoveries, literary genres, mathematical terms, healthy foods, figurative language devices, and sports.

Divide the class into teams of four to six, and begin the relay with two teams competing against each other for the longest list of phrases, synonyms, or terms associated with the topic or descriptions of the topic. The teams line up in front of the board. One member at a time goes to the board and adds to the list. That person then goes to the back of the line. Everyone on the team takes a turn adding to the brainstorming list. At the end of two minutes, the team with the most entries on the board wins the round. Then go to the next set of two teams, and finally have a playoff of the top two teams. Note that this is a highly motivating activity as students cheer each other on to generate the most words for their team task. To conclude, discuss the concept of generating ideas.

Order of Operations

To generate ideas, several mental operations must cause a FLOW.

First blast: Call out a burst of ideas; connect to the topic.

Long list: Add more words by associating and piggybacking on ideas.

Open mind: Anything goes; defer judgment, and go with the flow.

Working with the best: Select the best idea; target the one with the most potential.

For example, when generating ideas for a science project, eighth-grade students call out a first blast of ideas: simple machines and pendulums, electronics and robots, chemical compounds and reactions, and so on. Then, by associating and piggybacking on the growing list, new ideas emerge: one student, piggybacking on the electronics idea, may be inspired to name electronic game boards. Another, piggybacking on the simple machines idea, may think of Rube Goldberg inventions. Keeping an open mind so that there are no censors, students continue to generate ideas: environmental studies, human life adaptations. Finally, the students examine the list, looking for the best ideas. They may decide that the idea that seems to have the widest appeal for creativity and uniqueness is the Rube Goldberg machines. Pairs could target a task for the machine to perform and create their version of a Rube Goldberg device to accomplish the goal. For example, they could design a device to close a cupboard door, to turn on a light, or even to set off an alarm clock.

Instructional Strategy

Four-fold concept development is a differentiation tool used to understand a concept or idea and is a great tool to introduce the concept of *generate*. Divide the students into teams, and provide each team with a piece of poster paper. Instruct the students to fold the poster paper into four corner sections, and then make a small triangle fold with the folded corners (see figure 4.1). Once they open the poster, this triangle fold appears as a diamond shape within which students can write a focus word (a key learning concept word). Label the sections according to figure 4.1: (1) *list*, (2) *rank*, (3) *compare*, and (4) *illustrate*. Work with the students to develop their understanding of the focus word by moving from one section to the next in this order, and by performing the following tasks.

1. **List:** The students brainstorm synonyms or ideas for the focus word.
2. **Rank:** They look over the list and determine their top three words.
3. **Compare:** They use the sentence, "[Focus word] is like [concrete object] because both [give three comparisons and choose one]." For example, "Differentiation is like an elephant because both can be heavy on your mind."
4. **Illustrate:** They draw a visual metaphor or picture of the compared object.

A blank four-fold concept development form can be found in appendix A on page 216.

Assessment

Ask the students to count the number of words generated on their lists for a fluency score. Award extra points for original or novel ideas that appear only on one chart in the room.

Metacognitive Reflection

Ask the students to consider the following questions.

- How many ideas did you come up with in three minutes?
- Do you consider yourself fluent in generating ideas?

Classroom Content Lesson

In the Walk-Through, phase II, teachers practice the thinking skill within content-based lessons, providing guidance to ensure the proper application of the skill. ELA standard 10 recommends literature and instructional texts that are available for coupling with

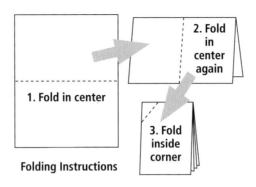

Folding Instructions

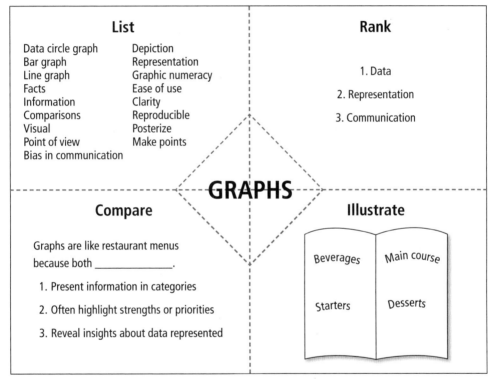

Figure 4.1: Four-fold concept development example.

*Visit **go.SolutionTree.com/instruction** for a free reproducible version of this figure.*

grade-level lessons (available at www.corestandards.org/ELA-Literacy/standard-10 -range-quality-complexity/).

▶ Elementary Level

Have students work in pairs and generate measurement data by measuring the length of six different objects of their choice in the classroom. Instruct the pairs to first generate a list of objects to measure and then measure each object to a fourth of an inch with a ruler. Then have the pair use another standard to measure the same objects. This can be a pencil, piece of chalk, footprint, hand size, and so on. Using these alternative measuring standards illustrates how early mankind may have created or used standards that showed consistency in their measurements.

Have students represent their measurements on a single piece of paper. In each pair, one student should use the ruler, and the other should record the figures on the piece of paper.

▶▶ Middle Level

Ask students to generate a web of "green ideas for the community." Divide the students into groups of three, and instruct each group to choose one idea, research it, find a community agency to sponsor or partner with the group, and plan a service project to put into action. These might include tree planting, beach cleanup, "Graffiti Gone" campaigns, and so on.

▶▶▶ Secondary Level

Ask freshmen to list all the factors that impact student achievement. Then, have them prioritize the factors by frequency or impact and select the top three factors to gather data on. Finally, invite students, in teams, to develop a student-friendly multimedia presentation to share with next year's incoming freshman class.

Teachers at all three levels (elementary, middle, and secondary) can inspire creative thinking by perfecting student use of the brainstorming process. Students can easily use the acronym DOVE to learn how best to generate a lot of items in a brainstorming session.

Don't outlaw any word; allow anything

Opt for outlandish, unusual words

Vast number of words preferred

Expand by piggybacking or association

CCR Performance Task Lesson

During the Drive-Through, phase III, the thinking skill is transferred to authentic applications using selected performance tasks from the state CCR standards, allowing educators to make a direct connection between the selected thinking skill and the new version of the standards. While North Dakota's state standard is presented as the example in this chapter (see "Examples From the State Standards: Generate," page 48), the Common Core

State Standards' *Appendix B: Text Exemplars and Sample Performance Tasks* (NGA & CCSSO, 2010b) is applied as a resource to the performance tasks in this section. There are almost always similarities among the state standards, and readers can consider the teaching of thinking skills within this example as they would their own state standards. The key is that the task requires a performance that demonstrates evidence of learning in concrete, meaningful, and real-world applications.

To deepen students' confidence with this skill, the teacher facilitates the student work, moving the students closer and closer to independent practice. Once the students are able to employ the skill independently, they are ready to transfer it across the curriculum. (For additional performance tasks, browse the state standards that appear in the References and Resources section, page 241.)

▶ Elementary Level

The following sample performance task illustrates the application of the ELA standard RI.4.4 (Reading: Informational Text, grade 4, standard 4):

> Students determine the meaning of domain-specific words or phrases, such as *crust*, *mantle*, *magma*, and *lava*, and important general academic words and phrases that appear in Seymour Simon's Volcanoes. (NGA & CCSSO, 2010b, p. 76)

▶▶ Middle Level

The following sample performance task illustrates the application of the ELA standard RL.6.6 (Reading: Literature, grade 6, standard 6):

> Students explain how Sandra Cisneros's choice of words develops the point of view of the young speaker in her story "Eleven." (NGA & CCSSO, 2010b, p. 89)

▶▶▶ Secondary Level

The following sample performance task illustrates the application of the ELA standard RI.11–12.9 (Reading: Informational Text, grades 11–12, standard 9):

> Students analyze Thomas Jefferson's Declaration of Independence, identifying its purpose and evaluating rhetorical features such as the listing of grievances. Students compare and contrast the themes and argument found there to those of other U.S. documents of historical and literary significance, such as the Olive Branch Petition. (NGA & CCSSO, 2010b, p. 171)

Technology Integration

> **Featured technology:** SMART Board, Canva (www.canva.com),
> Adobe Spark's poster maker (spark.adobe.com/make/posters/),
> Microsoft Word templates, Google Docs (https://docs.google
> .com) templates, Wordle (www.wordle.net), YouTube (www
> .youtube.com), SurveyMonkey (www.surveymonkey.com)

The following tasks provide guidance on incorporating technology into lessons using this chapter's instructional strategy.

Digital Integration Task

In the Instructional Strategy section (page 50), four-fold concept development requires students to expand their creative thinking and visualize an idea using a metaphor. Begin by identifying and clarifying the lesson outcome (students showing that they understand the abstract concept key word *differentiation*) and checking that students have a prior knowledge of *metaphor*. Divide students into collaborative teams of three, and provide teams with a collaborative rubric on which they will be scored.

Share and analyze the key word *differentiation* with the class. Instruct each team to generate three metaphorical ideas that depict the concept of *differentiation*. To demonstrate the task, give the example of a box of crayons, which contains many different-colored crayons. Have each team talk about how the abstract word and concrete words are alike (for example, the item comprises many crayons in a box) and different (for example, the box contains many different colors of crayons). After discussing each metaphor it generates, the team should agree on its best example and the reasons why it is "best."

Invite teams to present their work via an online poster-making tool, such as Canva, Adobe Spark's poster maker, Microsoft Word, or Google Docs. Conduct a mini-design lab to help teams learn how to design a poster layout with their selected online tool. Ask each team to include a visual and a word showing how the metaphorical example they selected shows differentiation. Invite teams to present and explain their metaphor to the class. Assess their work, and have teams assess each other, with a collaborative rubric. To conclude, ask each team to agree on what they learned about the word *differentiation*, and post their ideas on the SMART Board.

Grade-Level Digital Variations

The following sections provide grade-level variations for incorporating technology into lessons.

▶ Elementary Level

After completing the Instructional Strategy section's lesson on generating ideas (page 50), introduce students to Wordle (www.wordle.net), a popular word cloud generator. (You can find other options for word cloud generators online; see, for example, www.smashingapps.com/2011/12/15/nine-excellent-yet-free-online-word-cloud-generators.html [Jay, 2011]). With a familiar topic, model how to create a word cloud on your SMART Board. Have student teams make their own word clouds with words they generate about the comparison from the Instructional Strategy lesson.

▶▶ Middle Level

Initiate a product-making project in which students, alone or in teams, will create a public sculpture. Invite students to search online for examples of public sculpture. Via the Share function on Google Docs, have students work together to develop quality criteria for a public sculpture. Select a few criteria students should use to manage the size and cost of their creations. Next, have them design and make their own sculptures. Share a rubric to students' digital devices to assess their work. Determine the criteria you will use in this rubric (for example, includes three or more media, includes found objects, communicates message to the community, fits in location). To spark student interest, view "Anatomy of a Project: Kinetic Conundrum" (available at https://bit.ly/2QfjyjM; Edutopia, 2010) for an exemplary variation.

▶▶▶ Secondary Level

Invite your students to solve a community problem they identify via a class project. Have students create an online survey using SurveyMonkey (www.surveymonkey.com) and administer it to community stakeholders so they can identify local problems they feel are important to solve. (Please also see the lesson on problem solving, page 40.) Have students use these data to select and define the problem their project will attempt to solve. Next, use the procedures and technology for generating ideas identified in the middle-level lesson. Instruct students to plan as a class how they can solve the community problem, and arrange for the class to present the plan to the relevant local government council. Carry out the proposed plan, including creating needed documents and displays.

Reflection Questions

These questions are designed to enrich your learning from doing. Such reflection enables you to deepen your understanding of the lessons you have just provided. You might also consider modifying these questions to further guide your students' reflection on this thinking skill.

1. How, when, and why do you have students generate long lists of ideas?

2. How does your subject matter provide opportunities for students to generate, produce, or make something as evidence of their learning?

3. What takeaway from this chapter will enhance another lesson or unit you are doing?

4. Complete the following sentence: It is easy for me to generate many ideas when I . . .

5. Ask students what other relevant software might be helpful in generating ideas.

Chapter 5: Associate

2

Associate reverently, as much as you can, with your loftiest thoughts.

—Henry David Thoreau

———————

A youngster saw a seagull fly by in the summer sky, and his dad did what all parents do with their toddlers. He pointed to the seagull and said, "Bird."

The child mimicked his dad and pointed and said, "Bird."

"Yes, that's a bird. A bird flies in the sky."

Suddenly, a butterfly floated down to land on the child's arm, and he said, "Bird."

To the child's surprise, his dad said, "No, that's a butterfly."

Then a plane soared overhead, and the little one, making a natural connection again, deliberately pointed to the sky and said, "Bird."

But again, much to the child's disappointment and confusion, his dad said, "No. That's an airplane."

To associate ideas is to piggyback on them, unite and combine different ideas, and connect, relate, and link different ideas to each other. It is creativity at work. Brainstorming, imagining, inventing, and innovating are evidence that the mind is making cognitive connections through association of thoughts. The result is a new concept or idea.

Table 5.1 (page 58) provides examples of what this thinking skill looks and sounds like in the classroom.

Table 5.1: Associate Look-Fors and Sound Bites

Looks Like	Sounds Like
Students listing synonyms	"That reminds me of . . ."
Students connecting two ideas	"Your word makes me think of . . ."
Students charting antonyms	"Related to that idea is . . ."
Students bridging snapshots (images)	"What about the synonym or rhyming word . . . ?"
Partners alternating jotting down ideas	"I see another link between the . . ."

Concepts develop from a continuing association process, as illustrated in the vignette opening this chapter. Children learn by associating one idea with another. They connect thoughts and then apply and generalize the ideas to build new concepts. Building concepts through critical associations is a trial-and-error process as the concepts become more refined. This is how children develop big umbrella ideas about the world around them.

While it is a creative skill, associating ideas is also a critical skill in discerning similarities and differences. Learning how to identify associated types of problems in mathematics, to link cause with effect in the science lab, and to relate symptoms to an illness in the real world makes association a most worthy higher-order thinking skill for 21st century thinking.

Examples From the State Standards: Associate

Phonics and Word Recognition: 0.3.0.3. Know and apply grade-level phonics and word analysis skills in decoding words.

   a. Demonstrate basic knowledge of one-to-one letter-sound correspondences by producing the primary or many of the most frequent sound for each consonant.
   b. Associate the long and short sounds with common spellings (graphemes) for the five major vowels.

Geometry & Measurement: 9.3.1.3. Understand that quantities associated with physical measurements must be assigned units; apply such units correctly in expressions, equations and problem solutions that involve measurements; and convert between measurement systems.

   For example: 60 miles/hour = 60 miles/hour ° 5280 feet/mile ° 1 hour/3600 seconds = 88 feet/second.

Source for standards: Minnesota Department of Education, n.d.a, n.d.b.

Explicit Teaching Lesson

In the Talk-Through, phase I, the educator teaches the thinking skill explicitly. There are several elements to aid the teacher in this phase: motivational mindset, order of operations, instructional strategy, assessment, and metacognitive reflection.

To *associate* is to connect or bring together into relationship. Related terms include *unite*, *link*, *combine*, *align*, and *relate*.

Motivational Mindset

To introduce the skill of associating ideas, test students' familiarity with the grocery store. Ask students to write down the name of the aisle in which particular products are found and to hold up their responses. For example, ask students to name the aisle in which they might find toothpicks. Once everyone has held up a response, discuss the results. Then ask students to explain what associations they made in making their decision. Repeat the exercise with other items that may be difficult to locate, such as sliced almonds, popcorn, paper plates, and so on.

Order of Operations

Associating ideas often starts with a visual or mental scan of previously generated ideas. The brain literally makes a dendritic connection between ideas that are related (Willis, 2008). It is important at this point in the association process to just play along and not censor anything. Allow all ideas to flow. Anything goes. Review the list again to see if anything sparks; it is important to allow time for the piggybacking to take place. When you have exhausted the ideas, review the list, and keep the best ideas for development. This process can be summed up with SPARK.

Scan the list of ideas for associations.

Play along with connections made.

Allow anything.

Review again for more related ideas.

Keep the best for development.

A simple example of associating ideas is the formal brainstorming process. A middle school class is brainstorming fund-raising ideas for a field trip to Springfield, Illinois, to visit the state capitol. Ideas come fast and furious: cooking a spaghetti dinner, washing cars, hosting a candy sale, selling tickets to a play, creating a newspaper to distribute at a cost. Then there is a long pause as the entire class scans the list. Finally, someone makes a connection and says, "I'm going to piggyback on Shawn's idea about the car wash. How about offering yard work for the neighborhood? It's spring, and there are always yard cleanup jobs." Others jump in and add ideas: baby-sitting, dog walking, errands, and all kinds of neighborhood services.

"Yeah! What if we create a brochure of things we can do?"

"I love that idea."

"We could call it, 'Spring Into Spring With Springfield Services.'"

Instructional Strategy

ABC graffiti is an activity that requires the skill of associating. Essentially, the alphabet becomes an advance organizer for the creative process. Divide students into teams, and give each team a poster paper and markers of a certain color (for example, team 1 has all blue markers, team 2 has all red markers, and so on). In figure 5.1, the target focus appears at the top of the paper. In this case, it is World War II. Then, teams write the letters of the alphabet on their paper (see figure 5.1) and fill in as many ideas or associations for each letter of the alphabet as they can in three minutes. When time is up, students have one minute to go around to the other teams' posters and add new words using their own team colors. In the end, each team can see, because of the color coding, how many associations they have made beyond their initial efforts. Students can review and compare with the SPARK process. A blank ABC graffiti chart can be found in appendix A on page 217.

Assessment

Each team counts the number of entries on all the ABC graffiti papers in the room, scoring its results: two points for words on the team members' own paper and five points for their words on other teams' papers. More value is placed on associations beyond their original or first ideas. In this way, each team can check their poster and see how they did, and move around the room to see how helpful they were in associating ideas for others.

Metacognitive Reflection

Each team, using the SPARK order of operations, comes up with three possible ways that this strategy could be adapted using online technology (for example, an online tool to foster associating and connecting ideas is Google Share). This activity engages the metacognitive element as students discuss the benefits of piggybacking on ideas to expand their understandings.

World War II	
A	N
B	O
C	Pearl Harbor
D-Day	Q
E	Roosevelt
F	S
G	T
H	U
I	V
J	W
K	X
L	Y
M	Z

Figure 5.1: ABC graffiti example.

*Visit **go.SolutionTree.com/instruction** for a free reproducible version of this figure.*

Classroom Content Lesson

In the Walk-Through, phase II, teachers practice the thinking skill within content-based lessons, providing guidance to ensure the proper application of the skill. ELA standard 10 recommends literature and instructional texts that are available for coupling with grade-level lessons (available at www.corestandards.org/ELA-Literacy/standard-10-range-quality-complexity/).

▶ Elementary Level

Work with students to fill in an ABC graffiti chart (see figure 5.1). This can be used for any content area. For instance, students can use their prior knowledge to contribute to an ABC graffiti exercise on the topic of the Civil War or the branches of government in social studies class. They can use the ABC graffiti exercise in science class to unpack and classify living things or in mathematics class to examine strategies for solving problems.

▶▶ Middle Level

Complete an ABC graffiti chart with students about a current topic of study. Then have student teams delve into their textbooks to compare the information found there with what they have listed on the chart. The goal is to list as many ideas outside of those found in the textbook as possible.

▶▶▶ Secondary Level

Associating ideas using an ABC graffiti activity is useful for juniors and seniors in exploring career options or investigating options for college. Work with students to create an ABC graffiti chart of the most interesting career choices. Consider displaying the completed chart in the guidance office to spur the imagination of all high school students.

CCR Performance Task Lesson

During the Drive-Through, phase III, the thinking skill is transferred to authentic applications using selected performance tasks from the state CCR standards, allowing educators to make a direct connection between the selected thinking skill and the new version of the standards. While Minnesota's state standard is presented as the example in this chapter (see "Examples From the State Standards: Associate," page 58), the Common Core State Standards' *Appendix B: Text Exemplars and Sample Performance Tasks* (NGA & CCSSO, 2010b) is applied as a resource to the performance tasks in this section. There are almost always similarities among the state standards, and readers can consider the teaching of thinking skills within this example as they would their own state standards. The key is that the task requires a performance that demonstrates evidence of learning in concrete, meaningful, and real-world applications.

To deepen students' confidence with this skill, the teacher facilitates the student work, moving the students closer and closer to independent practice. Once the students are able to employ the skill independently, they are ready to transfer it across the curriculum. (For additional performance tasks, browse the state standards that appear in the References and Resources section, page 241.)

▶ Elementary Level

The following sample performance task illustrates the application of the ELA standard RL.4.7 (Reading: Literature, grade 4, standard 7):

> Students make connections between the visual presentation of
> John Tenniel's illustrations in Lewis Carroll's *Alice's Adventures*
> *in Wonderland* and the text of the story to identify how the

pictures of Alice reflect specific descriptions of her in the text.
(NGA & CCSSO, 2010b, p. 70)

▶▶ Middle Level

The following sample performance task illustrates the application of the ELA standard RL.8.2 (Reading: Literature, grade 8, standard 2):

> Students summarize the development of the morality of Tom
> Sawyer in Mark Twain's novel of the same name and analyze
> its connection to themes of accountability and authenticity by
> noting how it is conveyed through characters, setting, and plot.
> (NGA & CCSSO, 2010b, p. 89)

▶▶▶ Secondary Level

The following sample performance task illustrates the application of the ELA standard RL.9–10.2 (Reading: Literature, grades 9–10, standard 2):

> Students analyze in detail the theme of relationships between
> mothers and daughters and how that theme develops over the
> course of Amy Tan's *The Joy Luck Club*. Students search the text
> for specific details that show how the theme emerges and how
> it is shaped and refined over the course of the novel. (NGA &
> CCSSO, 2010b, p. 121)

Reflection Questions

These questions are designed to enrich your learning from doing. Such reflection enables you to deepen your understanding of the lessons you have just provided. You might also consider modifying these questions to further guide your students' reflection on this thinking skill.

1. How might you use ABC graffiti to explicitly teach students how to use the SPARK process to associate ideas when doing projects and tasks that require the creative flow of ideas and information?

2. Do you agree or disagree that the ability to associate ideas is intuitive—an innate gift—rather than a skill that can be learned? Justify your thinking.

3. What connections can you make between the explicit teaching of thinking skills and the state standards' goal to have every student career and college ready?

Chapter 6: Hypothesize

*The great tragedy of science is the slaying of a
beautiful hypothesis by an ugly fact.*

　　　　　　　　　　　　　　　　—Thomas Huxley

2

For their final performance assessment, students, working in teams of four, were
required to present their findings on the theory of why the dinosaurs became
extinct. As each team took a turn, the speaker for the team stood proudly;
showed the graphs, pictures, and research; and reported the hypothesis the team
had adopted. One hypothesis put forth was this: "It's only a working theory, but
we think the reason the dinosaurs disappeared from the earth is because of the
Ice Age that descended upon them. It wiped them out because there was no
vegetation left for them to eat and survive."

In the school setting, the thinking skill of hypothesizing may take on a weighty
cognitive role. It may be part of the formal scientific method seen in biology class,
it may be found in the plot predictions that English literature students make as they
read a novel, or it could even be part of the metacognitive thinking that students do
as they are anticipating their grade on an essay in history class. Table 6.1 (page 66)
provides examples of what hypothesizing looks and sounds like in the classroom.

It is not surprising that the CCSS cite the higher-order thinking skill of hypothesizing, as it appears in a number of high-yield instructional strategies (Costa & Kallick,
2000; Marzano, Pickering, & Pollock, 2001). Hypothesizing, guessing, and following
hunches are natural thinking paths for learners as they generate creative ideas and

Table 6.1: Hypothesize Look-Fors and Sound Bites

Looks Like	Sounds Like
Students estimating the distance objects will travel	"My best guess is . . ."
Students considering different possible stage directions	"I think if we try it this way . . ."
Students sketching possible plans to build a project	"I'm guessing . . ."
Students testing and measuring objects to see if they fit	"Let's assume for a minute that . . ."
Students pausing over a palette of paints	"What if we look at it another way?"

produce, invent, and innovate. In fact, this is the skill of the scientist, as famously noted in the scientific method:

1. Ask a question.

2. Do background research.

3. Construct a hypothesis.

4. Test your hypothesis by doing an experiment.

5. Analyze your data and draw a conclusion.

6. Communicate your results. (Science Buddies, n.d.)

Making a hypothesis is a natural component of any kind of problem solving, whether it is in the classroom or in real-life situations. Imagine that you are driving along and sense that there is something wrong with the steering. Immediately you think about the tires. As you pull over, you are already hypothesizing about when, where, and how you might have gotten a flat. Was it when you drove through the alley to take a shortcut? Did you pick up a nail? Could it have been from the long trip to Indiana last weekend? It was so hot that you may have worn the tires down from the excessive heat. The guessing goes on until you finally get out and see a nail in the tire.

Or, imagine the refrigerator has spontaneously defrosted, and you find a puddle of water on the kitchen floor. You automatically start hypothesizing. Did the power go off? Did the motor burn out in this old fridge? Did you forget to close the freezer door? Perhaps you bumped the temperature control switch on the inside wall. After close inspection, your final hypothesis is that the refrigerator defrosted because the motor stopped working, as nothing will restart it.

Hypothesizing is a huge part of what we do in our daily lives. If students are to become effective, successful problem solvers in all aspects of their lives, they need to have a formal look at this important thinking skill.

Examples From the State Standards: Hypothesize

Summarize, represent, and interpret data on a single count or measurement variable: S.ID.4. Use the mean and standard deviation of a data set to fit it to a normal distribution and to estimate population percentages. Recognize that there are data sets for which such a procedure is not appropriate. Use calculators, spreadsheets, and tables to estimate areas under the normal curve.

Statistics and Probability: 6.SP.1. Recognize a statistical question as one that anticipates variability in the data related to the question and accounts for it in the answers. For example, "How old am I?" is not a statistical question, but "How old are the students in my school?" is a statistical question because one anticipates variability in students' ages.

Source for standards: Oregon Department of Education, 2010.

Explicit Teaching Lesson

In the Talk-Through, phase I, the educator teaches the thinking skill explicitly. There are several elements to aid the teacher in this phase: motivational mindset, order of operations, instructional strategy, assessment, and metacognitive reflection.

To *hypothesize* means to believe enough to act, even though there is uncertain or tentative evidence. Related terms include *predict, develop, interpret, synthesize, estimate, anticipate, infer,* and *speculate.* Martin H. Fischer (n.d.) clarifies what a hypothesis is: "Don't confuse hypothesis and theory. The former is a possible explanation; the latter, the correct one. The establishment of theory is the very purpose of science."

Motivational Mindset

To spark students' interest and pique their curiosity, walk into the classroom with a box that is secured tightly, and place it front and center for all to see. Ask the students to discuss with a partner what they think is in the box. Students should support their hypotheses with the facts that they are using to guess. Allow about three minutes for this discussion.

Ask the pairs to share some of their thoughts about the box and give their rationale for the hypotheses they offer. Next, unveil the object inside the box. Depending on the subject you teach, you may select a bone, a laptop computer, field glasses, or anything that is somehow related to the next topic of study. Before introducing the topic, have the students hypothesize what this object has to do with what they are going to learn. Continue the conversation until the students close in on the topic.

Order of Operations

To hypothesize is to question and connect. First, focus on the idea, then make mental connections, and finally, concretize the hunch or prediction by verbalizing it. The AHA acronym is appropriate here.

Ask questions about the target idea or situation.

Harbor conscious connections.

Announce the hunch, and try to confirm it.

The act of generating a hypothesis is a skill that will serve students not only in school but also when they have left school and begun their careers. With reflective practice, students will be able to hone this skill so that a hunch becomes more than intuition and instead a cognitive strategy employable in a variety of situations.

Instructional Strategy

Poll Everywhere (www.polleverywhere.com) is a powerful software tool or app for handheld wireless devices (cell phones) or computers. Teachers can use this in the classroom to activate prior knowledge about the target concepts, skills, or topics. The questioner poses questions, and participants weigh in by voting online or via texting. They hypothesize or make predictions about an idea, and the results show up in graph format as a projected image. Questions can be posed in multiple-choice, true or false, and agree or disagree formats. Following are two examples.

1. Based on your experience, what is the best way to end bullying in our school?

    ▶ Tougher penalties for offenders

    ▶ More security personnel in the hallways

    ▶ Mandatory antibullying classes for everyone

    ▶ Mediation between offender and victim

2. Good grades are the primary reason to go to school.

    ▶ Agree

    ▶ Disagree

When learners hypothesize and predict outcomes, it piques their curiosity and motivates them to find the answers. They want to investigate to confirm or validate their thinking.

Assessment

Ask the students to create a Prediction Page to record their hypotheses of what might happen in their lives in the next month, by the end of the semester, and by the end of the year, and then verify them as time goes on.

Metacognitive Reflection

Ask students to discuss why it is important to hone the skill of hypothesizing and how it may apply to their lives outside school.

Classroom Content Lesson

In the Walk-Through, phase II, teachers practice the thinking skill within content-based lessons, providing guidance to ensure the proper application of the skill. ELA standard 10 recommends literature and instructional texts that are available for coupling with grade-level lessons (available at www.corestandards.org/ELA-Literacy/standard-10-range-quality-complexity/).

▶ Elementary Level

Bring in a large, odd-shaped sack, and have the students guess what is in the sack by asking questions similar to those on the game show *21* (for example, "Is it bigger than a frog?" "Does it make noise?" "Is it edible?"). Allow students to work in pairs to come up with questions, and invite them to guess what they think is in the sack only after they ask their questions. Some pairs will ask their questions early; others will wait to hear the results of the other questions.

▶▶ Middle Level

Assign students a short story to read, but do not provide the end. Have the students come up with possible endings to the story. Grade their hypotheses on their logical incorporation of existing facts gleaned from the part of the story they read.

▶▶▶ Secondary Level

Ask students to respond to one of the following five scenarios with an original hypothesis that they support with a rationale.

What if:

1. Germany had developed an atomic weapon and had won World War II?

2. Alcohol were illegal and marijuana were legal?

3. Seventy percent of elected officials in the United States were women and 30 percent were men?

4. Shakespeare were a modern-day author?

5. America had adopted the metric system in 1990?

CCR Performance Task Lesson

During the Drive-Through, phase III, the thinking skill is transferred to authentic applications using selected performance tasks from the state CCR standards, allowing educators to make a direct connection between the selected thinking skill and the new version of the standards. While Oregon's state standard is presented as the example in this chapter (see "Examples From the State Standards: Hypothesize," page 67), the Common Core State Standards' *Appendix B: Text Exemplars and Sample Performance Tasks* (NGA & CCSSO, 2010b) is applied as a resource to the performance tasks in this section. There are almost always similarities among the state standards, and readers can consider the teaching of thinking skills within this example as they would their own state standards. The key is that the task requires a performance that demonstrates evidence of learning in concrete, meaningful, and real-world applications.

To deepen students' confidence with this skill, the teacher facilitates the student work, moving the students closer and closer to independent practice. Once the students are able to employ the skill independently, they are ready to transfer it across the curriculum. (For additional performance tasks, browse the state standards that appear in the References and Resources section, page 241.)

▶ Elementary Level

The following sample performance task illustrates the application of the ELA standard RL.5.2 (Reading: Literature, grade 5, standard 2):

> Students summarize the plot of Antoine de Saint-Exupéry's *The Little Prince* and then reflect on the challenges facing the characters in the story while employing those and other details in the text to discuss the value of inquisitiveness and exploration as a theme of the story. (NGA & CCSSO, 2010b, p. 70)

▶▶ Middle Level

The following sample performance task illustrates the application of the ELA standard RST.6–8.9 (Science and Technical Subjects, grades 6–8, standard 9):

> Students construct a holistic picture of the history of Manhattan by comparing and contrasting the information gained from Donald Mackay's *The Building of Manhattan* with the multimedia

sources available on the "Manhattan on the Web" portal hosted by the New York Public Library. (NGA & CCSSO, 2010b, p. 100)

▶▶▶ Secondary Level

The following sample performance task illustrates the application of the mathematics standard HSS.MD.3 (Statistics and Probability, high school, standard 3):

> Develop a probability distribution for a random variable defined for a sample space in which theoretical probabilities can be calculated; find the expected value. For example, find the theoretical probability distribution for the number of correct answers obtained by guessing on all five questions of a multiple-choice test where each question has four choices, and find the expected grade under various grading schemes. (NGA & CCSSO, 2010c, p. 83)

Reflection Questions

These questions are designed to enrich your learning from doing. Such reflection enables you to deepen your understanding of the lessons you have just provided. You might also consider modifying these questions to further guide your students' reflection on this thinking skill.

1. In your learning community, how might you focus on the skill of valuing hunches, generating hypotheses, predicting outcomes, and estimating results as part of your focus on student success?

2. How might you build one opportunity for hypothesizing into your lessons in mathematics? Science? Social studies? Language arts? Technology?

3. Hypothesize the effects of the CCSS being implemented with fidelity throughout the United States. Compare your prediction with a colleague's.

Complex Thinking

The concept of complex thinking is complex in itself. Complexity involves the sophistication of language used, including word choice and sentence structure, as well as the level of discipline-based concepts. With complex thinking, the student is expected to not only read with literal clarity but also interpret what is implied. Complex thinking requires skill in determining the author's perspective and purpose, the inherent bias, the nuance of tone and tenor, and the real meaning of the words on the page as crafted by the author, with intended or unintended persuasion. Complex thinking can be seen as the ability to cut through the abstract ideas presented in order to discern them in concrete ways. It helps the student grasp the underlying meaning of the concept.

All too often, texts are complex in vocabulary and concepts, and students with little background knowledge are lost before they begin the comprehension process. When narrative or informational texts combine discipline-specific vocabulary, sophistication in structure, subtle tonality, dense meaning, and intentional nuance, they can create frustrating barriers to student understanding.

This proficiency includes three skills: (1) clarify, (2) interpret, and (3) determine. Each of these thinking skills is a tool to examine complex text in both narrative and informational sources.

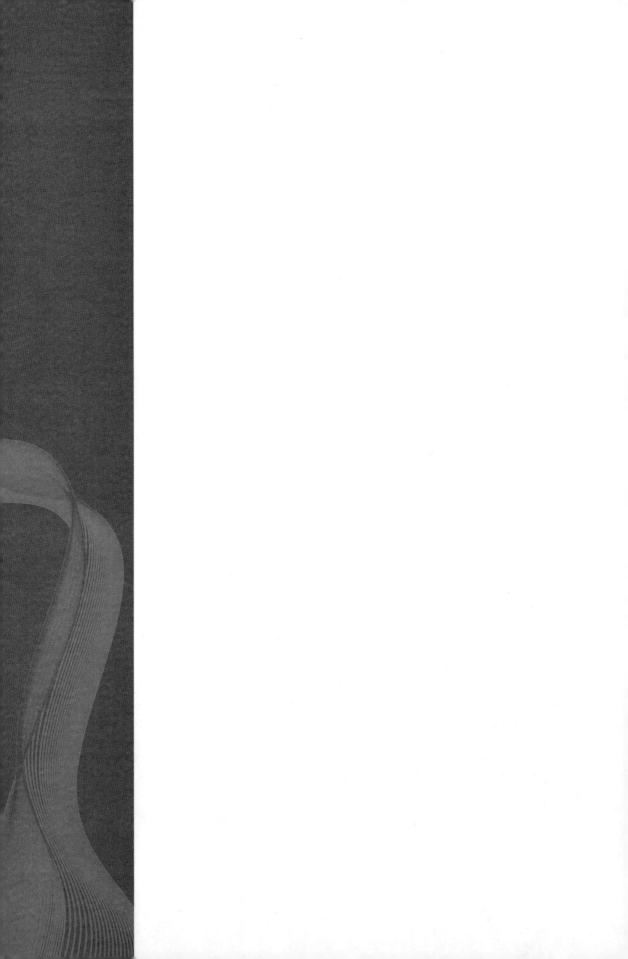

Chapter 7: Clarify

Clarity is the counterbalance of profound thoughts.
—Marquis de Vauvenargues

A senior in high school, excited about the sciences and determined to go into the field of biochemistry, decided to talk to a neighborhood friend who had an advanced degree in biochemistry. While they were talking, the graduate mentioned that he had done his dissertation on the topic of chemical bonding. Enthusiastically, the young friend asked, "Can I read it?"

"Wow! I would love that. No one has ever even asked me the title of my dissertation. Let me get it. You can take as long as you want with it."

The senior was eager and started reading as soon as he got home. After the first few pages, he realized that he was stumbling and sputtering his way through the text. He was surprised by the complexity of what he was trying to understand, including unknown words, confusing passages, and intricate diagrams.

Upon returning the tightly bound book to its owner, the high school student reluctantly confessed, "Quite honestly, I wasn't able to really grasp this. It is really complicated stuff."

"Hey, no worries. Of course it is tough to read at this point in your studies. That's why you're going to college. You need more background in this area. Your classes will be able to clarify all of this for you."

"Thanks for the encouraging words. I was feeling pretty stupid."

The skill of clarifying can involve a number of interwoven tasks, such as:

- Analyzing vocabulary
- Simplifying questions

- Illustrating with examples to explain a point
- Paraphrasing
- Referencing a relevant source
- Illuminating a significant phrase

As delineated in the CCSS, clarifying the meaning of complex text involves knowledge of three tiers of vocabulary: (1) everyday words, (2) words encountered most often in written work rather than spoken communications, and (3) words that are content specific to a discipline or area. In addition to clarifying for meaning, word choice and the tenor and tone of words may need clarification.

Clarifying also involves understanding complex sentence structure; compound sentences; adverbial phrases; parenthetical notations; and intricate, long, and meandering passages. Metaphorically, clarifying is running a fine-tooth comb through the passage to reveal tangles that need smoothing. Table 7.1 provides examples of what this thinking skill looks and sounds like in the classroom.

Table 7.1: Clarify Look-Fors and Sound Bites

Looks Like	Sounds Like
Students participating in peer editing	"Let me paraphrase."
Students revising their papers	"Let me say it in my words."
Students finding the precise word	"It may not be clear."
Students shortening a long sentence	"A better way to express this is . . ."
Students diagramming a sentence	"If I could clarify my statement . . ."

If there is one skill that serves as a foundation for many of the more sophisticated skills, such as making inferences and generalizing, it is this skill of clarifying. Clarifying an idea put forth in verbal or written form is the essence of understanding, comprehending, or making meaning. It is one of the most foundational steps in becoming a literate learner. Without the ability to clarify—to see clearly what the author intends—much communicated information becomes misconstrued. Clarifying is an essential thinking skill for literacy and learning across all disciplines.

Explicit Teaching Lesson

In the Talk-Through, phase I, the educator teaches the thinking skill explicitly. There are several elements to aid the teacher in this phase: motivational mindset, order of operations, instructional strategy, assessment, and metacognitive reflection.

To *clarify* is to make something, such as an idea or statement, clear or intelligible. Related terms include *explain, illuminate, elucidate, make transparent, unpack,* and *tell.*

> ## Examples From the State Standards: Clarify
>
> **§110.15. (15) Writing/Writing Process.** Students use elements of the writing process (planning, drafting, revising, editing, and publishing) to compose text. Students are expected to:
>
> (C) revise drafts to clarify meaning, enhance style, include simple and compound sentences, and improve transitions by adding, deleting, combining, and rearranging sentences or larger units of text after rethinking how well questions of purpose, audience, and genre have been addressed;
>
> **§110.15. (27) Research/Synthesizing Information.** Students clarify research questions and evaluate and synthesize collected information. Students are expected to improve the focus of research as a result of consulting expert sources (e.g., reference librarians and local experts on the topic).

Source for standards: Texas Education Agency, n.d.b.

Motivational Mindset

To introduce the idea of clarifying, divide the students into pairs. Have them decide who is student A and who is student B. Assign A the role of illustrator and B the role of communicator. Give the communicator a picture of an object (for example, a bike, backpack, or geometric figure), and have the communicator describe the picture to the illustrator, who draws exactly what is being described. When the drawing is complete, invite the pairs to compare the drawing with the original picture. Have students discuss what was and was not clear in the instructions. End the exercise with a brief comment on clarity and why clarifying is such an important skill in reading, writing, seeing, and listening.

Order of Operations

The skill of clarifying begins with a search for meaning, a crystal-clear understanding of what is being said or read. Then, one expresses significant words or phrases in his or her own way. The final step is articulating the idea in its simplest terms to expose its essence. This process is represented with the acronym SEE.

Seek the meaning of words and phrases.

Express this in your own words.

Expose the essence of the idea in the simplest terms.

For example, students consider the following Joe Wayman (1980) quote:

> If words remain words and sit quietly on the page; if they remain
> nouns and verbs and adjectives, then we are truly blind. But if
> words seem to disappear and our innermost self begins to laugh
> and cry, to sing and dance and finally to fly . . . if we are trans-
> formed in all that we are, to a brand new world, then, and only
> then, can we READ. (p. 46)

The students first look at the words and phrases that seem important (*transformed,
truly blind, innermost self*) and figure out what they are stating. Next, they paraphrase
and express the meaning in their own words: *readers must be involved in the reading,
not just word calling*. Finally, they expose the essence clearly, in the simplest terms, to
bring a final clarity: *reading takes the reader to a new place in his or her mind*.

Instructional Strategy

Post the Preamble to the U.S. Constitution for all students to see:

> We, the people of the United States, in order to form a more
> perfect union, establish justice, insure domestic tranquility, pro-
> vide for the common defense, promote the general welfare, and
> secure the blessings of liberty to ourselves and our posterity, do
> ordain and establish this Constitution of the United States of
> America. (NGA & CCSSO, 2010b, p. 93)

Also post the following four instructions.

1. Select three vocabulary words to clarify.

2. Write a clarifying question about a confusing phrase.

3. Paraphrase the Preamble in your own words.

4. Give a clear, simple, in-a-nutshell summary of the Preamble.

Have each student fold a piece of paper into fourths, number the quadrants from
1 to 4, and write the corresponding instruction in each quadrant (see figure 7.1).
Divide the students into teams of four, and assign each student within the team a
number from 1 to 4. All students follow the instructions and write their responses to
each of the four questions on their papers. When they finish, have students tear their
papers into the four sections and pass all the responses to instruction 1 to student
1 on the team, all the answers to instruction 2 to student 2 on the team, and so on.
Each student then prepares an oral summary of the four responses. Invite students
to share their team's responses in a sharing round, and finish with a final debriefing
of the activity (Pete & Fogarty, 2010).

1. Select three vocabulary words to clarify.	2. Write a clarifying question about a confusing phrase.
3. Paraphrase the Preamble in your own words.	4. Give a clear, simple, in-a-nutshell summary of the Preamble.

Figure 7.1: Example exercise for the skill of *clarify*.

Assessment

Have the students choose one phrase from the Preamble (for example, "insure domestic tranquility," "provide for the common defense," or "secure the blessings of liberty to ourselves"). Invite students to explain its meaning and restate the phrase to make it clearer to contemporary readers.

Metacognitive Reflection

Ask the students to compare clarifying the Preamble as a small group to understanding it on their own.

Classroom Content Lesson

In the Walk-Through, phase II, teachers practice the thinking skill within content-based lessons, providing guidance to ensure the proper application of the skill. ELA standard 10 recommends literature and instructional texts that are available for coupling with grade-level lessons (available at www.corestandards.org/ELA-Literacy/standard-10-range-quality-complexity/).

▶ Elementary Level

Clarifying meaning can be done quite successfully through dialogue. Divide students into pairs, and have them play the game *Tell and Retell*. Looking at a picture book, one student begins by telling the other student what is happening in the picture. Then the other student restates it in his or her own words. As the students work, monitor the activity and ask probing questions to help them go beyond simple recall and realize the depth of clarification. This demonstrates to students that they can clarify the ideas they see, hear, or read by paraphrasing or stating the ideas in their own words. If they can say it, they own it! Then have the pairs practice with the same picture book, but this time, they will read a page or paragraph to play the game.

▶▶ Middle Level

Practice the skill of clarifying by using optical illusions so you encourage students to look closely and examine the image for telling details. Optical illusions are highly motivational for teens, and they encourage participation because they are nonjudgmental. Use M. C. Escher's drawings or search "optical illusions" online for a wealth of resources that range in difficulty for age appropriateness. Use the experience to move to clarifying text as students read and notice clues and cues to the meaning of texts.

▶▶▶ Secondary Level

Have students read the following story problem and solve it using a graph with "Distance from home" represented on the y-axis and "Total time" on the x-axis. Ensure students use precision when specifying units of measurement and labeling axes so they clarify the representation of quantities in the problem.

> **Problem:** Sara starts walking from her home to the store. Ten minutes later, when she is halfway to the store, she realizes she forgot to bring money, so she turns around and returns home. She then walks all the way to the store in the next fifteen minutes.

CCR Performance Task Lesson

During the Drive-Through, phase III, the thinking skill is transferred to authentic applications using selected performance tasks from the state CCR standards, allowing educators to make a direct connection between the selected thinking skill and the new version of the standards. While Texas's state standard is presented as the example in this chapter (see "Examples From the State Standards: Clarify," page 77), the Common Core State Standards' *Appendix B: Text Exemplars and Sample Performance Tasks* (NGA & CCSSO, 2010b) is applied as a resource to the performance tasks in this section. There are almost always similarities among the state standards, and readers can consider the teaching of thinking skills within this example as they would their own state standards. The key is that the task requires a performance that demonstrates evidence of learning in concrete, meaningful, and real-world applications.

To deepen students' confidence with this skill, the teacher facilitates the student work, moving the students closer and closer to independent practice. Once the students are able to employ the skill independently, they are ready to transfer it across the curriculum. (For additional performance tasks, browse the state standards that appear in the References and Resources section, page 241.)

▶ Elementary Level

The following sample performance task illustrates the application of the ELA standard RL.2.5 (Reading: Literature, grade 2, standard 5):

> Students describe the overall story structure of *The Thirteen Clocks* by James Thurber, describing how the interactions of the characters of the Duke and Princess Saralinda introduce the beginning of the story and how the suspenseful plot comes to an end. (NGA & CCSSO, 2010b, p. 53)

▶▶ Middle Level

The following sample performance task illustrates the application of the ELA standard RL.6.6 (Reading: Literature, grade 6, standard 6):

> Students explain how Sandra Cisneros's choice of words develops the point of view of the young speaker in her story "Eleven." (NGA & CCSSO, 2010b, p. 89)

▶▶▶ Secondary Level

The following sample performance task illustrates the application of the ELA standard RL.11–12.7 (Reading: Literature, grades 11–12, standard 7):

> Students compare two or more recorded or live productions of Arthur Miller's *Death of a Salesman* to the written text, evaluating how each version interprets the source text and debating which aspects of the enacted interpretations of the play best capture a particular character, scene, or theme. (NGA & CCSSO, 2010b, p. 163)

Technology Integration

> **Featured Technology:** SMART Board, ShareFile (www.sharefile.com/fileshare), Microsoft Word, Twitter (https://twitter.com), Sticky Notes, Google Docs (https://docs.google.com) folders, RubiStar (http://rubistar.4teachers.org)

The following tasks provide guidance on incorporating technology into lessons using this chapter's instructional strategy.

Digital Integration Task

For a technology-infused multiday lesson, post the reading selection from the Instructional Strategy section on page 78 (the U.S. Constitution's Preamble), along with the four instructions, on the SMART Board. After students, alone or in teams, have completed the instructions' vocabulary selection step and written a clarifying question about a confusing phrase, have them share their work in Google Drive (drive.google.com). Identify confusing phrases, and distribute them throughout the class. Remind the students that the best questions ask for examples—for instance, "What is an example of a 'more perfect union' in this context?"

List the questions on a new SMART Board screen. Use these questions to guide explanations and discussion about the Preamble. After you clarify all the questions, instruct the students to open Microsoft Word or Google Docs to compose a summary of the Preamble in their own words, alone or in teams. Show an example summary to point out the features of a strong summary.

Ask each student to reduce his or her team's summary to a nutshell statement of the Preamble in his or her own words using Twitter, text messaging, or email. You may choose for students to share these summaries with you alone, or you may choose to project them onto the SMART Board and invite the authors to stand and hear constructive feedback from their peers (for example, "What I like about this summary is . . ." or "I think this is a good summary because . . .").

Grade-Level Digital Variations

The following sections provide grade-level variations for incorporating technology into lessons.

▶ Elementary Level

Show students how they can use online sticky notes (see note.ly) to ask clarifying questions about the narrative or informational text between partner teams. Model clarifying questions they could ask using the 5Ws and the H (who, what, when, where, why, and how). Instruct teams to ask three clarifying questions, each on a different sticky note, and send the notes through Google Share to their partner team for responses. When teams have finished answering these questions, have the teams send them back. Share some sample responses from the class.

▶▶ **Middle Level**

Develop students' clarifying skills by asking each team to email its completed electronic summary to the team sitting to its right. Have that team review the summary and pose clarifying questions. Invite teams to reply to the email with their questions so the original team can answer them.

▶▶▶ **Secondary Level**

In this long-term assignment (three to six weeks), direct students to make an e-folder in Google Docs to store the feedback they receive on their summaries. Continue each week with short essays or informational articles as the reading material. Have students work within their teams to ask clarifying questions and then share a teacher-made guiding rubric (created using RubiStar at rubistar.4teachers.org) to the team members' computers so together they may assess their use of clarifying questions with each other.

Reflection Questions

These questions are designed to enrich your learning from doing. Such reflection enables you to deepen your understanding of the lessons you have just provided. You might also consider modifying these questions to further guide your students' reflection on this thinking skill.

1. Where do you rank this thinking skill of clarifying in terms of urgency for your students in their reading and writing? (Place a check mark next to your answer.)

   _____ Very high

   _____ High

   _____ In the middle

   _____ Low

   _____ Very low

2. What habit of mind (Costa & Kallick, 2000) is most prevalent when clarifying ideas? Why? (Place a check mark next to your answer.)

   _____ Persistence

   _____ Tolerance for ambiguity

   _____ Precision and accuracy

3. Complete the following.

   ▶ My best strategy for clarifying text is . . .

   ▶ I like or don't like reading primary source text because . . .

Chapter 8: Interpret

Everyone is of course free to interpret the work in his own way. I think seeing a picture is one thing and interpreting it is another.

—Jasper Johns

An eight-year-old asked his mom a question: "When I was watching a rerun of the old *Mork & Mindy* show, Mom, Mork said that a traffic light has a green light that means *go*, a red light that means *stop*, and a yellow light that means *step on the gas*. Doesn't the yellow light mean *slow down*?"

His mom explained, "Yes, the yellow light means *slow down*, but Mork was interpreting what he had been observing. Sometimes drivers do step on the gas for a yellow light as they try to get through the light before it turns red. He said it as a playful joke on a comedy show. You misinterpreted what he meant."

"Oh, I get it. He was saying it as a joke."

"Yes, he described what he saw happening, but it was the opposite of what was supposed to be happening."

A reader needs a sophisticated level of understanding of complex text in order to interpret the author's meaning using the text itself and peripheral information. Interpreting meaning is a personalized approach to the text and presumes that the reader's scrutiny is heightened. Personal bias or point of view may influence that interpretation. Interpretation of complex works calls for a level of sophistication in "sensing" the meaning. It is not merely a literal summation of the words and syntax, but a rendering of the impression that the complex work transmits through the words and the syntax. It is this subtle but critical difference between clarifying and interpreting that makes the explicit teaching of the two skills essential.

For example, consider the phrase, "That's great!" How would you interpret its meaning? Is it a positive assessment, or is it a sarcastic comment? Without a known context, the interpretation may vary. In addition, the reader's level of cynicism may influence the interpretation, as one reader might assume a cynical viewpoint, while another assumes a complimentary one.

Consider another example: "The contents of the will came as quite a surprise to the heirs gathered in the room." This sentence could be interpreted as a good thing or a bad thing based on past experiences of various readers. If their prior experience of the reading of a will has primarily been with diabolical mysteries in novels or television dramas, they may see this as a warning of ominous things to come. But if they have had a family experience of a surprise inheritance, they may interpret this line as a sign of wonderful news.

These examples illustrate the intricacies of interpreting what one reads or hears. On the surface, it seems clear, but with nuance and innumerable extenuating circumstances, a more involved interpretation takes shape.

Table 8.1 provides examples of what this thinking skill looks and sounds like in the classroom.

Table 8.1: Interpret Look-Fors and Sound Bites

Looks Like	Sounds Like
Students collaborating with a peer	"Their performance was insightful."
Students changing symbols to words	"I think the message was confusing."
Students observing an object from many angles	"The data tell a story."
Students completing a mind map of key phrases from a speech	"His character was not convincing."
Students examining pictures of faces and naming the emotions expressed	"Here is what I think he is saying."

In the words of Mike Tyson (n.d.), "It's good to know how to read, but it's dangerous to know how to read and not how to interpret what you're reading." Readers cannot be word callers—focused only on the letters of the word and not the semantics. They must read *and* interpret the meaning of what they are reading.

> ## Examples From the State Standards: Interpret
>
> **Vocabulary Acquisition and Use: L.6.5.** Demonstrate understanding of figurative language, word relationships, and nuances in word meanings.
>
>   a. Interpret figures of speech (e.g., personification) in context.
>
> **Represent and interpret data: 1.MD 4.** Organize, represent, and interpret data with up to three categories; ask and answer questions about the total number of data points, how many in each category, and how many more or less are in one category than in another.

Source for standards: State of Idaho Department of Education, n.d.a, n.d.b.

Explicit Teaching Lesson

In the Talk-Through, phase I, the educator teaches the thinking skill explicitly. There are several elements to aid the teacher in this phase: motivational mindset, order of operations, instructional strategy, assessment, and metacognitive reflection.

To *interpret* means to explain, to provide the meaning of something. Related terms include *construe*, *disclose*, *elucidate*, *explicate*, and *illustrate*.

Motivational Mindset

To introduce the skill of interpreting, play a sample piece of music, and ask the students to interpret the mood of the piece. They must support their interpretations with an explanation. Use three extremely different musical examples. This sets the scene to talk about interpretation and the personalization that plays a role.

Order of Operations

The process for interpreting can be summed up with the acronym XRAY.

EXamine and express the gist.

Rank key words and phrases.

Account for tenor and tone.

Yield a personal opinion or interpretation.

When interpreting text according to the standards, an initial read is needed to examine the entire piece for the gist of the idea. For example, students determine that the main idea of the following passage is that the writer must write:

"Words on paper!" he told himself. "Words in the air don't matter. If I don't have words on paper I'm not a writer. I'm a talker! No words on paper, how can I improve a sentence? No words on paper, what's to work with, what's to send the publisher, Budgeron?"

"So simple. No mystery. Words on paper!" (Bach, 2002, pp. 16–17)

With that message in mind, students take a closer look at the words and phrasing. Words that jump out in this piece and that students rank as significant are *improve* and *publisher*, implying that the author is a professional writer. The phrase "words in the air" is an interesting way to describe talking rather than writing.

A student shares his personal interpretation or opinion of the text: "I think the author is saying that good writers write. I might also add that, in my opinion, this is a great piece to share with aspiring authors who need to spend more time writing than talking about their writing."

Instructional Strategy

The *one-minute write* is a great strategy to use to practice the skill of interpreting. Tell the students to get ready to write for one minute, uninterrupted, on a selected topic. They are to begin writing on the signal, "Begin!" They are to stop on the signal, "Hold up your pens!" Conduct the exercise as explained, timing exactly one minute.

When they have finished the task, ask them to count the number of words they wrote and put the number on their paper. Now ask them to set a goal for the next one-minute write on the same topic. They are to expand on the topic and, at the same time, try for a personal best in terms of fluency and word count. Conduct the second exercise just as you did the first. Afterward, have students count their words to determine if they met their goal and share both their writings with a partner, who will follow the steps of XRAY.

Assessment

Have half the class watch a famous political speech with the sound off, while the other half reads the speech. Those who watch the speech base their interpretation of what was said only on the visuals; those students who read the speech base their interpretation of what was said on the words only, without nonverbal clues.

Metacognitive Reflection

Ask students to discuss with a partner or group how interpreting is different from clarifying when reading complex text.

Classroom Content Lesson

In the Walk-Through, phase II, teachers practice the thinking skill within content-based lessons, providing guidance to ensure the proper application of the skill. ELA standard 10 recommends literature and instructional texts that are available for coupling with grade-level lessons (available at www.corestandards.org/ELA-Literacy/standard-10-range -quality-complexity/).

▶ Elementary Level

Have students prepare a series of role plays about scientific phenomena by "becoming" a thing and interpreting that thing through drama. For example, students could become a magnet, a mammal, a cell dividing, a pendulum, a molecule, an atom, a plant, a bee, electricity, light, or energy.

Next, in pairs, have them read a selected short passage in the science text and interpret the reading. Then ask them to compare how they interpreted their thing in a dramatic way with how they interpreted the reading. Make the point that both interpretations involved making personal meaning.

▶▶ Middle Level

Require students to find an opinion-page editorial about a local, state, or national concern that involves a civic issue. Have them read the article and interpret the article's meaning. Ask them to include the source, to define significant words and phrases, and to provide their opinion of the tenor and tone of the piece. Let them share their interpretation with a partner. Sample a few interpretations with the whole class.

▶▶▶ Secondary Level

Using a statistical graph from the stock market that shows the behavior of a particular stock, have student pairs research the company, read the graph, and interpret their findings, stating their opinion of the stock's potential. During the lesson, supply the student pairs with updated financial information so they are continually being challenged to justify their interpretation with real-time research.

CCR Performance Task Lesson

During the Drive-Through, phase III, the thinking skill is transferred to authentic applications using selected performance tasks from the state CCR standards, allowing educators to make a direct connection between the selected thinking skill and the new version of the standards. While Idaho's state standard is presented as the example in this chapter (see "Examples From the State Standards: Interpret," page 87), the Common Core State Standards' *Appendix B: Text Exemplars and Sample Performance Tasks* (NGA & CCSSO, 2010b) is applied as a resource to the performance tasks in this section. There are almost always similarities among the state standards, and readers can consider the teaching of thinking skills within this example as they would their own state standards. The key is that the task requires a performance that demonstrates evidence of learning in concrete, meaningful, and real-world applications.

To deepen students' confidence with this skill, the teacher facilitates the student work, moving the students closer and closer to independent practice. Once the students are able to employ the skill independently, they are ready to transfer it across the curriculum. (For additional performance tasks, browse the state standards that appear in the References and Resources section, page 241.)

▶ Elementary Level

The following sample performance task illustrates the application of the ELA standard RI.4.7 (Reading: Informational Text, grade 4, standard 7):

> Students interpret the visual chart that accompanies Steve Otfinoski's *The Kid's Guide to Money: Earning It, Saving It, Spending It, Growing It, Sharing It* and explain how the information found within it contributes to an understanding of how to create a budget. (NGA & CCSSO, 2010b, p. 76)

▶▶ Middle Level

The following sample performance task illustrates the application of the ELA standard RI.6.8 (Reading: Informational Text, grade 6, standard 8):

> Students trace the line of argument in Winston Churchill's "Blood, Toil, Tears and Sweat" address to Parliament and evaluate his specific claims and opinions in the text, distinguishing which claims are supported by facts, reasons, and evidence, and which are not. (NGA & CCSSO, 2010b, p. 93)

▶▶▶ Secondary Level

The following sample performance task illustrates the application of the ELA standard RI.11–12.4 (Reading: Informational Text, grades 11–12, standard 4):

> Students analyze how the key term *success* is interpreted, used, and refined over the course of G. K. Chesterton's essay "The Fallacy of Success." (NGA & CCSSO, 2010b, p. 171)

Reflection Questions

These questions are designed to enrich your learning from doing. Such reflection enables you to deepen your understanding of the lessons you have just provided. You might also consider modifying these questions to further guide your students' reflection on this thinking skill.

1. How do you interpret student behavior based on your personal understandings of students in your discipline? What are your key triggers for forming an opinion?

2. Which habit of mind (Costa & Kallick, 2000) seems most relevant when interpreting ideas? Why? (Place a check mark next to your answer.)

   _____ Thinking flexibly

   _____ Posing questions

   _____ Thinking about thinking

3. If you were to write a note to yourself about teaching your students the skill of interpreting and mail it today, what would the note say? For example, it might say, "I commit to teaching my students the explicit skill of interpreting what they hear and what they read."

4. Complete the following sentence: The most fascinating thing I learned in this chapter was . . .

Chapter 9: Determine

You can determine what you want. You can decide on your major objectives, targets, aims, and destination.

—W. Clement Stone

A youngster was asked to choose between two options. He could begin with one cent and have his money doubled each day for thirty days, or he could have $100,000 immediately. Even though the $100,000 seemed like a whole lot of money, he determined that it was probably a trick question, so he reluctantly chose the option of one cent a day, doubled. Once he had determined his choice, the teacher asked him to predict or estimate what the total might be. When he calculated the actual earnings of his choice, he was astonished at the total. And he was so proud that he had followed his hunch and taken the risk against his natural inclination. He had outsmarted the teacher on this one, and it felt like a victory.

The thinking skill of determining is advanced often in the CCSS. Students are asked to determine relationships, to determine key attributes, to determine the appropriate response, and to determine the central idea or theme. They are asked to determine the slope, determine the answer, and determine the mood of the story. They are also asked to determine the appropriate ratio, the best method for experimenting in the lab, and the subtleties of the relationship between the author and the point of view represented.

In essence, this skill of determining dictates the ability to see similarities and differences, to make sound judgments based on the perceived facts, and to venture a best guess with skill and grace. Make no bones about it; to determine is to risk an opinion, to see the implications of that determination, and to act on it.

To determine something in the course of reading, writing, speaking, or listening, the student must be actively involved in complex thinking. For example, the reader of a well-constructed short story must be immersed in rich details and compelled to go deeper into meaning, nuance, specifics, and word choices the author has made in order to verify or determine the author's intent. Complex text hones the skill of determining.

Table 9.1 provides examples of what this thinking skill looks and sounds like in the classroom.

Table 9.1: Determine Look-Fors and Sound Bites

Looks Like	Sounds Like
Students using a decision tree graphic	"This makes the difference."
Students comparing and contrasting	"I think it is a competitive relationship."
Students labeling load-bearing supports in a model	"It's hard to decide."
Students identifying who is the most valuable member of a science team	"A subtle difference is . . ."
Students highlighting text	"It's difficult to see any distinction, but . . ."

To determine is a resolute act that is woven throughout everyday life, a skill used by people who are able to thoughtfully and quickly navigate the options presented in any situation.

Examples From the State Standards: Determine

Geometry & Measurement (GM): 3.GM.3.2. Determine the solutions to problems involving addition and subtraction of time in intervals of 5 minutes, up to one hour, using pictorial models, number line diagrams, or other tools.

Vocabulary: 5.4.R.2. Students will use word parts (e.g., affixes, Greek and Latin roots, stems) to define new words and determine the meaning of new words.

Source for standards: Oklahoma State Department of Education, 2016a, 2016b.

Explicit Teaching Lesson

In the Talk-Through, phase I, the educator teaches the thinking skill explicitly. There are several elements to aid the teacher in this phase: motivational mindset, order of operations, instructional strategy, assessment, and metacognitive reflection.

To *determine* is to settle by an authoritative or conclusive decision. Related terms include *resolve, adjust, verify, arbitrate, decide, mediate,* and *referee.*

Motivational Mindset

To set the scene for teaching the skill of determining, conduct a few *right-and-wrong exercises*. Humans face these basic determinations on a fairly regular basis. Have students weigh in on one or several of the following sample dilemmas and discuss what helped them determine their opinion. Is it right or wrong:

- To double-dip with your chip?
- To borrow something without permission?
- To not invite a friend to an event?
- To tell a white lie or omit the truth?
- To refuse an invitation, or to go and not participate?

Order of Operations

Determining is a sophisticated skill that involves both analytical and evaluative thinking. When determining something, the brain is scanning for similarities and differences; at the same time, it is evaluating the options offered. While the student is determining a relationship between two arguments or weighing the differences between two economic philosophies, the brain holds the thoughts in balance. A systematic series of steps occur as a determination or decision is being made. To determine similarities and differences when making a judgment or decision, a reader or listener must put all options on the table, note the key points in each idea being considered, analyze and weigh the various choices, and, finally, express the selected option.

Determining could be used when verifying point of view in a story, when deciding who is at fault in a legal case, or when resolving which compound caused a chemical reaction. This process is represented with the acronym NOTE.

Note key points.

Observe options.

Think it through and identify possibilities.

Express personal choice.

For example, as a student determines the relationship between two leaders, Lincoln and Douglass, in a historical debate, he notes the key points of each speech. Then he analyzes the opposing views for similarities and differences. The student determines the extent of the adversarial relationship between the two and draws some conclusions about their arguments in order to think through the options being offered. Finally, he clearly expresses his determination.

Instructional Strategy

Use this interactive strategy to determine relevance, relationship, nuance, central theme, and bias, or, as in this case, areas of concern. Post a target topic, such as college and career options. Have individual students generate comments or concerns about their own college and career options and write them on sticky notes. Then help them determine what overall themes they are facing. Have all the students look over the collection of comments generated by their classmates, noting similarities and differences, and place the sticky notes into clusters with similar themes on a large board. Then, invite the entire group to determine all-encompassing, generalizable labels for the various clusters. In order to determine the labels for the various clusters that emerge, let the conversations revolve around the essence of each category. As this discussion moves forward with clarification, watch the ideas crystallize and specific headers emerge. Finally, have the students create a verb for each label to indicate the needed action.

Assessment

Ask students to determine the value of the following skills by jotting them on sticky notes and placing them in rank order.

- Analyzing
- Evaluating
- Clarifying
- Interpreting
- Deciding
- Synthesizing

Have the students discuss their reasons for the ranking with a partner and then work to cluster the skills into at least two categories and label the clusters appropriately. Then have them add a verb to create a final label. The ranking or sequencing of the skills or ideas deepens their understanding of each as the students have to identify, evaluate, communicate, and come to consensus. Clustering the ideas around a theme and labeling that group models the act of determination.

Metacognitive Reflection

Have the students discuss the difficulty of determining labels for the clusters. What was hardest to do? Easiest? Why?

Classroom Content Lesson

In the Walk-Through, phase II, teachers practice the thinking skill within content-based lessons, providing guidance to ensure the proper application of the skill. ELA standard 10 recommends literature and instructional texts that are available for coupling with grade-level lessons (available at www.corestandards.org/ELA-Literacy/standard-10-range -quality-complexity/).

▶ Elementary Level

Have the students collect rocks from the playground or park using egg cartons for the collection boxes. Students must each have a dozen rocks for the activity. Once back in the classroom, divide the students into pairs, and have them sort their twenty-four rocks into two, three, or four different categories. Then ask them to determine a name for each category. Invite each pair to share with another pair and discuss how they determined the names for their groupings and which was the hardest and the easiest to do.

▶▶ Middle Level

Assign various decades to student teams in social studies class. Ask the teams to research their designated decade and to plan and present their findings. They must determine five categories as their organizing framework and develop their presentation around those designations. Quiz the students on how they determined which categories to use to organize their presentation framework.

▶▶▶ Secondary Level

In mathematics class, ask students to brainstorm their concerns about mathematics in a nutshell statement, using sticky notes—for example, fear of failure. Then ask them to cluster the concerns that seem to go together and determine the labels for the clusters. Discuss their decision-making process in determining the headings.

CCR Performance Task Lesson

During the Drive-Through, phase III, the thinking skill is transferred to authentic applications using selected performance tasks from the state CCR standards, allowing educators to make a direct connection between the selected thinking skill and the new version of the standards. While Oklahoma's state standard is presented as the example in this chapter (see "Examples From the State Standards: Determine," page 94), the Common Core State Standards' *Appendix B: Text Exemplars and Sample Performance Tasks* (NGA & CCSSO, 2010b) is applied as a resource to the performance tasks in this section. There are almost always similarities among the state standards, and readers can consider the teaching of thinking skills within this example as they would their own state standards. The key is that the task requires a performance that demonstrates evidence of learning in concrete, meaningful, and real-world applications.

To deepen students' confidence with this skill, the teacher facilitates the student work, moving the students closer and closer to independent practice. Once the students are able to employ the skill independently, they are ready to transfer it across the curriculum. (For additional performance tasks, browse the state standards that appear in the References and Resources section, page 241.)

▶ Elementary Level

The following sample performance task illustrates the application of the ELA standard RI.4.2 (Reading: Informational Text, grade 4, standard 2):

> Students determine the main idea of Colin A. Ronan's "Telescopes" and create a summary by explaining how key details support his distinctions regarding different types of telescopes. (NGA & CCSSO, 2010b, p. 76)

▶▶ Middle Level

The following sample performance task illustrates the application of the ELA standard RI.7.4 (Reading: Informational Text, grade 7, standard 4):

> Students determine the figurative and connotative meanings of words such as *wayfaring*, *laconic*, and *taciturnity* as well as of phrases such as *hold his peace* in John Steinbeck's *Travels With Charley: In Search of America*. They analyze how Steinbeck's specific word choices and diction impact the meaning and tone of his writing and the characterization of the individuals and places he describes. (NGA & CCSSO, 2010b, p. 93)

▶▶▶ Secondary Level

The following sample performance task illustrates the application of the ELA standard RST.11–12.4 (Science and Technical Subjects, grades 11–12, standard 4):

> Students determine the meaning of key terms such as *hydraulic*, *trajectory*, and *torque* as well as other domain-specific words and

phrases such as *actuators*, *antilock brakes*, and *traction control* used in Mark Fischetti's "Working Knowledge: Electronic Stability Control." (NGA & CCSSO, 2010b, p. 183)

Reflection Questions

These questions are designed to enrich your learning from doing. Such reflection enables you to deepen your understanding of the lessons you have just provided. You might also consider modifying these questions to further guide your students' reflection on this thinking skill.

1. How is the skill of determining like deciding? How is it different?

2. Discuss with your team or professional learning community how the skill of determining might be used effectively.

3. Complete the following sentence: When I have to come to a determination, I work best when I am . . .

3

Comprehensive Thinking

When applied to how people think, the adjective *comprehensive* signals the type of thinking that is both broad and deep—all-encompassing. Comprehensive thinking provides us with a full grasp of the subject matter. In short, comprehensive thinking enables us to get the whole picture and understand it fully. For instance, if the topic of a seminar investigates the relationship of two different cultures, attendees will need to think comprehensively to understand the topic's full ramifications, infer connections that are not immediately apparent, and compare or contrast the cultures. In these ways, attendees discover the full meaning of the relationship between the two cultures.

The three thinking skills in this proficiency are essential for the development of student comprehension: (1) understand, (2) infer, and (3) compare and contrast. The first, *understand*, is the skill that enables the student to dig deeply into a significant topic or to answer a big question. The skill leads to the "I got it" element regarding the relationship between content and process.

The second skill, *infer*, is a sophisticated part of that basic understanding process. As students infer, or draw conclusions about what they can't see directly, they are forced to draw on secondary evidence by guessing or sniffing out the minute and sometimes invisible clues that let them read between the lines. They must rely on what they have stored in their brains from prior experiences so they can pinpoint the distinguishing factors that subtly define an idea or object and make it distinct from others.

The third skill that contributes to comprehensive thinking is *compare and contrast*. This is a dual-sided thinking skill that good readers may employ naturally but that benefits from careful nurturing. From their first years in

school, students must compare and contrast colors, shapes, sizes, word shapes, and sounds; good and bad characters in a story; and what is safe and what is not. In the upper grades, they compare and contrast civilizations, properties of matter, geometric shapes, story tone and tenor, and even the credibility, validity, and reliability of information they study.

Sometimes these three skills stand alone. Oftentimes, however, the full comprehension of a situation calls for their interaction. These three skills work together to provide students with not only a basic comprehension but also a deep understanding of the texts they read and study.

Chapter 10: Understand

All truths are easy to understand once they are discovered; the point is to discover them.

—Galileo

Teacher: "What don't you understand about the word *no*?"

Student: "I don't know."

Understanding goes beyond just having a sense of what is going on; with understanding, the student *knows* in a deeper way—a way that enables him or her to explain and elaborate on the idea, concept, or skill under study. To make sense, to make meaning, is implied when a student understands and comprehends.

Understanding is that foundational level of thinking that opens the doorway for more analysis, evaluation, scrutiny, and critical thinking about the topic. First, the student must grasp the meaning, getting the gist of what is there; then he or she can make determinations that are more sophisticated. With a basic understanding, students can compare and contrast, categorize, prioritize, predict, infer, and generalize.

In language arts, teachers want students to read an informational text or a fictional story with a sharp mind, identifying parts such as characters, events, symbols, and important scenes; examining characters' words and actions; finding the connections among the parts, words, and actions; and then communicating the ideas they have developed. In mathematics, teachers want to know how students have solved problems, why they reasoned in a certain way, and why that way ended in a logically defensible solution. Thus, *understanding* implies a deeper comprehension with the ability to not only explain but also use and apply that understanding appropriately.

The many applications of the skill *understand* all point to the same kind of thinking: making meaning of, making sense of, knowing in a deep way, getting the gist of, or knowing the essence of the information. To understand is all of the above, with the implied ability to share that understanding in some way. Table 10.1 provides examples of what this thinking skill looks and sounds like in the classroom.

Table 10.1: Understand Look-Fors and Sound Bites

Looks Like	Sounds Like
Students completing a mathematical equation on the board Students celebrating after a science experiment Students winning a debate Students completing a complex task	"I did this because . . ." "The reason for doing it this way was . . ." "The clues I used were . . ." "You will find the evidence on page . . ." "The most important ideas include . . ."

If students can't, don't, or won't read to understand, it affects everything else they do in the school arena. This leaves little doubt that understanding is most definitely a skill to teach explicitly to students as they approach narrative and informational text, as well as the speaking and listening situations that prevail in most classrooms. If students don't understand what they read or what they hear, the communication arts are not useful or productive. Understanding is the first measure of critical and creative literacy for students of all ages.

Examples From the CCSS: Understand

Presentation of Knowledge and Ideas: SL.5.4. Report on a topic or text or present an opinion, sequencing ideas logically and using appropriate facts and relevant, descriptive details to support main ideas or themes; speak clearly at an understandable pace.

Functions: 8.F.A.1. Understand that a function is a rule that assigns to each input exactly one output. The graph of a function is the set of ordered pairs consisting of an input and the corresponding output.

Source for standards: NGA & CCSSO, 2010a, 2010c.

Explicit Teaching Lesson

In the Talk-Through, phase I, the educator teaches the thinking skill explicitly. There are several elements to aid the teacher in this phase: motivational mindset, order of operations, instructional strategy, assessment, and metacognitive reflection.

To *understand* is to perceive the meaning of or grasp the idea of something. Related terms include *be aware of, be conscious of, comprehend, discern, fathom,* and *figure out.*

Motivational Mindset

To introduce the skill of understanding, ask students to pair up and tell each other a story about a time when they were expected to understand something and what happened when they did or didn't. Have them choose a topic from the following.

- To understand directions to visit a friend or a college
- To understand a joke
- To understand how to cook a hamburger
- To understand a decision that was made for them
- To understand . . . (choice option)

When finished, ask the students to identify what contributes to understanding. Make an all-class web, and add the responses.

Order of Operations

To understand an idea that he or she reads or hears, the student grasps the meaning of the main idea. Next, he or she identifies the details that support the main idea and tries to rephrase the information to make sense of it. Finally, he or she confirms the understanding by making a summary that captures the key ideas. To understand, a student must get the GIST.

Get the big idea, main idea, or theme.

Identify details to support the main idea.

Say it in your own words.

Test by creating a summary.

As students progress toward graduation from high school, the standards guide what they learn. Each year, the standards become increasingly complex. By the end of each grade, however, the grade standards return students to the same point—a deeper understanding of the curriculum content.

From the simple stories of kindergarten to the complex texts of the upper grades, it is essential that students sharpen the skill of understanding year by year so they can better grasp the fullest meaning of what they read. That sharpened skill is their key to success in the next year and in the world beyond their school's walls.

Instructional Strategy

The National Council of Teachers of English website ReadWriteThink (www .readwritethink.org) offers several interactive tools that focus on the various aspects of understanding and can help teachers develop their students' understanding. For example, the Cube Creator (grades 3–12) is especially popular with students. Teachers can use the cube to teach understanding of biography, fiction, historic stories, or science time lines. By starting with student-created autobiographies, teachers can use the cube to investigate what makes a good life story, one that projects meaning to the reader and reflects GIST.

Assessment

Prior to the strategy selected from ReadWriteThink, provide students with an age-appropriate rubric based on the GIST strategy (see figure 10.1 for an example). Ask them to read a preselected piece and use the rubric to decide how well they understood what they read via the GIST order of operations.

Understanding	Not at All	Some	Most	The Full Picture
Get Big Idea	No vision	Blurry vision	20–20 vision	Laser-like vision
Identify Details	Hands empty	Hands full	Arms full	Wheelbarrow full
Say It in Own Words	Communicated confusion	Created more questions than answers	Made the central point clear	Persuaded others on the subject
Test It	Nothing connected	One detail visible	Key details exposed	All details exposed

Figure 10.1: Example rubric for GIST.

Metacognitive Reflection

Ask students to complete the following two sentences.

1. I understand best when . . .

2. When reading a fiction story, I think I deepen my understanding when I . . .

Classroom Content Lesson

In the Walk-Through, phase II, teachers practice the thinking skill within content-based lessons, providing guidance to ensure the proper application of the skill. ELA standard 10 recommends literature and instructional texts that are available for coupling with grade-level lessons (available at www.corestandards.org/ELA-Literacy/standard-10-range-quality-complexity/).

▶ Elementary Level

Provide students with the following problem.

> **Problem:** Gina's mother told her that she could go online on her new iPad for twenty minutes. First, she went onto her Facebook page for seven minutes. Then she video chatted with a friend for one minute. Then they played a video game for eight minutes. How much longer can Gina stay online?

Solve the problem on the board, using a mathematical equation.

▶▶ Middle Level

Provide an age-appropriate graphic organizer for student trios. Allow each team to pick a story to read. In response to the ELA College and Career Readiness anchor standard 10 for reading (CCSS.ELA-LITERACY.CCRA.R.10), "Read and comprehend complex literary and informational texts independently and proficiently" (NGA & CCSSO, 2010a, p. 10), provide the students with time to read independently in class. Have each student complete the assigned graphic organizer alone before pooling ideas with the team. As a final product, ask teams to show their understanding by creating a poster that promotes the book with reasons why all students of this age should read it.

▶▶▶ Secondary Level

Select one to two days a week, or several minutes each day, for silent reading. Assign a book for all in the class to read independently. After all have done the reading, have each student complete a twenty-minute knowledge questionnaire about the main characters in the book.

Student teams can create their own questionnaires using SurveyMonkey (www.surveymonkey.com) and exchange them with another team. Use the information you gather from the surveys as a formative assessment for the next stage of this task. Divide the class into teams of five based on the assessment results. Differentiate assignments for each team.

- **Team 1, lowest performers:** Pick one object in the story that might be a symbol of the story's theme. Use a web to identify what characters do or say and what activities happen that support the symbol selection.

- **Teams 2, 3, and 4, average performers:** Identify one character in the story, and determine what his or her characteristics are. Compare one character to a person on the team, and create a Venn diagram showing similarities and differences.

- **Team 5, highest performers:** Pick one character from the story. Identify his or her key attributes. Select a character from a current TV show as a comparison. Identify the shared attributes, and prepare a five- to seven-page essay.

CCR Performance Task Lesson

During the Drive-Through, phase III, the thinking skill is transferred to authentic applications using selected performance tasks from the state CCR standards, allowing educators to make a direct connection between the selected thinking skill and the new version of the standards. While New Hampshire's CCSS-based state standard is presented as the example in this chapter (see "Examples From the CCSS: Understand," page 104), the Common Core State Standards' *Appendix B: Text Exemplars and Sample Performance Tasks* (NGA & CCSSO, 2010b) is applied as a resource to the performance tasks in this section. There are almost always similarities among the state standards, and readers can consider the teaching of thinking skills within this example as they would their own state standards. The key is that the task requires a performance that demonstrates evidence of learning in concrete, meaningful, and real-world applications.

To deepen students' confidence with this skill, the teacher facilitates the student work, moving the students closer and closer to independent practice. Once the students are able to employ the skill independently, they are ready to transfer it across the curriculum. (For additional performance tasks, browse the state standards that appear in the References and Resources section, page 241.)

▶ Elementary Level

The following sample performance task illustrates the application of the ELA standard RL.1.2 (Reading: Literature, grade 1, standard 2):

> Students *retell* Arnold Lobel's *Frog and Toad Together* while *demonstrating* their *understanding of a central message or lesson of the story* (e.g., how friends are able to solve problems together or how hard work pays off). (NGA & CCSSO, 2010b, p. 28)

▶▶ Middle Level

The following sample performance task illustrates the application of the ELA standard RST.6–8.7 (Science and Technical Subjects, grades 6–8, standard 7):

Students *integrate* the *quantitative or technical information expressed* in the *text* of David Macaulay's *Cathedral: The Story of Its Construction* with the information conveyed by the *diagrams* and *models* Macaulay *provides*, developing a deeper understanding of Gothic architecture. (NGA & CCSSO, 2010b, p. 100)

▶▶▶ Secondary Level

The following sample performance task illustrates the application of the ELA standard RL.11–12.3 (Reading: Literature, grades 11–12, standard 3):

Students *analyze* the first impressions given of Mr. and Mrs. Bennet in the opening chapter of *Pride and Prejudice*, based on *the setting* and how the *characters are introduced*. By comparing these first impressions with their later understanding based on how *the action is ordered* and the *characters develop* over the course of the novel, students understand the *impact* of Jane Austen's *choices* in *relating elements of a story*. (NGA & CCSSO, 2010b, p. 163)

Technology Integration

4

> **Featured technology:** SMART Board, Google Docs Network feature, ReadWriteThink (www.readwritethink.org) interactives, Adobe Flash, online journals (for example, dayoneapp .com), Book Adventure (http://bookadventure.com)

The following tasks provide guidance on incorporating technology into lessons using this chapter's instructional strategy.

Digital Integration Task

Open ReadWriteThink (www.readwritethink.org), and use the Search by Keyword box to find the Cube Creator activity (grades 3–12) from this chapter's Instructional Strategy section (page 106). Decide on the standards-aligned writing task you intend to teach by integrating this digital tool, and study the instructions for Cube Creator. Have students open Cube Creator on their computers. (You may need to help students install Adobe Flash onto their computers so they can open the activity.) Share with the students the GIST rubric (figure 10.1, page 106) for the process of understanding.

After students have completed the writing task with Cube Creator, ask each to complete the following prompt: "Generating many ideas before writing is a good idea because. . ." Invite students to each anonymously share their response on your SMART Board. Display all the responses, and highlight what is similar and different. At the end of the lesson, invite students to self-assess with the GIST rubric and your feedback.

Grade-Level Digital Variations

The following sections provide grade-level variations for incorporating technology into lessons.

▶ Elementary Level

ReadWriteThink provides a host of ready-to-go activities that promote deeper understanding throughout the primary grades. For younger students, the activity A Journal for Corduroy: Responding to Literature is a favorite.

▶▶ Middle Level

Provide students with digital (video, print, and audio) autobiographies about middle school–age students from diverse countries (http://bookadventure.com). ReadWriteThink's (n.d.a) interactive Bio Cube tool (https://bit.ly/2QfjyjM) helps students organize and synthesize information for use when writing an autobiography. Online versions of graphic organizers called *sequence charts* (https://bit.ly/2W0oGOC) can help students plan out their life stories. Extend your students' interest in the task by inviting them to illustrate their autobiographies. Use ReadWriteThink to engage students in critical thinking skills to deepen their reading comprehension. Help students transfer these ideas to their own lives by inviting them to write autobiographies.

▶▶▶ Secondary Level

Go to ReadWriteThink's (n.d.a) Bio Cube page (www.readwritethink.org/classroom -resources/student-interactives/cube-30057.html), and find the lesson for writing epitaphs for characters from plays and novels (www.readwritethink.org/classroom -resources/lesson-plans/analyzing-character-hamlet-through-956.html?tab=4). The site suggests students focus on epitaphs of characters who died, but the provided drama maps (www.readwritethink.org/files/resources/interactives/dramamap) can fit any character, living or dead. Conclude the lesson by displaying the epitaphs on trifold poster board or slideware.

Reflection Questions

These questions are designed to enrich your learning from doing. Such reflection enables you to deepen your understanding of the lessons you have just provided. You might also consider modifying these questions to further guide your students' reflection on this thinking skill.

1. What texts do I want to select so that my students have the opportunity to increase their understanding with increasingly difficult books?

2. How can I differentiate instruction for students who are learning to read for understanding with my selection of books?

3. What other ways can I differentiate instruction about this thinking skill?

4. When teaching for understanding in my subject area, what other thinking skills do I want to stress because they are connected to understanding?

4

Chapter 11: Infer

Scientific method, although in its more refined forms it may seem complicated, is in essence remarkably simple. It consists in observing such facts as will enable the observer to discover general laws governing facts of the kind in question. The two stages, first of observation, and second of inference to a law, are both essential, and each is susceptible to almost indefinite refinement.

—Bertrand Russell

4

"You are so wrong!" Kerry hollered at her sister. "When you don't have proof, you shouldn't infer that I did something I didn't. I didn't break your iPod."

"Says you," retorted Cali. "And besides, you don't know what you are talking about. The word you want is *imply*, not *infer*."

"What are you two arguing about now?" the girls' mother asked as she walked into the room.

"Two things: she broke my iPod, and her vocabulary stinks," snorted Cali.

"I did not, and my vocabulary is fine. She thinks she knows everything. I do know that a speaker or writer implies, and a listener or reader infers."

"You're right on that," their mother said. "So, Cali, what's your evidence that it was Kerry who broke your iPod?"

Sherlock Holmes is the master inference maker. He is the ultimate detective, finding clues most others miss, putting them together in ways no one else would think of, and discovering conclusions that always solve the deepest mystery. The scientist follows the same thinking regimen. Starting with a theory, based first on facts, the scientist gathers more and more evidence until he or she reaches a verifiable conclusion, or inference, with a sufficient amount of reliable data.

Authors, especially poets, turn the table on students. What they imply challenges their readers to infer. In one sense, readers have to assume the Sherlock Holmes role and go looking for clues about what they are reading. When they find the clues, they deepen their enjoyment of and involvement with the fictional word by making judgments about the characters and events.

Nonfiction writers are less circumspect. Rather than ask the reader to infer meaning from clues, the nonfiction writer presents the facts and guides the reader to a preordained conclusion. It is up to the reader to judge whether the literal data provided are necessary and sufficient for the stated conclusion.

Inferring is often referred to as "reading between the lines." It searches for the meaning that is sometimes hidden below the surface of the text. Inferred meaning is hinted at, implicit, not the predominant melody but background notes that weave through the piece.

Table 11.1 provides examples of what inferring looks and sounds like in the classroom.

Table 11.1: Infer Look-Fors and Sound Bites

Looks Like	Sounds Like
Students examining a fossil to determine its age	"My best guess is . . ."
Students improvising with another actor	"Reading between the lines, I . . ."
Students discussing the meaning of a poem	"I concluded . . ."
Students reading body language	"The clues tell me that . . ."

Making sound and reliable inferences is one of the most difficult challenges young people face in and out of school. In school, students are required to infer almost daily in literature, science, social science, and mathematics. Fiction writers often plant hidden clues to paint the distinctions that separate one character from another, often revealing key attributes. Lady Macbeth's bloody hands declare her role in the murder, but they also give clues about the depth of her guilt. In science, social science, and mathematics, students encounter facts and numbers that they must add up or put together to draw logical conclusions; they have to make inferences from stated and observed information.

Outside school, drawing inferences is no less important. From the earliest crib days, young children learn to read the faces of parents and siblings. As they grow older, they learn to study the words and actions of their peers. With these clues, they learn to form friendships or go a different way. Reading between the lines also helps people determine whether they should trust what they read, hear, or see.

Essentially, inferring is the skill of gathering data, reading situations or people, and making sense of what one sees, feels, and hears. It is a necessary skill for all learners. With a sharp ability to draw valid and logical conclusions from available evidence, students are ready to figure out the complexities of the world around them.

Examples From the State Standards: Infer

Draw informal comparative inferences about two populations:
NC.7.SP.3. Compare two sets of data within a single data display such as a picture graph, line plot, or bar graph.

Word Recognition/Vocabulary: 4.1.02. Infer word meanings from taught roots, prefixes, and suffixes to decode words in text to assist comprehension.

Source for standards: North Carolina Department of Public Instruction, 2017; Public Schools of North Carolina, n.d.a.

Explicit Teaching Lesson

In the Talk-Through, phase I, the educator teaches the thinking skill explicitly. There are several elements to aid the teacher in this phase: motivational mindset, order of operations, instructional strategy, assessment, and metacognitive reflection.

To *infer* is to come to a logical explanation or conclusion based on observations or facts. Related terms include *conjecture*, *deduce*, *derive*, *glean*, and *reason*.

Motivational Mindset

To pique students' interest in the skill of inferring, come to school wearing a T-shirt or hat from a special event (for example, a concert, a charity run, or a theater performance). Invite the students to share what they can infer about you from your choice of clothing.

Order of Operations

Inferring means looking beyond the obvious to understand the spin or slant put on the information. Students must investigate the facts, note the details, find a common thread, and explain the connections made that lead to a conclusion. This process is represented with the acronym INFER.

Investigate the facts.

Note all details.

Find the common thread.

Explain the connections.

Reach your conclusion.

In Shakespeare's Sonnet 18, he compares his lover to a summer's day, providing the reader with a list of comparisons that justify this love. It is the reader's job not only to enjoy the words, the metaphors, the rhymes, and the clever use of iambic pentameter but also to glean how all the comparisons are tied together as an impassioned plea for her love. Once that thread is apparent, it becomes easy for the reader to deduce how all the poem's parts fit together to show the author's deep expression for his beloved.

In the Shakespeare example, the reader must investigate the facts for meaning, note all the details of language that lend credence to the words, find the common thread of passion and love, explain the connection between passion and love, and reach the conclusion that this love will defy even death.

Instructional Strategy

Select an appropriate grade-level poem from the list that standard 10 of the CCSS recommends. Display the poem for the whole class to see, and read the poem. After the reading, ask the students to tell you what the poem says, to explain what the author implies, and to determine what they can infer. Highlight the words *say*, *imply*, and *infer* in your questions before making a list of their responses for all to see. Discuss the importance of each word, especially in language arts. Have the students apply the INFER process to see what makes sense, even if it is not explicitly stated.

Assessment

Invite students to share self-assessments of how they make inferences. Ask for explanations about the cues and clues they use to make inferences when they read, and ask them to share what they find difficult when trying to draw an inference. Have them use INFER as a guide to help them make this assessment specific.

Metacognitive Reflection

Have students complete the following sentence: When I read between the lines, I find it most helpful to . . .

Classroom Content Lesson

In the Walk-Through, phase II, teachers practice the thinking skill within content-based lessons, providing guidance to ensure the proper application of the skill. ELA standard 10 recommends literature and instructional texts that are available for coupling with grade-level lessons (available at www.corestandards.org/ELA-Literacy/standard-10-range-quality-complexity/).

▶ Elementary Level

In the classroom, on the playground, and in other appropriate locations in the school, post clues about characters in a book that all the students have read. Send the students on a clue search. Once they have brought back the clues, invite students to try to match their clues by character. Provide a poster board for each character so that students can attach the corresponding clues. After all clues are attached, randomly assign each student to a poster board. Ask the students to explain what the clues say about their character and to connect their ideas to what they have read in the story, making inferences that make sense from the information. Hang an INFER poster to which they can refer on a regular basis.

▶▶ Middle Level

After your students have read an age-appropriate, teacher-selected novel, divide them into teams of three, and ask them to create an *attribute web* on a large sheet of newsprint. The central shape of the web is a symbol that the team believes represents the character. The rays shooting out from the symbol are the words and phrases in the text that support the use of this symbol with this character. Have teams post or share their webs in preparation for a carousel discussion, during which they can cite specific textual evidence to support their conclusions.

▶▶▶ Secondary Level

Ask teams of students to select an age group in the community (no duplicates). As a class, prepare a health survey that covers all the groups, and determine a number of persons to survey. Have the teams select a sampling method they have studied and collect data from members of the community. After gathering the data, instruct each team to use the data to estimate the mean, and chart these means on poster board. Invite the class to ask appropriate questions about each team's methodology and the team to defend its selected sampling method. When each question session is done, encourage the focus team to draw a conclusion or inference about its sampling method and return to an assessment via INFER.

CCR Performance Task Lesson

During the Drive-Through, phase III, the thinking skill is transferred to authentic applications using selected performance tasks from the state CCR standards, allowing educators to make a direct connection between the selected thinking skill and the new version of the standards. While North Carolina's state standard is presented as the example in this chapter (see "Examples From the State Standards: Infer," page 115), the Common Core State Standards' *Appendix B: Text Exemplars and Sample Performance Tasks* (NGA & CCSSO, 2010b) is applied as a resource to the performance tasks in this section. There are almost always similarities among the state standards, and readers can consider the teaching of thinking skills within this example as they would their own state standards. The key is that the task requires a performance that demonstrates evidence of learning in concrete, meaningful, and real-world applications.

To deepen students' confidence with this skill, the teacher facilitates the student work, moving the students closer and closer to independent practice. Once the students are able to employ the skill independently, they are ready to transfer it across the curriculum. (For additional performance tasks, browse the state standards that appear in the References and Resources section, page 241.)

▶ Elementary Level

The following sample performance task is an example of the application of the ELA standard RL.4.1 (Reading: Literature, grade 4, standard 1):

> Students explain the selfish behavior by Mary and make inferences regarding the impact of the cholera outbreak in Frances Hodgson Burnett's *The Secret Garden* by explicitly referring to details and examples from the text. (NGA & CCSSO, 2010b, p. 70)

▶▶ Middle Level

The following sample performance task illustrates the application of the ELA standard RL.6.1 (Reading: Literature, grade 6, standard 1):

> Students cite explicit textual evidence as well as draw inferences about the drake and the duck from Katherine Paterson's *The Tale of the Mandarin Ducks* to support their analysis of the perils of vanity. (NGA & CCSSO, 2010b, p. 89)

▶▶▶ Secondary Level

The following sample performance task illustrates the application of the ELA standard RL.11–12.1 (Reading: Literature, grades 11–12, standard 1):

Students cite strong and thorough textual evidence from John Keats's "Ode on a Grecian Urn" to support their analysis of what the poem says explicitly about the urn as well as what can be inferred about the urn from evidence in the poem. Based on their close reading, students draw inferences from the text regarding what meanings the figures decorating the urn convey as well as noting where the poem leaves matters about the urn and its decoration uncertain. (NGA & CCSSO, 2010b, p. 164)

Reflection Questions

These questions are designed to enrich your learning from doing. Such reflection enables you to deepen your understanding of the lessons you have just provided. You might also consider modifying these questions to further guide your students' reflection on this thinking skill.

1. What rubrics can you build to guide your observations of students developing their inference skills?

2. What can you say or do to help parents appreciate the value of the thinking skill of making inferences?

3. Complete the following sentence: It is important for students to develop inference skills in my class because . . .

4

Chapter 12:
Compare and Contrast

Under the surface of contradiction lies similarity.
                                    —Asif Jordan

———————————

"My favorite sport? I'm not sure," said Thomas.

"Thomas likes any sport. As long as he can move." His mom chuckled.

"He plays hockey more than any other—all year round," his sister Anna said.

"Well, when you compare how much time I spend on each sport, I guess hockey is my favorite."

In their first months, babies recognize an increasing number of faces. Very early on, they distinguish the features of their parents from those of others who pick them up. When young children begin to read, they discriminate letters and sounds, recognize complex emotions that signal different reactions, and determine detailed similarities and differences in pictures. Progressing through the school years, children sharpen their abilities to compare and contrast all that they capture with their senses. Whether in mathematics, science, fine arts, literature, or social sciences, their minds group likenesses and separate differences in what they see, hear, and read.

Most children come to find it easy to pick the precise words for grouping objects that are alike. They learn to sort by color, shape, odor, size, number, and texture. They can create attribute webs or lists focused on a single quality in multiple examples: "Which objects in this room are blue? Round? Long? Short?" Even when contrasting two similar objects, young students often find it simple to list the characteristics that make the difference and note that "this is a pencil and that is a pen because . . ."

In the middle grades, as students move to more abstract thinking, some begin to experience difficulty with comparisons. For instance, when asked to complete a Venn diagram showing the similarities and differences between Asian and African elephants, many find it easy to note the physical traits they see or hear. But beyond the obvious, some students struggle with finding anything to say about the subtler likenesses and differences. There are those students who have not yet developed the abstract thinking processes needed to perceive anything beyond the concrete similarities (such as size, shape, and color). They are trapped in the literal. For instance, when asked to compare two characters in a story, students who have not developed their inferring skills may struggle to name any characteristics that relate to how the character might be feeling or how the character thinks and plans.

The ELA standards not only call for students to employ these twin skills of comparing and contrasting, but raise the ante to ensure that students will show the progress they have made in being able to apply these skills in increasingly complex learning tasks.

Table 12.1 provides examples of what the compare-and-contrast thinking skill looks and sounds like in the classroom.

Table 12.1: Compare-and-Contrast Look-Fors and Sound Bites

Looks Like	Sounds Like
Students completing a Venn diagram	"I see how they are alike."
Students sorting science specimens	"The opposing point is . . ."
Students labeling for classification	"I see how they are different."
Students debating an issue	"This is not exactly the same because . . ."
	"A different point of view is . . ."

The compare-and-contrast thinking skill is a basic cognitive skill. It is learned in the earliest years of life, determines early success in school, and leads the way to development of the mega skill of understanding. It doesn't stand alone; it relies on other thinking skills, such as inferring, analyzing, synthesizing, and evaluating. In its subtler form, compare and contrast suggests distinguishing or differentiating.

The compare-and-contrast skill has application in every phase of students' lives. When they go to the grocery store, they do comparison shopping. When they walk home, they differentiate their house from the neighbors' homes. They compare and contrast clothes, test scores, smartphones, grades, and TV shows they like.

In school, students can't advance without developing the skill of comparing and contrasting. In fact, Robert Marzano et al. (2001) declare the skill of finding similarities and differences to be a top-ten skill in terms of high-yield strategies in student achievement.

Examples From the State Standards: Compare and Contrast

Integration of Knowledge and Ideas: 1.9. Compare and contrast the adventures and experiences of characters in stories.

Craft and Structure: 9–10.6. Compare the point of view of two or more authors for how they treat the same or similar topics, including which details they include and emphasize in their respective accounts.

Source for standards: Louisiana Department of Education, n.d.b.

Explicit Teaching Lesson

In the Talk-Through, phase I, the educator teaches the thinking skill explicitly. There are several elements to aid the teacher in this phase: motivational mindset, order of operations, instructional strategy, assessment, and metacognitive reflection.

To *compare* is to show likeness or similarities, to note sameness. Related terms include *equate*, *liken*, *match*, *correspond*, and *parallel*. To *contrast* is to show the differences between two or more things. Related terms include *differ*, *deviate*, *vary*, and *separate*.

Motivational Mindset

To pique students' interest in the skill of compare and contrast, ask them to work with a partner and determine how they are alike and different. After the pairs find their similarities and differences, ask them to talk about which was easier to do—compare or contrast.

Order of Operations

When comparing and contrasting ideas, objects, people, and events, there are a number of critical thinking steps, represented by the acronym ALIKE.

Account for literal similarities and differences.

Look again; don't miss the obvious.

Investigate the hidden details of likeness and difference.

Know the categories.

Express in alternating or dual descriptions.

For example, students complete a very brief comparison of two cars—a Ford and a Toyota—using the ALIKE process. They first account for the obvious similarities and differences: the Ford is bigger and a brighter color than the Toyota; the Ford is more expensive. Then they look again for more data: the Toyota is a hatchback, and the Ford has a normal trunk space. Investigating further, they find that the Ford is made in America by an American company, and the Toyota is made in America by a Japanese company. The Toyota is in a category of "all options included," while the Ford is in the category of "all options extra." The students express their summary of the two: the Ford is more expensive with fewer amenities, while the Toyota is more appealing to the eye and has lots of desirable options. While this is a simplistic example of the ALIKE process, it demonstrates the thinking that is involved in comparing and contrasting.

Instructional Strategy

Divide the students into cooperative teams of three, and assign them two wild animals. Allow students to conduct research on the animals, both in print and online. Then ask the teams to create a Venn diagram comparing and contrasting the two animals and prepare to present their work to the whole class.

Assessment

Prior to the teams' work on their Venn diagrams, present an assessment rubric that will identify how many differences and similarities they should find and what evidence they should pick to illustrate both.

After student teams complete their Venn diagrams, invite one team to post its diagram for all to see. After noting what the first team presented and its match to the rubric, invite at least two other teams to present and contrast their diagrams so the class can build a final diagram that represents the most complete set of comparisons and contrasts.

Metacognitive Reflection

Ask the students to answer the following questions.

- When you were comparing the two animals, what clues were most important?

- When you were contrasting the Venn diagrams from the different teams, what clues did you look for?

- How did the Venn diagrams help make more complete and precise comparisons or contrasts?

Classroom Content Lesson

In the Walk-Through, phase II, teachers practice the thinking skill within content-based lessons, providing guidance to ensure the proper application of the skill. ELA standard 10 recommends literature and instructional texts that are available for coupling with grade-level lessons (available at www.corestandards.org/ELA-Literacy/standard-10-range-quality-complexity/).

▶ Elementary Level

Assign the students to groups of three. Provide a sufficient number of stories so each group has its own book with at least three characters. Invite the students to take turns reading the story aloud to each other before each selects a character to act out in a different voice. After they demonstrate their story to their group, ask the students to explain why they selected the different voices and prepare a presentation that compares and contrasts the voices.

▶▶ Middle Level

Give students twelve separate mathematics problems: four of them use only digits, four of them are story problems, and four of them use geometric shapes. Have the students solve all twelve and then, in pairs, compare and contrast attributes of the three different formulas. Ask them to answer the questions, "Which was the easiest to solve, and why? Which was the hardest to solve, and why? Which formula is most practical for real-world applications, and why?" To facilitate the students' thinking, walk among the pairs to listen and ensure they are answering the questions asked.

▶▶▶ Secondary Level

Divide the class into teams, and have each team choose a novel from a list of important books that have movie versions. Tell the team to read the novel first, with each person on the team concentrating on one character. Afterward, have students review their character in the movie by focusing on what the character says and does and what others say about the character. Instruct students to use a Venn diagram to collect the information. When they are finished, invite students to make a poster board contrasting the presentation of the character in each medium.

CCR Performance Task Lesson

During the Drive-Through, phase III, the thinking skill is transferred to authentic applications using selected performance tasks from the state CCR standards, allowing educators to make a direct connection between the selected thinking skill and the new version of the standards. While Louisiana's state standard is presented as the example in this chapter (see "Examples From the State Standards: Compare and Contrast," page 123), the Common Core State Standards' *Appendix B: Text Exemplars and Sample Performance Tasks* (NGA & CCSSO, 2010b) is applied as a resource to the performance tasks in this section. There are almost always similarities among the state standards, and readers can consider the teaching of thinking skills within this example as they would their own state standards. The key is that the task requires a performance that demonstrates evidence of learning in concrete, meaningful, and real-world applications.

To deepen students' confidence with this skill, the teacher facilitates the student work, moving the students closer and closer to independent practice. Once the students are able to employ the skill independently, they are ready to transfer it across the curriculum. (For additional performance tasks, browse the state standards that appear in the References and Resources section, page 241.)

▶ Elementary Level

The following sample performance task illustrates the application of the ELA standard RL.5.9 (Reading: Literature, grade 5, standard 9):

> Students compare and contrast coming-of-age stories by Christopher Paul Curtis (*Bud, Not Buddy*) and Louise Erdrich (*The Birchbark House*) by identifying similar themes and examining the stories' approach to the topic of growing up. (NGA & CCSSO, 2010b, p. 70)

▶▶ Middle Level

The following sample performance task illustrates the application of the ELA standard RL.7.9 (Reading: Literature, grade 7, standard 9):

> Students compare and contrast Laurence Yep's fictional portrayal of Chinese immigrants in turn-of-the-twentieth-century San Francisco in *Dragonwings* to historical accounts of the same period (using materials detailing the 1906 San Francisco earthquake) in order to glean a deeper understanding of how authors use or alter historical sources to create a sense of time and place as well as make fictional characters lifelike and real. (NGA & CCSSO, 2010b, p. 89)

▶▶▶ Secondary Level

The following sample performance task illustrates the application of the ELA standard RL.11–12.9 (Reading: Literature, grades 11–12, standard 9):

Students compare and contrast how the protagonists of Herman Melville's *Billy Budd* and Nathaniel Hawthorne's *Scarlet Letter* maintain their integrity when confronting authority, and they relate their analysis of that theme to other portrayals in nineteenth- and early-twentieth-century foundational works of American literature they have read. (NGA & CCSSO, 2010b, p. 163)

Reflection Questions

These questions are designed to enrich your learning from doing. Such reflection enables you to deepen your understanding of the lessons you have just provided. You might also consider modifying these questions to further guide your students' reflection on this thinking skill.

1. How could you reinforce the ALIKE process with your students?

2. Analyze the grade-level curriculum, and brainstorm ways to intensify the explicit instruction of compare and contrast.

3. What additional strategies can you use to develop your students' skills at understanding similarities and differences?

4

Collaborative Thinking

While collaboration is an acknowledged skill of the global community, it is also an essential skill of the school community. In fact, according to well-established and often repeated studies (Johnson & Johnson, 1975, 2010, 2014; Joyce & Weil, 1996; Kagan, 1994; Marzano et al., 2001; Sharan, 1990; Slavin, 1996), it is the number-one proficiency in terms of student achievement. Collaboration as a skill leads to its own benefits—including problem solving and leadership—but it also facilitates the implementation of other high-yield classroom strategies, like comparing and contrasting (Gokhale, 1995). Note that more recent studies add problem solving and research to the mix (Johnson & Johnson, 2014; Texas A&M University, 2013).

Several essential component parts of collaboration contribute to a successful structure—specifically, teamwork, communication, leadership, and conflict resolution. Teamwork skills relate to invested members working toward a common goal; communication skills foster a back-and-forth sharing of ideas; leadership skills showcase the strengths and talents of each member; and conflict resolution skills allow teams to move forward despite differences. Open-ended and challenging tasks, which students cannot complete alone but rather require students to think and make decisions to solve complex problems together, are a hallmark of effective collaborative learning (Texas A&M University, 2013).

Embedded in this atmosphere of collaboration are three specific skills that affect the results of the group effort: (1) explain, (2) develop, and (3) decide. To *explain* implies a two-way communication between the explainer and the receiver of the explanation and confirmation of message received. To *develop* implies that the explanations result in collaborative, ongoing progress. Finally, to *decide* implies that a sound outcome results from fruitful collaborations.

Chapter 13: Explain

If you can't explain it simply, you don't understand it well enough.

—Albert Einstein

Lamenting the lack of skill and understanding students have about algebra, middle school teacher Mr. Pedley said, "The question asked for students to show their work. This is what I got from Peter."

Name: *Peter*

Question #6

Expand: (a + b) – y

$$= (a+b) - y$$
$$= (a + b) - y$$
$$= (a + b) - y$$
$$= (a + b) - y$$

Ms. Meyers enjoyed the unexpected response of the student and got a good laugh, but sensing her colleague's frustration, she tried to respond appropriately: "Thanks for sharing your story. That picture tells it all. You must be a bit exasperated, but you have to admit, he tried."

"Yeah, he tried, but my worry is, it's either a hilarious joke on me or a very sad note on the state of affairs in my algebra class."

"Well, either way, as the English teacher, I love it. You know what they say,
'Stories stick and stay, but facts fade away.' It makes the mark in my book for a
great explanation on his part. He showed the skill as he understood it."

In developing the cooperative skills and collaborative spirit of teamwork, the ability
to listen attentively is important. To listen with attention means that the conversation
sometimes involves paraphrasing, affirming, clarifying, and testing options. When an
explanation is given in a collaborative process, there are explicit, attentive listening
techniques that should accompany the explanation.

A closer look shows that paraphrasing is the key to understanding. When students
can repeat or paraphrase in their own words, they anchor the learning. Another listening technique is affirming what someone is saying, signaling that the listener is
with the speaker. That occasional nod or intermittent "uh-huh" lets the speaker know
that the listener is there and hearing what the speaker is saying. Clarifying questions
also act as a signal that the communication is being received. The questions serve to
push the explanation to more detail and elaboration. The concept of testing options
is a final tool for attentive listening. Testing options sounds like "What if . . . ?" or
"Yes, but . . ." or "What about . . . ?" While explaining is an essential skill for collaboration, attentive listening is a natural partner in the discussion.

Both *how* and *why* explanations support deep thinking about complex texts and
help students in their collaborative tasks. Table 13.1 provides examples of what
explaining looks and sounds like in the classroom.

Table 13.1: Explain Look-Fors and Sound Bites

Looks Like	Sounds Like
Students talking using hand gestures	"I'm wondering why . . ."
Students talking to a partner	"Let me show you."
Students using a story as an example	"First, . . . , second, . . . , and third, . . ."
Students pointing to a time line and talking	"That explains it for me."
Students using a manipulative to show an example	"Your explanation is not clear to me."

The skill of explaining is found in most real-world communications and is essential
to productive and meaningful collaborations. It is used in giving directions ("Let me
explain how to get there"), in describing processes or products ("Can you explain
how this works?"), and in clarifying communications ("I want to explain in terms
that are understandable to all").

Examples From the CCSS: Explain

Key Ideas and Details: RL.4.1. Refer to details and examples in a text when explaining what the text says explicitly and when drawing inferences from the text.

Algebra: HSA.SSE.B.3. Choose and produce an equivalent form of an expression to reveal and explain properties of the quantity represented by the expression.

Source for standards: NGA & CCSSO, 2010a, 2010c.

Explicit Teaching Lesson

In the Talk-Through, phase I, the educator teaches the thinking skill explicitly. There are several elements to aid the teacher in this phase: motivational mindset, order of operations, instructional strategy, assessment, and metacognitive reflection.

To *explain* is to make something plain or clear, understandable or intelligible. Related terms include *articulate, tell, comment on, illuminate, illustrate, interpret, justify, make more explicit*, and *paraphrase*. In practice, when students are required to show their work and state the steps they used in solving a problem, they are actually being asked to explain their thinking in an explicit way and to track it on paper.

Motivational Mindset

To begin the lesson on the skill *explain*, provide each student with a cartoon. Have students, in pairs, explain to their partner what is happening in their cartoon. The partner can either add to what has been said or ask a question. Then, instruct students to change roles. Make the point that explaining is a basic communication skill that needs to be honed for use in many different circumstances.

Order of Operations

Under examination, explicitly teaching the skill of explaining seems to be a simple process. The explanation begins with a statement of the big idea, which is usually supported with a telling detail or two. The explainer adds any other details necessary for clarity. Finally, the explainer listens for any questions and responds appropriately. The process is represented by the acronym TELL.

Tell the big idea.

Express supporting statements.

Look for more details.

Listen for questions, and respond.

For example, after class on Friday, a student explains to a friend how to get to the campground. He says, "The quickest, most direct way to get there is to go by the corner gas station and take the first right." He continues with a supporting statement: "You'll notice a little sign that says, 'Caroga Lake,' just as you turn onto that road." He pauses as he tries to think of any other details. He then says, "I can't remember the name for sure, but I think it might say, 'Route 10.'" His friend asks, "How far is it from there? And, is it on the right or left?" The student then provides this additional information.

Instructional Strategy

Have your students practice the TELL order of operations by creating portmanteaus, or *sandwich words*. Choose a topic and, with the class, brainstorm a list of words that are relevant to the topic (for example, if the selected topic were friendship, generated words might include *buddy, trust, loyal, longtime, honest, reliable, fun, comfortable, time, patient, play, interests, dependable, partner, understanding, Facebook, long lasting, laughter, support, listener,* and *kind*). Have student pairs create a new word by combining two words from the list to create a big idea. The new word needs an explanation, so have the pairs provide a pseudo-dictionary definition. Invite students to imagine questions the sandwich word might raise, and add details to create a full description, complete with an example sentence.

Sandwich word 1: Plartner (combining *play* and *partner*)

Definition: Plartner (noun)—a good friend who will always be your partner during playtime

Example sentence: When it is time for recess, Bobby and I go together because we are plartners.

Sandwich word 2: Buddstanding (combining *buddy* and *understanding*)

Definition: Buddstanding (noun)—the ability of good friends to always comprehend what the other is saying or feeling

Example sentence: What Betty said may not have made sense to you, but I understood her perfectly because of our buddstanding.

Assessment

Ask the students to explain to a partner why it is important to know the history of words and their meanings.

Metacognitive Reflection

Have students write their responses to these questions: Was this open-ended assignment easier or harder than an assignment from the book? Why or why not?

Classroom Content Lesson

In the Walk-Through, phase II, teachers practice the thinking skill within content-based lessons, providing guidance to ensure the proper application of the skill. ELA standard 10 recommends literature and instructional texts that are available for coupling with grade-level lessons (available at www.corestandards.org/ELA-Literacy/standard-10 -range-quality-complexity/).

▶ Elementary Level

Have students work in pairs to read a picture book. Explain that one student should read a passage, and then the other should explain how the picture in the book supports what the author has written. Instruct pairs to take turns reading and explaining until the end of the book. Then invite the pairs to think of a story they both know and explain to each other what pictures would be appropriate to include in the story.

▶▶ Middle Level

Provide students with the following problem.

> **Problem:** How many different text messages can you make with the following emojis? Explain your answer to your partner using a mathematical equation.

▶▶▶ Secondary Level

Divide the class into pairs. Have the students scan a text for significant words and compile a list of ten to twenty. Ask them to cluster the words, create two sandwich words, and write an explanation of what the words mean, following the

TELL process. Once they finish, have them share their words and explanations with other teams.

Debrief the class with what makes a good, great, and grand explanation. What are the factors that matter? Then apply the skill of explaining to an illuminating episode in the text.

CCR Performance Task Lesson

During the Drive-Through, phase III, the thinking skill is transferred to authentic applications using selected performance tasks from the state CCR standards, allowing educators to make a direct connection between the selected thinking skill and the new version of the standards. While Delaware's CCSS-based state standard is presented as the example in this chapter (see "Examples From the CCSS: Explain," page 133), the Common Core State Standards' *Appendix B: Text Exemplars and Sample Performance Tasks* (NGA & CCSSO, 2010b) is applied as a resource to the performance tasks in this section. There are almost always similarities among the state standards, and readers can consider the teaching of thinking skills within this example as they would their own state standards. The key is that the task requires a performance that demonstrates evidence of learning in concrete, meaningful, and real-world applications.

To deepen students' confidence with this skill, the teacher facilitates the student work, moving the students closer and closer to independent practice. Once the students are able to employ the skill independently, they are ready to transfer it across the curriculum. (For additional performance tasks, browse the state standards that appear in the References and Resources section, page 241.)

▶ Elementary Level

The following sample performance task illustrates the application of the ELA standard RL.3.7 (Reading: Literature, grade 3, standard 7):

> Students explain how Mark Teague's illustrations contribute to what is conveyed in Cynthia Rylant's *Poppleton in Winter* to create the mood and emphasize aspects of characters and setting in the story. (NGA & CCSSO, 2010b, p. 53)

▶▶ Middle Level

The following sample performance task illustrates the application of the ELA standard RH.6–8.5 (History/Social Studies, grades 6–8, standard 5):

> Students describe how Russell Freedman in his book *Freedom Walkers: The Story of the Montgomery Bus Boycott* integrates

and presents information both sequentially and causally to explain how the civil rights movement began. (NGA & CCSSO, 2010b, p. 100)

▶▶▶ Secondary Level

The following sample performance task illustrates the application of the ELA standard RST.11–12.1 (Science and Technical Subjects, grades 11–12, standard 1):

Students analyze the concept of mass based on their close reading of Gordon Kane's "The Mysteries of Mass" and cite specific textual evidence from the text to answer the question of why elementary particles have mass at all. Students explain important distinctions the author makes regarding the Higgs field and the Higgs boson and their relationship to the concept of mass. (NGA & CCSSO, 2010b, p. 183)

 # Technology Integration

> **Featured technology:** SMART Board, Google Share, Wikipedia (www.wikipedia.org), Thesaurus.com (www.thesaurus.com), digital tree charts, virtual libraries, kid-friendly databases, topical URLs, Wordle (www.wordle.net), Teacher Toolkit (www.theteachertoolkit.com) resources, random word generators

The following tasks provide guidance on incorporating technology into lessons using this chapter's instructional strategy.

5

Digital Integration Task

To infuse digital skill development into the sandwich word strategy (described in the Instructional Strategy section, page 134), introduce your students to Wikipedia, which provides access to many topics. Have each team select a topic word or article using Wikipedia. After they choose a topic word, instruct students to read the article and select two key words from the first paragraph. These two key words will form the front and back halves of the sandwich. Have the team members also access Thesaurus.com (www.thesaurus.com) and explore age-appropriate, fun ways they can use it to play with and understand the key words selected for each team's sandwich.

Share the acronym TELL with student trios at their computer stations. Instruct students to think about and explain how TELL connects with the thinking they are doing in this sequence of activities. Invite the teams to search online for the words in the acronym and record synonyms from several different word sources. Give each team an age-appropriate digital tree chart to organize its results (available online at www.edrawsoft.com/template-blank-tree-chart.php; EdrawSoft, n.d.). For young students, provide a large sheet of poster paper and markers or crayons to each team so they can produce their tree. Add the branches as you introduce such terms as *definition*, *synonym*, and so on, and remind them to connect this activity to TELL. Let older students determine their major branch names. Then, invite each team to present their completed trees to the class. Each team member should have an equal turn to explain their chart and how what their group did fits with TELL.

Grade-Level Digital Variations

The following sections provide grade-level variations for incorporating technology into lessons.

▶ Elementary Level

Virtual libraries, such as the Kentucky Virtual Library (www.kyvl.org/?b=p), can help students take notes so students can explain what they mean by a word. Virtual libraries allow students to search kid-friendly databases, such as Grolier Online (http://emea.scholastic.com/en/grolier-online), so that they can find information that is appropriate for their reading level and age level and then construct explanations of a topic that make sense to all.

▶▶ Middle Level

Once students are familiar with sandwich words, spice up the sandwiches by sharing portmanteaus with the class (for examples, see https://bit.ly/2M6aajO; Vappingo, n.d.). Invite student trios to brainstorm possible related words and then build word clouds using Wordle (www.wordle.net) to share the words. Have the teams post these word clouds in a gallery walk (see https://bit.ly/1ConhN3; Teacher Toolkit, n.d.), and follow up with the discussion techniques from the Teacher Toolkit (see www.theteachertoolkit.com/index.php/tool/3-2-1).

▶▶▶ Secondary Level

To take the boredom out of vocabulary study, search for a free random word generator (such as https://randomwordgenerator.com). Give student trios a key vocabulary word from a lesson, or let teams select their own key words from the text or a STEM informational article. Share the random word generator with the teams, demonstrate and guide practice on how to use it with their words, and send them off to make their lists. On other days, assign a word cloud for discussion (https://bit.ly/1ConhN3; Teacher Toolkit, n.d.), fill in a free Friday with games of *Scrabble* or *Mad Libs*, or follow up with a creative writing activity (from https://bit.ly/1ConhN3; Teacher Toolkit, n.d.) as alternative vocabulary study methods.

Reflection Questions

These questions are designed to enrich your learning from doing. Such reflection enables you to deepen your understanding of the lessons you have just provided. You might also consider modifying these questions to further guide your students' reflection on this thinking skill.

1. An effective way to teach or explain concepts is by storytelling. How can teachers use storytelling in their explanations embedded in their lessons? Share an example of how you already teach using storytelling.

2. Have you ever considered that a disciplinary measure may be an opportunity to teach students the skill of explaining? How might you turn a disciplinary measure into such a teachable moment?

3. Considering that an explanation given by someone not familiar with the topic can be time consuming, how can the skill of explaining fit into a crowded classroom curriculum?

5

Chapter 14: Develop

An acquaintance that begins with a compliment is sure to develop into a real friendship.

—Oscar Wilde

A mom called to her son, who was in his bedroom, "Why do you read about those dinosaurs all the time? You need to get out and do things with your friends."

The son called back, "I don't do it all the time, just when I have some time."

"But why is it so important to you that you can't take a minute to socialize and enjoy the day? You have your head buried in a book or are online every waking hour of the weekend."

"Mom, you know what I told you before. To become an expert at something takes ten thousand hours of study and practice. If I want to develop into a prize-winning champion, I'll have to practice intensely for ten years. Well, I want to be an archaeologist, and to be the best one, I have to put in the time."

"What are you talking about? You're eleven."

"Yeah, but that means if I keep working hard, I'll be twenty-one when I am expert enough."

The more the individuals in a group work together, the more their collaborative expertise develops and grows. There is a developmental path that often occurs as collaborations advance through various stages. The four stages of developing skillful collaborations include (1) forming, (2) norming, (3) storming, and (4) performing (Bellanca & Fogarty, 2003; Tuckman, 1965). In fact, it is much like the path that professional learning communities often follow. The first stage is formally putting the group together or forming the collaborative team. Then, once the team begins to collaborate, the norming process evolves, and norms develop as the accepted behaviors of the group. As the collaborations develop into specific tasks, with robust and rigorous conversations, a third stage of the collaborative process emerges: storming. This is when the team members are struggling to reach a consensus and finding ways to agree to disagree and move on. Ironically, storming is a sign of healthy collaborations, because it demonstrates the development from placating people to offering different perspectives and different views. The final stage in the process of developing a sound team is the performing stage. Performing as a tightly knit team of individuals requires commitment and dedication to the higher cause.

Table 14.1 provides examples of what this thinking skill looks and sounds like in the collaborative classroom.

Table 14.1: Develop Look-Fors and Sound Bites

Looks Like	Sounds Like
Students with their heads together in conversation	"What about this idea?"
A student leaning in toward a partner	"I like what I am hearing."
Students gathering at a table	"I agree."
Students listening attentively	"You're exactly right."
A student indicating a point on a chart	"Yes, but . . ."

The story at the beginning of the chapter explores the concept of developing as an expert, which is somewhat different from developing as part of collaboration. In either case, the concept of developing requires mindfulness. Developing an idea is much different from simply having an idea, and this real-world skill of knowing how to develop one's thoughts is sorely needed for student work in all disciplines. Students must learn how to take an initial idea and develop it in full detail and to take the idea to completion. Voicing an opinion on the op-ed page of the local newspaper or on a favorite blog is very different from tweeting a 140-character thought about it.

Examples From the State Standards: Develop

Text Types and Purposes: W.7.3. Write narratives to develop real or imagined experiences or events using effective technique, relevant descriptive details, and well-structured event sequences.

Using Probability to Make Decisions HSS-MD.A.3. Develop a probability distribution for a random variable defined for a sample space in which theoretical probabilities can be calculated; find the expected value. *For example, find the theoretical probability distribution for the number of correct answers obtained by guessing on all five questions of a multiple-choice test where each question has four choices, and find the expected grade under various grading schemes.*

Source for standards: State of New Jersey Department of Education, 2016a, 2016b.

Explicit Teaching Lesson

In the Talk-Through, phase I, the educator teaches the thinking skill explicitly. There are several elements to aid the teacher in this phase: motivational mindset, order of operations, instructional strategy, assessment, and metacognitive reflection.

To *develop* is to bring out the capabilities or possibilities of something or to bring to a more advanced or effective state. Related terms include *disclose, elaborate, evolve, exhibit, form, materialize, untwist, unwind,* and *achieve*.

Motivational Mindset

Have the students imagine that a textbook has been invented that has all the answers to every question any student will ever need to know to complete his or her education and graduate. Their quick assignment is to develop a title and a slogan for the book.

Order of Operations

Developing ideas or strategies can be an independent endeavor, but in this discussion, it is placed in the context of collaborative thinking and teamwork. The acronym MAKE illustrates how collaborative teams develop ideas beyond the talking stage and into realized goals.

5

Meet to discuss the issue.

Ask questions.

Kick ideas around.

Express the goal and plan.

To develop ideas, team members must first find a time and location in which to meet and discuss the issue. Once the issue is on the table, team members more often than not will start to ask relevant and pertinent questions to develop the idea further. That usually leads to a more heated exchange in which ideas are kicked around to develop a fuller picture, which, sooner or later, must develop into a fully expressed, well-articulated plan if meaningful results are to occur.

Instructional Strategy

Problem scenarios are often used to express a challenge or problem that needs attention. Using "students trying to find balance between schoolwork and extracurricular activities" as the target topic, lead a whole-group discussion about this issue. Ask clarifying questions and help students see the idea from many perspectives. Then, divide the students into groups of five, and have them create a problem scenario around one of the ideas they discussed as a class. Instruct them to title the scenario, write a short description, and then develop three possible solutions.

For example, a scenario may be titled "Join Every Club." The description may be, "You are concerned that your GPA and entrance exams will not be enough to get you into your dream school, so to beef up your résumé, you decide to join some clubs. Soon, you find that all your time is spent preparing to attend or attending meetings. Your schoolwork is beginning to suffer. What will you do?"

Explain that the groups must use the MAKE strategy when developing both the scenario and the solutions.

Assessment

Develop a student-designed handbook for incoming high school freshmen that will help them with the pressure of college preparation.

Metacognitive Reflection

Give students the beginning of a story line, and ask them to develop a surprise or unexpected ending to the situation presented. Use picture book stories, historical scenarios, or current events that are playing out in the news. The idea is to have them develop an ending that is plausible but not necessarily probable.

Classroom Content Lesson

In the Walk-Through, phase II, teachers practice the thinking skill within content-based lessons, providing guidance to ensure the proper application of the skill. ELA standard 10 recommends literature and instructional texts that are available for coupling with grade-level lessons (available at www.corestandards.org/ELA-Literacy/standard-10-range-quality-complexity/).

▶ Elementary Level

Teach the students how to create problem scenarios, and then assign them to create their own problem scenarios based on a unit of study in science or social studies. Assign the students roles: "You are . . . What will you do?" Have students discuss the situations and try to come up with alternative solutions.

For example, in a science class, student teams are asked to create possible problem scenarios that an explorer may encounter when traveling to the Arctic. They then exchange scenarios and provide three possible solutions.

▶▶ Middle Level

Instruct two students working collaboratively to develop a uniform probability model for the following problem by assigning equal probability to all outcomes. Then, have the students use the model to determine probabilities of events.

> **Problem:** If a student is selected at random from a class, find the probability that Devon will be selected and the probability that a girl will be selected.

▶▶▶ Secondary Level

Ask pairs of students to develop scenarios about careers or college using stakeholder roles and open-ended questions: "You are a . . . What will you do?" In the next period, have them exchange scenarios with another pair and develop responses to the scenario, which will be included in a presentation.

CCR Performance Task Lesson

During the Drive-Through, phase III, the thinking skill is transferred to authentic applications using selected performance tasks from the state CCR standards, allowing educators to make a direct connection between the selected thinking skill and the new version of the standards. While New Jersey's state standard is presented as the example in this chapter (see "Examples From the State Standards: Develop," page 143), the Common Core

State Standards' *Appendix B: Text Exemplars and Sample Performance Tasks* (NGA & CCSSO, 2010b) is applied as a resource to the performance tasks in this section. There are almost always similarities among the state standards, and readers can consider the teaching of thinking skills within this example as they would their own state standards. The key is that the task requires a performance that demonstrates evidence of learning in concrete, meaningful, and real-world applications.

To deepen students' confidence with this skill, the teacher facilitates the student work, moving the students closer and closer to independent practice. Once the students are able to employ the skill independently, they are ready to transfer it across the curriculum. (For additional performance tasks, browse the state standards that appear in the References and Resources section, page 241.)

▶ Elementary Level

The following sample performance task illustrates the application of the ELA standard RL.1.1 (Reading: Literature, grade 1, standard 1):

> Students (with prompting and support from the teacher), when listening to Laura Ingalls Wilder's *Little House in the Big Woods*, ask questions about the events that occur (such as the encounter with the bear) and answer by offering key details drawn from the text. (NGA & CCSSO, 2010b, p. 28)

▶▶ Middle Level

The following sample performance task illustrates the application of the ELA standard RL.6.6 (Reading: Literature, grade 6, standard 6):

> Students explain how Sandra Cisneros's choice of words develops the point of view of the young speaker in her story "Eleven." (NGA & CCSSO, 2010b, p. 89)

▶▶▶ Secondary Level

The following sample performance task illustrates the application of the ELA standard RL.11–12.3 (Reading: Literature, grades 11–12, standard 3):

> Students analyze the first impressions given of Mr. and Mrs. Bennet in the opening chapter of *Pride and Prejudice* based on the setting and how the characters are introduced. By comparing these first impressions with their later understanding based on how the action is ordered and the characters develop over the course of the novel, students understand the impact of Jane Austen's choices in relating elements of a story. (NGA & CCSSO, 2010b, p. 163)

Reflection Questions

These questions are designed to enrich your learning from doing. Such reflection enables you to deepen your understanding of the lessons you have just provided. You might also consider modifying these questions to further guide your students' reflection on this thinking skill.

1. Read this quote: "You must take action now that will move you towards your goals. Develop a sense of urgency in your life" (H. Jackson Brown, Jr. Quotes, n.d.). How might your professional learning community or team develop a sense of urgency in the school about 21st century skills? Why would you do that?

2. Using a standards-based traditional lesson, write a problem scenario for students. How might you invite them into the investigation and turn the lesson into an inquiry lesson?

3. Complete the following sentence: I would like to develop . . .

5

Chapter 15: Decide

Nothing is more difficult, and therefore more precious, than to be able to decide.

—Napoleon Bonaparte

———————————

Two high school students were moving a piano for the music director. They were asked to put it somewhere out of the way until after the parent conferences. As they moved down the hallway, headed for the stairwell, they were noticeably laboring and struggling with the weight and size of the piano. One of the boys said, "I don't think we are ever going to get this thing up to the fourth floor."

His partner said, "Up? I thought we were taking it down."

Moral of the story: decide where you are going, or you won't know when you get there.

To decide—to plan and settle on a final outcome—is an act of evaluation, prioritization, and commitment. Decision making is no easy task as one must weigh the pros and cons, or the strengths and weaknesses, of the various options, but to do this in a collaborative environment, in which multiple opinions abound, is even more difficult. Deciding as a team involves a complex matrix of effective communication, clarity of thought, effective arguments, and willingness to compromise, and the decision requires commitment if it is to succeed fully.

Table 15.1 (page 150) provides examples of what this thinking skill looks and sounds like in the collaborative classroom.

Table 15.1: Decide Look-Fors and Sound Bites

Looks Like	Sounds Like
Students creating charts of pros and cons	"How many agree?"
Students filling out a T-chart for strengths and weaknesses	"Let's look at the options."
Students participating in team meetings	"What are the pros? Cons?"
Students putting their heads together	"My decision is based on . . ."
Students voting	"I prefer this one because . . ."

Deciding is a necessary skill if students are to become productive problem solvers and creative innovators, both in and out of school. There is no college, career, or life situation in which decision making does not play a role.

Examples From the State Standards: Decide

Understand congruence in terms of rigid motions: G-CO.B.6. Use geometric descriptions of rigid motions to transform figures and to predict the effect of a given rigid motion on a given figure; given two figures, use the definition of congruence in terms of rigid motions to decide if they are congruent. (DOK 1,2)

Make inferences and justify conclusions from sample surveys, experiments, and observational studies: S-IC.B.5. Use data from a randomized experiment to compare two treatments; use simulations to decide if differences between parameters are significant. (DOK 2,3)

Source for standards: Iowa Department of Education, 2010.

Explicit Teaching Lesson

In the Talk-Through, phase I, the educator teaches the thinking skill explicitly. There are several elements to aid the teacher in this phase: motivational mindset, order of operations, instructional strategy, assessment, and metacognitive reflection.

To *decide* is to solve or conclude a question, controversy, or struggle by giving victory to one side. Related terms include *resolve, award, choose, conclude, decree,* and *establish.*

Motivational Mindset

To introduce the skill of deciding, ask students to pair up and talk about their decision-making processes. They should share the answers to the following questions.

- How do you balance work and play?
- What is your favorite thing to do when you have free time?
- What is your decision-making process?

This activity works best if each partner talks about the first question before moving on to the second question and so on, so there is more back-and-forth conversation about making decisions.

Order of Operations

Decision making is a process that embraces a series of steps to arrive at that final decision. It is often a time-consuming task that requires robust interactions to understand the entire situation. The KNOW acronym delineates this process.

Know all the options.

Note the pluses and minuses, pros and cons.

Outline probable, possible, and preferable solutions.

Welcome a decision, and celebrate.

Everyone, including students, makes decisions automatically as part of everyday life. Being aware of that decision-making process and being able to reflect on and improve that process is another issue entirely.

Instructional Strategy

Create a *differentiated lesson* on the Civil War that requires students to make decisions about how they will represent what they have learned. The assignment is to write an essay about the Civil War using one of four focuses: (1) the people, (2) the causes, (3) the outcomes, or (4) the battles. Have students decide which will be their focus using the KNOW process. For example, first, ensure the students are aware of the topic options: the people, the causes, the outcomes, and the battles. Then, have students note the pluses and minuses of each possible option by listing the pros and cons. Next, instruct students to outline probable obstacles to overcome, possible resources they can depend on, and preferable solutions. Finally, allow them to select their preferred topic and begin their essay with the focus they have decided on.

The decision-making process continues at this point. For example, if a student chooses to write an essay with a focus on the people, he or she will have to decide whether to write about a group of people, a specific family, or an individual. He or she will need to decide whether these people represented the North or the South, if they were historically significant, or if they were simply representatives of a type of people who contributed to the history of the Civil War.

Each step of the way, require the students to use the KNOW order of operations to work through their decisions and to make clear their thinking processes, in addition to writing the final essay on the Civil War.

Assessment

Have students apply the KNOW decision-making process in another assignment they already did in another subject area, giving details of how it might have improved the final assignment.

Metacognitive Reflection

Have students respond to the question, Do you agree or disagree with the statement "A good decision-making process always results in a good decision"? Why or why not?

Classroom Content Lesson

In the Walk-Through, phase II, teachers practice the thinking skill within content-based lessons, providing guidance to ensure the proper application of the skill. ELA standard 10 recommends literature and instructional texts that are available for coupling with grade-level lessons (available at www.corestandards.org/ELA-Literacy/standard-10-range -quality-complexity/).

▶ Elementary Level

Ask students, in a whole-group discussion, to decide on the top five most popular books for their grade level by using the KNOW process. Allow all students to nominate books for consideration with a justification statement, which is then followed by a group discussion. Then help the students decide on the winners by voting with secret ballots. Initiate a celebration by featuring the covers of all five chosen books on a poster and hanging it on the bulletin board for Parent Night.

▶▶ Middle Level

Have students research and decide, using the KNOW process, which five U.S. government documents are most important for teenagers to be familiar with. Instruct students to nominate and justify their document choice with three valid reasons. Facilitate discussions and question-and-answer sessions, and follow these with secret ballot voting, allowing students to rate each candidate document on a scale of 1 to 10. Add up the ballots' votes to decide the winning five. Initiate a celebration for the decision by reading the first paragraphs of the five winning documents over the school's PA system.

▶▶▶ Secondary Level

Have the students research and decide, using the KNOW process, which are the five most important scientific discoveries to impact the world as we know it. Direct students to present each candidate discovery in a team presentation that includes vital information. Help students decide on the top five through discussions of the pros and cons of each and then by a final and secret ballot vote. Share the winning five in an artistic display in the entrance hall showcase.

CCR Performance Task Lesson

During the Drive-Through, phase III, the thinking skill is transferred to authentic applications using selected performance tasks from the state CCR standards, allowing educators to make a direct connection between the selected thinking skill and the new version of the standards. While Iowa's state standard is presented as the example in this chapter (see "Examples From the State Standards: Decide," page 150), the Common Core State Standards' *Appendix B: Text Exemplars and Sample Performance Tasks* (NGA & CCSSO, 2010b) is applied as a resource to the performance tasks in this section. There are almost always similarities among the state standards, and readers can consider the teaching of thinking skills within this example as they would their own state standards. The key is that the task requires a performance that demonstrates evidence of learning in concrete, meaningful, and real-world applications.

To deepen students' confidence with this skill, the teacher facilitates the student work, moving the students closer and closer to independent practice. Once the students are able to employ the skill independently, they are ready to transfer it across the curriculum. (For additional performance tasks, browse the state standards that appear in the References and Resources section, page 241.)

▶ Elementary Level

The following sample performance task illustrates the application of the ELA standard RI.K.4 (Reading: Informational Text, grade K, standard 4):

> Students ask and answer questions about animals (e.g., hyena, alligator, platypus, scorpion) they encounter in Steve Jenkins and Robin Page's *What Do You Do With a Tail Like This?* (NGA & CCSSO, 2010b, p. 36)

▶▶ Middle Level

The following sample performance task illustrates the application of the ELA standard RL.6.1 (Reading: Literature, grade 6, standard 1):

5

Students cite explicit textual evidence as well as draw inferences about the drake and the duck from Katherine Paterson's *The Tale of the Mandarin Ducks* to support their analysis of the perils of vanity. (NGA & CCSSO, 2010b, p. 89)

►►► Secondary Level

The following sample performance task illustrates the application of the ELA standard RI.11–12.6 (Reading: Informational Text, grades 11–12, standard 6):

Students determine Richard Hofstadter's purpose and point of view in his "Abraham Lincoln and the Self-Made Myth," analyzing how both Hofstadter's style and content contribute to the eloquent and powerful contrast he draws between the younger, ambitious Lincoln and the sober, more reflective man of the presidential years. (NGA & CCSSO, 2010b, p. 171)

Reflection Questions

These questions are designed to enrich your learning from doing. Such reflection enables you to deepen your understanding of the lessons you have just provided. You might also consider modifying these questions to further guide your students' reflection on this thinking skill.

1. List ten on-your-feet decisions you made today.

2. Use the KNOW process on a personal decision, such as a big-item purchase, vacation plans, or a career choice. Then have your students do the same kind of activity with their parents.

3. Rank your personal experience with decision making by completing this sentence: Decision making is _____ for me because . . . (Fill in the blank with one of the following.)

   ► A breeze

   ► Relatively easy

   ► Deliberative

   ► Relatively hard

   ► Agonizing

Communicative Thinking

What do researcher Michelle Dawson, inventor Temple Grandin, composer Hikari Ōe, wildlife illustrator Dylan Pierce, and Australian author Donna Williams have in common? All these brilliant minds are challenged with autism. In their younger years, these famous individuals struggled to communicate by the spoken word with most people who met them. The fault was not in the listeners, nor in the speakers. Each one of these people with a high-functioning mind found it difficult to speak with precise language just what was on his or her mind.

Although these are special cases, there are many students who are inhibited by one challenge or another when explaining what they want others to understand. Communication doesn't work well. Sometimes the break is with the spoken word. Other times, it is with the written word.

Teachers may often assume that this inability to communicate is due to the person's mental ability. However, this is seldom the case. Some students have difficulty gathering the information they need to understand an idea. Blind and dyslexic students face this challenge. Others lack skill in processing information. Others still struggle with communicating. Teachers can help these students strengthen their communicative skills, especially in classrooms that intentionally adopt project-based learning and active inquiry instruction. Both models provide teachers with multiple opportunities to integrate written and spoken communication for daily instruction and practice.

The three skills described in this chapter—(1) reasoning, (2) connecting, and (3) representing—are critical to the expression of meaning. These communicative skills appear in all subject areas as essential means for presenting information to another's ears or eyes. The ability to *reason* is to be able to make logical sense of ideas as the first step toward communicating ideas. In like manner, *connecting* is a highly relevant skill that synthesizes facts, data, and other inputs into meaningful patterns. These chunks of information help students consolidate ideas, create relevant findings, and present the findings to others. Finally, the third skill, *representing*, allows the presenter to transform words into images or vice versa so listeners and readers can picture the concept or fact. All three are directly connected to making sense of information and sharing that interpretation with others.

Chapter 16: Reason

People are generally better persuaded by the reasons which they have themselves discovered than by those which have come into the mind of others.

—Blaise Pascal

———————————————

After Julie dropped the bus fare in the box, she took the third aisle seat. To her astonishment, the passenger in the window seat addressed her: "Well, Mrs. Peterson, where are you going today?"

Julie asked the lady if they had met before.

"Oh, no. I never laid eyes on you before you got on the bus."

"Then how do you know my name?" Julie asked.

"Oh, that is easy," the lady responded. "The tag on your satchel gives your name, and the ring on your finger says you are married. It's simple logic, and I'm good at reasoning."

The act of reasoning has rules. A must follow B with a sufficient line of evidence. All the facts selected must contribute to the argument. No facts may be extraneous or unconnected. Each one says something, and when they are connected, we reach a conclusion.

"What's your reason?" or "Why do you think that?" is the most important question teachers can ask after students have presented an answer. In providing their reason, students must explain a situation or circumstance that made certain results seem possible or appropriate. Sometimes the reason is tight and clear, as in the case of cause and effect—the weak center support collapsed, causing the bridge to fall.

In other instances, the connection evidence is weak or muddled. When some of the facts prove to be unconnected to the effect or result, or when there are not enough valid facts, a reason is weak.

Reasoning is a two-step act. First, the student uses logic to arrive at a conclusion. Second, he or she communicates that reasoning to others to convince them of the conclusion. Table 16.1 provides examples of what this thinking skill looks and sounds like in the classroom.

Table 16.1: Reason Look-Fors and Sound Bites

Looks Like	Sounds Like
A student proving a mathematical equation	"What's your reasoning?"
Students engaged in a mock trial	"Are these facts connected to this case?"
A student describing how he solved a puzzle	"What facts are we missing?"
A student team discussing which project to choose	"What is your evidence?"
A student offering a conclusion for a failed experiment	"What is your justification?"

Reasoning is what humans do. We take clues and draw conclusions. Challenges to reason well are found in every life situation and career field. After employing reason to make logical sense of a situation or challenge, the person is often called on to explain the line of reasoning taken.

Doctors reason as they diagnose mysterious illnesses: "What do the facts tell me? Can I read these facts and find a reasonable answer that will restore my patient's health?" They sit with the patient, explain the diagnosis, and communicate the reasons for a proposed line of treatment.

Police reason as they look at the clues at a crime scene: "What details do I see? Can I read these clues and find the guilty party?" Later in court, the officer must communicate to the judge the logical thinking that put the clues together to prove a person's guilt.

Brokers reason as they follow the financial trends: "What is happening that will give me proof that I should buy or sell?" After a trade, brokers explain their rationale to their clients. Communication is the key to the transaction.

Plumbers reason as they search for the source of a leak: "How do I systematically follow this trail to the most likely source?" Once it is found, they communicate what work is required and the reasons for doing that work on a specific schedule.

Computer programmers reason as they follow a logical code to write a new software solution: "What are the rules that I must follow to do this?" After writing the new code, they communicate it to their client.

Teenagers reason as they argue for new rights: "If I am old enough to drive a car, then I must be old enough to stay out an extra hour." Again, communication is key to the interaction.

In these many different situations, the individuals call on the power of reasoning to reach a logical conclusion and then persuade others of the conclusion's rationality.

Examples From the State Standards: Reason

Integration of Knowledge and Ideas: RI.9–10.8. Delineate and evaluate the argument and specific claims in a text, assessing whether the reasoning is valid and the evidence is relevant and sufficient; identify false statements and fallacious reasoning.

Statistical and Probabilistic Reasoning (SPR): QR.SPR.3. Represent numerical summaries and visual displays of real-world data to make informed decisions. Reason, communicate, and describe strengths, limitations, and fallacies of various displays.

Source for standards: Arizona Department of Education, n.d., 2018.

Explicit Teaching Lesson

In the Talk-Through, phase I, the educator teaches the thinking skill explicitly. There are several elements to aid the teacher in this phase: motivational mindset, order of operations, instructional strategy, assessment, and metacognitive reflection.

To *reason* is to come to a conclusion by thinking logically and to communicate a position based on logic. Related words include *argue, deduce, derive, advocate, surmise, rationalize, contend,* and *assert.*

Motivational Mindset

A quick and motivating way to introduce the thinking skill of reasoning is with the game *Give Me a Reason.* In this game, brief interactions highlight reasoning skills as part of everyday conversations and negotiations. Direct student pairs to role-play, with person A acting as the adult (parent, teacher, or coach) and person B acting as the student. Use the following as examples.

Partner B asks, "May I stay at my friend's house tonight?"

Partner A replies, "Give me a reason that makes sense."

Partner B says, "I want to go to college out of state."

Partner A replies, "Give me a reason that makes sense."

———————————

Partner B asks, "Is it OK if I miss practice tomorrow?"

Partner A replies, "Give me a reason that makes sense."

———————————

Partner B says, "I want an after-school job."

Partner A replies, "Give me a reason that makes sense."

Discuss as a class some reasons that students give in these dialogues, and judge which truly make sense.

Order of Operations

As with all higher-order thinking processes, reasoning requires a series of steps. The first step is to look at the facts and determine what's important and what's not. Then it's helpful to offer connecting details that support the initial facts gleaned about the situation. Next, gather obvious and not-so-obvious explanations that seem logical. Identify the most likely reason, the one that makes the most sense with the evidence at hand. Finally, conclude with what seems to be the best reason for the outcome, and communicate that conclusion in some way. Use the acronym LOGIC to remember this process.

Look at all the facts.

Offer connecting details.

Gather explanations.

Identify the most sensible reason.

Conclude and communicate.

For example, two students are arguing about what constitutes a lie. One contends that lying is explicitly speaking a mistruth, while the other insists that not telling something you know is the same as lying. To add a little more to their cases, the students offer details to support their arguments. The first one claims that lying is an action, while the other says that a lie can be implied. They then gather explanations from each side. The first says, "If you asked me whether I liked your outfit and I said I did, but I really didn't, I'd be telling an outright lie." The second student retorts, "I agree, but if you didn't like it and you didn't say anything at all because you didn't want to hurt my feelings, you'd be lying by withholding the truth." Now they identify the best explanation: "If we agree that lying is intentional and deceitful, both of our examples fit the category." Finally, they can conclude and communicate this logic: it is a lie to intentionally deceive, whether the lie is explicit or implicit.

Instructional Strategy

A fun activity with which to engage students in the skill of reasoning is a *comic strip activity*. Pass out a six-frame comic strip template to each student (for a free reproducible version of this template, see appendix A, page 218).

Read the first half of a selected story. Have students fill in the first three scenes on their comic strips based on what was read and then trade with a partner. Then ask them to fill in the last three scenes, predicting, based on the facts, what will happen in the second half of the story. All should prepare reasons for their selections based on textual evidence. When all have completed the task, read the second half of the story to see what happens.

Assessment

Ask students to create a rubric based on their discussions of what they now think are good reasons for taking an action. Brainstorm a list of ideas, and then vote to get the top four. Save this rubric for the metacognitive reflection.

Metacognitive Reflection

Ask students to think about the following questions and then provide specific examples with their answers.

- How reasonable are you when you are arguing your point of view on something?

- Do you use facts or emotion to make your case?

- How do you measure up to the criteria on our class rubric when you are trying to prove a point?

Classroom Content Lesson

In the Walk-Through, phase II, teachers practice the thinking skill within content-based lessons, providing guidance to ensure the proper application of the skill. ELA standard 10 recommends literature and instructional texts that are available for coupling with grade-level lessons (available at www.corestandards.org/ELA-Literacy/standard-10-range-quality-complexity/).

6

▶ Elementary Level

Identify a controversial issue in your classroom, such as cell phone use. Using a pros-versus-cons chart, engage in a whole-group discussion. When all points seem to have been made, have the students determine whether they are for or against the issue and give reasons for their conclusions.

▶▶ Middle Level

Ask students to agree or disagree with the concept of gender-specific classes in their middle school. Have them list the pros and cons and provide logical arguments for their conclusions.

▶▶▶ Secondary Level

Divide the class into groups of three students. Give each student a worksheet containing three different linear equations. Have the students each solve the three equations on their sheet and then pass their work to another student in their group. Instruct the students to take turns interpreting their fellow student's logic and sharing the reasoning process they believe their peer used in solving the linear equations. Invite each student to explain just one of the three problems until all three students have interpreted a problem. Finally, have the three students reflect on their conversation and note how the properties of equality enable one to rewrite an equation in an equivalent form.

CCR Performance Task Lesson

During the Drive-Through, phase III, the thinking skill is transferred to authentic applications using selected performance tasks from the state CCR standards, allowing educators to make a direct connection between the selected thinking skill and the new version of the standards. While Arizona's state standard is presented as the example in this chapter (see "Examples From the State Standards: Reason," page 159), the Common Core State Standards' *Appendix B: Text Exemplars and Sample Performance Tasks* (NGA & CCSSO, 2010b) is applied as a resource to the performance tasks in this section. There are almost always similarities among the state standards, and readers can consider the teaching of thinking skills within this example as they would their own state standards. The key is that the task requires a performance that demonstrates evidence of learning in concrete, meaningful, and real-world applications.

To deepen students' confidence with this skill, the teacher facilitates the student work, moving the students closer and closer to independent practice. Once the students are able to employ the skill independently, they are ready to transfer it across the curriculum. (For additional performance tasks, browse the state standards that appear in the References and Resources section, page 241.)

▶ Elementary Level

The following sample performance task illustrates the application of the ELA standard RI.4.8 (Reading: Informational Text, grade 4, standard 8):

> Students explain how Melvin Berger uses reasons and evidence in his book *Discovering Mars: The Amazing Story of the Red Planet* to support particular points regarding the topology of the planet. (NGA & CCSSO, 2010b, p. 76)

▶▶ Middle Level

The following sample performance task illustrates the application of the ELA standard RI.6.8 (Reading: Informational Text, grade 6, standard 8):

> Students trace the line of argument in Winston Churchill's "Blood, Toil, Tears and Sweat" address to Parliament and evaluate his specific claims and opinions in the text, distinguishing which claims are supported by facts, reasons, and evidence, and which are not. (NGA & CCSSO, 2010b, p. 93)

▶▶▶ Secondary Level

The following sample performance task illustrates the application of the ELA standard RI.11–12.8 (Reading: Informational Text, grades 11–12, standard 8):

> Students delineate and evaluate the argument that Thomas Paine makes in *Common Sense*. They assess the reasoning present in his analysis, including the premises and purposes of his essay. (NGA & CCSSO, 2010b, p. 171)

Reflection Questions

These questions are designed to enrich your learning from doing. Such reflection enables you to deepen your understanding of the lessons you have just provided. You might also consider modifying these questions to further guide your students' reflection on this thinking skill.

1. When is student reasoning most evident in your classroom?

2. Descartes said, "I think, therefore I am." How does his statement apply to your teaching of the skill of reasoning?

3. As you look back over your facilitation of this thinking skill, what have you learned about the teaching of reasoning, and how can you improve?

Chapter 17: Connect

*Believing that the dots will connect down the road
will give you the confidence to follow your heart, even
when it leads you off the well-worn path.*

—Steve Jobs

"You're making no sense. What do you mean, I stood you up?" Tom asked.

"You were supposed to meet me at the music counter. We were going to look at the new white iPhone," Leo responded.

"Couldn't be. My schedule says I was supposed to be at kung fu practice. That's my guide for the day. It's how I make my schedule, my connections. You know, like connecting the dots for the sequence of the day."

"Well, somehow, you missed a dot, and you missed our connection!"

In essence, connecting is a skill in combining, synthesizing, and interpreting how various elements go together. Connecting is discerning patterns, seeing likenesses and differences, and finding the perfect slot for the new idea.

Written and spoken words not only communicate what they mean but also suggest other meanings. In each context, the thinking person has to combine all the clues in order to make sense of the situation. In narrative text, an inflection, a nod, a smile, or a frown connects to other clues to change the meaning of a single word. In informational text, connections between people, places, and things are relevant to the communicated meaning. How are the people connected in this historical event? What does the place at which people shop have to do with their food choices? How do the cause-and-effect connections play out in this science experiment?

6

The mind must make connections and associations to consolidate and chunk information for storage and subsequent retrieval. Thus, making critical connections in reading, writing, speaking, and listening is an active part of the communication process.

The skill of making connections can be taught explicitly, practiced endlessly, and honed in all grade levels and across all content areas. It is important to recognize that students make sense of new information by making connections, connecting the dots, perceiving relationships, and noticing how ideas are associated. Making connections is a high-level cognitive process that is very different from memorizing facts. The brain is a meaning-making machine, searching through patterns to find a fit for the new information. Time is well spent when teachers stir up prior knowledge to help the brain make these connections.

Through experience, students learn to view information with questioning eyes and to ask, "How does all this connect?" rather than impulsively jumping to a conclusion. As students consider all the facts, including their own prior experiences, they learn to select those details that seem to have the closest and strongest connections. When they have as complete a picture as possible, they communicate to others the reasons for each connection. Table 17.1 provides examples of what connecting looks and sounds like in the classroom.

Table 17.1: Connect Look-Fors and Sound Bites

Looks Like	Sounds Like
Students completing graphic organizers	"The picture is clear if these are linked."
Students linking two ideas from two different chapters	"I see the connection."
Student teams color-coding a textbook	"I think that this goes with this."
Students tracing ideas on a wall map	"They go in this order."
Students labeling lines on an organizational chart	"I see how A and B match."

In connecting ideas, students learn to ask questions such as "How are causes related to effects?" and "How are events connected in time, place, and type?" In answering such questions, students go far beyond memorized facts. While making connections makes learning in the daily curriculum easier and more successful, students may also use this skill outside school, noting how incidents in the neighborhood or political events are connected, for instance.

> ## Examples From the State Standards: Connect
>
> **Meaning, Context, and Craft (MCC): 2.1.1.** Explore print and multimedia sources to write opinion pieces that introduce the topic, state an opinion and supply reasons that support the opinion, use transitional words to connect opinions and reasons, and provide a concluding statement or section.
>
> **Structure and Expression: A1.ASE.3.** Choose and produce an equivalent form of an expression to reveal and explain properties of the quantity represented by the expression.
>
>   a. Find the zeros of a quadratic function by rewriting it in equivalent factored form and explain the connection between the zeros of the function, its linear factors, the x-intercepts of its graph, and the solutions to the corresponding quadratic equation.

Source for standards: South Carolina Department of Education, 2015a, 2015b.

Explicit Teaching Lesson

In the Talk-Through, phase I, the educator teaches the thinking skill explicitly. There are several elements to aid the teacher in this phase: motivational mindset, order of operations, instructional strategy, assessment, and metacognitive reflection.

To *connect* is to join, link, or associate, to bring together as a whole. Related terms include *attach*, *bridge*, *conjoin*, *correlate*, *hook up*, *interface*, and *couple*.

Motivational Mindset

To introduce students to the thinking skill of connecting, play a game called *Bricks and Mortar*. The bricks represent big ideas, and the mortar is the glue that holds the ideas together.

Using subject-specific topics, name a topic, and have students supply comprehensive sentences related to the topic, noting contextual connections. For example, the topic, or brick, is "legislative." The mortar that the first student mentions is "It's one of the three branches of government." The second student, who must make another connection, says, "It makes the laws in the two houses of Congress." This contextual gluing continues for several rounds, to build meaningful connections to the topic.

Order of Operations

Making connections involves several mental operations. Students must judge the information that is important, observe obvious connections that the mind races to, identify the pattern that fits, and name the connection that makes sense. The acronym for this process is JOIN.

Judge the new information for telling facts.

Observe obvious connections.

Identify patterns and find a fit.

Name the connection that makes sense.

For example, a high school class reads the following poem:

> *The well-made book,*
> *climbs from the shelf,*
> *it says*
> *I'm here*
> *because somebody gave a damn*
> *and worked with someone else*
> *who gave a damn,*
> *and together they made me possible*
> *and says all this quietly,*
> *albeit firmly.*
> *It has texture and depth*
> *so that it almost breathes.*
> *It is filled with the dignity*
> *of common labor,*
> *and somewhat mirrors human fallibility:*
> *there is no perfect book.*
>
> —Anonymous

The students first look for facts in the poem: "It's about the collaborative labor that goes into writing a book." Then, to make sense of this, the students make obvious connections. They may turn their minds to a familiar book and think about how it appealed to them from the library or bookstore shelf. Now, they identify a pattern it fits with: "This is a narrative poem that tells a story." Finally, as they grasp the meaning, they name the connection that makes sense to them: "I have never really thought about how much work goes into a book and that there are others involved to make the whole thing happen. It's like the work that goes into my writing and the feedback I get from peer editing and from the teacher."

Instructional Strategy

The *KWL chart*, attributed to Donna Ogle (1986), is an effective tool to access prior knowledge for making explicit connections. It is meant to act as a graphic organizer for whole-group or small-group interactions.

Choose a topic from your current unit of study. Provide each table team with a KWL chart (a blank KWL chart can be found in appendix A, page 219). Have teams complete the chart by listing five to seven things they know about the topic in the first column, What I Know. This is where they will connect to their knowledge and understanding from prior experiences and background knowledge. Then, ask teams to list five to seven things that they want to learn about the topic in the second column, What I Want to Know. Here, students will connect what they know with questions they have and curiosities that stirring up their prior knowledge has aroused.

Once they have completed the two columns, have them share and compare with another group. If circumstances allow, revisit the KWL chart at the end of the class and complete the third column, What I Learned, as a whole class.

Assessment

Have the students complete the following prompts as journal entries.

- The KWL can help me . . .
- If I were to make a checklist about connecting prior knowledge, I would include . . .
- The most important thing I learned from this lesson about making connections is . . .

Metacognitive Reflection

Ask students to consider the following question: When you are puzzled about something you don't understand, what do you do to help you make the appropriate connections?

Classroom Content Lesson

In the Walk-Through, phase II, teachers practice the thinking skill within content-based lessons, providing guidance to ensure the proper application of the skill. ELA standard 10 recommends literature and instructional texts that are available for coupling with grade-level lessons (available at www.corestandards.org/ELA-Literacy/standard-10 -range-quality-complexity/).

▶ Elementary Level

Take the students on a walk in the neighborhood around the school. Point out important buildings (stores, churches, homes, and so forth). Back in the classroom, give students a template sketch of the blocks walked. Ask them to sketch in the important buildings they saw. Invite them to share with a partner one specific building in the neighborhood and their personal connection to it. After partner talk, sample several student answers, and debrief the class on the value of making personal connections to the experience.

▶▶ Middle Level

Plan a research project that aligns with a grade-appropriate ELA standard and allows for students to present to the class. For instance, assign groups of three to investigate the life of a historic character. Teach them to do library or online research about the character. After the research, have each student make a personal connection to the character under study and write a paragraph about the connection, which he or she will present to the class. Discuss how making connections—text to another text, text to a world situation, or text to self—is a reading strategy that helps students connect to the text with real understanding (Anderson, Hiebert, Scott, & Wilkinson, 1984).

▶▶▶ Secondary Level

Ask student trios to select a poem. (See a list of age-appropriate text suggestions in Common Core ELA standard 10, available at www.corestandards.org/ELA-Literacy /standard-10-range-quality-complexity/.) Invite the students to identify an important metaphor or analogy in the poem; interpret the selection with evidence from the poem and the author's life, beliefs, and times; and make and explain a visual display (poster, website, multimedia) of how that metaphor connects to a timely issue today. Have a class display with presentations.

CCR Performance Task Lesson

During the Drive-Through, phase III, the thinking skill is transferred to authentic applications using selected performance tasks from the state CCR standards, allowing educators to make a direct connection between the selected thinking skill and the new version of the standards. While South Carolina's state standard is presented as the example in this chapter (see "Examples From the State Standards: Connect," page 167), the

Common Core State Standards' *Appendix B: Text Exemplars and Sample Performance Tasks* (NGA & CCSSO, 2010b) is applied as a resource to the performance tasks in this section. There are almost always similarities among the state standards, and readers can consider the teaching of thinking skills within this example as they would their own state standards. The key is that the task requires a performance that demonstrates evidence of learning in concrete, meaningful, and real-world applications.

To deepen students' confidence with this skill, the teacher facilitates the student work, moving the students closer and closer to independent practice. Once the students are able to employ the skill independently, they are ready to transfer it across the curriculum. (For additional performance tasks, browse the state standards that appear in the References and Resources section, page 241.)

▶ Elementary Level

The following sample performance task illustrates the application of the ELA standard RI.K.3 (Reading: Informational Text, grade K, standard 3):

> Students (with prompting and support from the teacher) describe the connection between drag and flying in Fran Hodgkins and True Kelley's *How People Learned to Fly* by performing the "arm spinning" experiment described in the text. (NGA & CCSSO, 2010b, p. 36)

▶▶ Middle Level

The following sample performance task illustrates the application of the ELA standard RL.8.2 (Reading: Literature, grade 8, standard 2):

> Students summarize the development of the morality of Tom Sawyer in Mark Twain's novel of the same name and analyze its connection to themes of accountability and authenticity by noting how it is conveyed through characters, setting, and plot. (NGA & CCSSO, 2010b, p. 89)

▶▶▶ Secondary Level

The following sample performance task illustrates the application of the ELA standard RI.9–10.3 (Reading: Informational Text, grades 9–10, standard 3):

> Students analyze how Abraham Lincoln in his "Second Inaugural Address" unfolds his examination of the ideas that led to the Civil War, paying particular attention to the order in which the points are made, how Lincoln introduces and develops his points,

6

and the connections that are drawn between them. (NGA & CCSSO, 2010b, p. 130)

Reflection Questions

These questions are designed to enrich your learning from doing. Such reflection enables you to deepen your understanding of the lessons you have just provided. You might also consider modifying these questions to further guide your students' reflection on this thinking skill.

1. How do you go about using a standard to guide the design of an activity or lesson that connects to students in a relevant way?

2. How might you work with a partner or two to design a project that will challenge students to focus on making connections between two different subject areas? You should require that a presentation of their project explain the way their ideas connect the two subjects.

3. Complete the following sentence: I connect best with my students when I . . .

Chapter 18: Represent

In order to represent life on the stage, we must rub elbows with life, live ourselves.

—Marie Dressler

———————————

"Look, Mother! A rainbow. Isn't it beautiful?"

"Yes," said the mother. "And do you know what it represents?"

The boy shook his head.

"It means that you are going to have nothing but good luck for the next year."

"Oh wow!" exclaimed the boy. "For real?"

"Well, yes and no," his mother said. "The rainbow is real. It is made by the sun's reflection off water droplets in the sky. But it is also just a fairy tale. Some people believe that the rainbow represents good luck. It's a symbol for them. It gives them hope and joy."

The skill *represent* requires one to show, illustrate, or provide a rendition of information. Drawings, illustrations, webpages, dramas, role plays, PowerPoint presentations, iMovie videos, collages, dioramas, inventions, podcasts, posters, symbolic figures and codes, and cartoons—all can be acceptable representations that demonstrate evidence of learning. When students are given options for providing evidence of learning, they own the learning.

It is important to note that even though this skill of representing works through various modalities, *represent* is not explicitly stated as a high-frequency ELA word. However, the skills of producing and presenting, illustrating, and showing results are prevalent in many standards. Words that might allude to this same thinking skill of representing information within the ELA standards include *demonstrate, produce, depict, illustrate, show, prove, reproduce,* and *draw.*

Represent appears often in the mathematics standards. In this context, it refers to showing how a mathematical operation can be demonstrated or illustrated in different forms to clarify and exhibit understanding.

Students have many means of representing their understanding at their fingertips. The more skillful they become in representing their ideas, the more skillful their communication skills become. It is most definitely a skill that needs attention.

Table 18.1 provides examples of what this thinking skill looks and sounds like in the classroom.

Table 18.1: Represent Look-Fors and Sound Bites

Looks Like	Sounds Like
Students creating a storyboard of the events in a novel	"I forgot the symbol for greater than."
Students acting out the process of metamorphosis	"I need the symbolic language for pi."
Students building a scale model of the solar system	"This geometric shape changes to . . ."
	"How do you show area and perimeter?"
	"This collage tells them what they need to know."

Representing information is a critically important skill for students. One reason involves *receptive language skills,* and the other targets *expressive language skills.* Receptive language skills—the taking in of information through either reading, sensing, or listening—involve the knowledge and understanding of representational language, symbols and signs that are embedded in text. Symbolic language is extremely abstract, yet it is extremely critical to understanding as one reads or views incoming information that is in code. When receiving these codes, perhaps a series of dots and dashes or a photo of a red rose, the receiving person has to call on layers of prior experience and mix and match them until arriving at the hidden or suggested meaning.

Using expressive language skills to represent one's ideas is just as essential. A picture is indeed worth a thousand words, and the presentation of information is enhanced in innumerable ways when accompanied by illustrations, pictures, charts, graphs, and visual media of all kinds.

With this in mind, it is easy to make the case for teaching students how to understand text from representational symbols, and how to infuse their own products with representations of the facts that simply and clearly communicate their knowledge and understanding.

Developing representational thinking skills extends into the wonderful world of commanding language, and the ability to produce a rich expression of language opens up various career possibilities and choices—journalism, marketing, communications, science, writing, advertising, singing, art, the list goes on and on.

Examples From the State Standards: Represent

Integration of Knowledge and Ideas: RL.9–10.7. Analyze the representation of a subject or a key scene in two different artistic mediums, including what is emphasized or absent in each treatment (e.g., Auden's "Musée des Beaux Arts" and Breughel's *Landscape with the Fall of Icarus*).

Number and Operations in Base Ten: 1.NBT.A.1. Count to 120, starting at any number less than 120. In this range, read and write numerals and represent a number of objects with a written numeral.

Source for standards: Ohio Department of Education, 2017a, 2017b.

Explicit Teaching Lesson

In the Talk-Through, phase I, the educator teaches the thinking skill explicitly. There are several elements to aid the teacher in this phase: motivational mindset, order of operations, instructional strategy, assessment, and metacognitive reflection.

Represent means to stand for, symbolize, or depict. Related terms include *delineate, denote, describe, display, express, hint, illustrate, outline, picture, portray, render,* and *reproduce.*

Motivational Mindset

It is important to break students' propensity to interpret the world around them literally. They must learn to make the distinction between the literal and the figurative. A start is to invite students to take a look at international road signs and have them discuss with a partner what each sign represents. Visit www.ideamerge.com /motoeuropa/roadsigns (Idea Merge, n.d.) for images of European road signs.

6

Order of Operations

Representing information is a communication skill that students use in every class at one time or another. To help them develop this skill, walk them through the process using the acronym SHOW.

Select the idea to represent.

Hunt for significant elements.

Organize elements to show meaning.

Weed for accuracy and impact.

For example, eighth-grade students participate in an exercise about reading body language during which they use the SHOW order of operations. Student pairs are given the task of reading their partner's body language. To do so, they hunt for the elements of body language that portray meaning. They combine these elements to come up with an interpretation of the other student's nonverbal representation. They discuss the consequences of misreading this representation and then role-play such situations.

Instructional Strategy

Optical illusions offer a marvelous way of representing both obvious and elusive ideas. Figure 18.1 represents a humorous before-and-after look at the concept of marriage. Using SHOW as the guide, walk the class through the investigation of this illusion.

Figure 18.1: Optical illusion example.

Assessment

Have the students make a checklist of the steps in the SHOW order of operations and then assess if and how they used each step with the optical illusion.

Metacognitive Reflection

Divide students into trios, and ask them to discuss times when they could use SHOW in their mathematics studies.

Classroom Content Lesson

In the Walk-Through, phase II, teachers practice the thinking skill within content-based lessons, providing guidance to ensure the proper application of the skill. ELA standard 10 recommends literature and instructional texts that are available for coupling with grade-level lessons (available at www.corestandards.org/ELA-Literacy/standard-10-range-quality-complexity/).

▶ Elementary Level

Use place value and three-digit numbers in a mathematics lesson to illustrate representation. Use a place value chart to demonstrate that the numeral 145 can be represented as one hundred, four tens, and five ones. Complete the chart to show other combinations (representations). Provide the students with other three-digit numbers, and have them work out the possible combinations in pairs.

▶▶ Middle Level

Design an inquiry lesson that asks students to explore the ways they represent themselves and their values to their peers. The lesson should end with partners sharing with each other a brief presentation of how they represent themselves.

▶▶▶ Secondary Level

Ask students to prepare a presentation that represents their interests, talents, and strengths in reference to college choices and career aspirations. Have them include a section on how they will represent these skills in a college or job interview. Ask them to share their representations with partners.

CCR Performance Task Lesson

During the Drive-Through, phase III, the thinking skill is transferred to authentic applications using selected performance tasks from the state CCR standards, allowing educators to make a direct connection between the selected thinking skill and the new version of the standards. While Ohio's state standard is presented as the example in this chapter (see "Examples From the State Standards: Represent," page 175), the Common Core State Standards' *Appendix B: Text Exemplars and Sample Performance Tasks* (NGA & CCSSO, 2010b) is applied as a resource to the performance tasks in this section. There are almost always similarities among the state standards, and readers can consider the teaching of thinking skills within this example as they would their own state standards. The key is that the task requires a performance that demonstrates evidence of learning in concrete, meaningful, and real-world applications.

To deepen students' confidence with this skill, the teacher facilitates the student work, moving the students closer and closer to independent practice. Once the students are able to employ the skill independently, they are ready to transfer it across the curriculum. (For additional performance tasks, browse the state standards that appear in the References and Resources section, page 241.)

▶ Elementary Level

The following sample performance task illustrates the application of the ELA standard RL.3.6 (Reading: Literature, grade 3, standard 6):

> When discussing E. B. White's book *Charlotte's Web*, students distinguish their own point of view regarding Wilbur the Pig from that of Fern Arable as well as from that of the narrator. (NGA & CCSSO, 2010b, p. 53)

▶▶ Middle Level

The following sample performance task illustrates the application of the ELA standard RI.8.2 (Reading: Informational Text, grade 8, standard 2):

> Students provide an objective summary of Frederick Douglass's *Narrative*. They analyze how the central idea regarding the evils of slavery is conveyed through supporting ideas and developed over the course of the text. (NGA & CCSSO, 2010b, p. 93)

▶▶▶ Secondary Level

The following sample performance task illustrates the application of the ELA standard RL.9–10.7 (Reading: Literature, grades 9–10, standard 7):

> Students analyze how artistic representations of Ramses II (the pharaoh who reigned during the time of Moses) vary, basing their analysis on what is emphasized or absent in different treatments of the pharaoh in works of art (e.g., images in the British

Museum) and in Percy Bysshe Shelley's poem "Ozymandias."
(NGA & CCSSO, 2010b, p. 122)

 # Technology Integration

> **Featured technology:** SMART Board, Google Share, place value
> chart, Microsoft Word tables feature, place value games, email,
> Google Slides (https://docs.google.com/presentation), Google
> Sheets (https://docs.google.com/spreadsheets)

The following tasks provide guidance on incorporating technology into lessons using this chapter's instructional strategy.

Digital Integration Task

Download an age-appropriate place value chart (several options are available online at https://bit.ly/2JDkwph [Sample Templates, n.d.]) so student teams can construct mathematical place values. Or have teams design their own chart in Microsoft Word by clicking the Insert tab and creating a table. Make sure students understand that place value refers to the position of a number, which represents what value it is assigned.

According to Shumate (2017), "Place value provides the foundation for regrouping, multiple-digit multiplication, and more in the base ten (decimal) system and is a starting point for the understanding of other base systems." For this technology integration lesson, show your selected chart on the SMART Board, and share it to the students' devices via Google Share. Guide the teams to complete the chart before they discuss with you the place values you asked them to represent. Next, add the place values. Monitor the teams at work and coach those who have difficulty.

Grade-Level Digital Variations

The following sections provide grade-level variations for incorporating technology into lessons.

▶ Elementary Level

Despite its simple definition, young students may find place value a challenging concept to grasp. As Shumate (2017) explains, "Regardless of whether Mom is in the kitchen, the living room, or the garage, she is always Mom. However, if the digit 5 is in different locations (the tens or hundreds place, for example), it means something different." What is the difference? To help students understand, line up three different

6

chairs found in your classroom (yours, a student desk-chair, and a side chair). Divide the class into thirds, and instruct each third to surround one chair, creating three groups. Number each group (from one to three). Then, assign one student in each group the role of recorder, and give him or her a large piece of chart paper and three dark-colored markers. Display a 5 × 8 column matrix on your SMART board with the following headers: *part*, *#1*, *#2*, *#3*, and *special features*. In the *part* column, list various parts or features of a chair (seat, back, four legs, in classroom, and so on). The rest of the matrix should be blank. Invite the recorders to copy the chart onto their pieces of paper.

Each recorder will put a check in its relevant # column when all in the group agree a part or feature is present on their chair. Next, groups will agree on other observations they can make about their chair (for example, "It is soft and fluffy"; "It is blue"). Recorders should list these observations in the *special features* column. When each team has enough observations to fill all eight rows, stop the group work (some teams may have more than eight observations listed). Hang the finished charts on a wall, and ask students to find items that are on all three lists. Circle these features.

When done, ask, "What features do all chairs have in common?" or "What makes a chair different from other pieces of furniture?" Follow by asking, "How do you make a chair 'special' or unique?" Then, introduce students to Canva (www.canva.com) so they can follow its instructions with your coaching to make a poster for selling a unique chair they will design in pairs. Pairs must include all the required features of a chair, but may add their own to make it unique.

▶▶ Middle Level

Provide students with access to a variety of place value games of your choice (for options, visit www.math-play.com/place-value-games.html), and have them play the games. To ensure they learned from play, ask them to respond to writing prompts via email, telling you what they specifically learned about representing place value.

▶▶▶ Secondary Level

Ask students to prepare a presentation using Google Slides. The presentation should explain their talents, their interests, or both. Provide a presentation rubric to guide their work and discussion after the presentation. Invite students to couple this presentation with a résumé (created using Google Sheets) or college application that features their talents in a field of their choice or one related to your subject.

Reflection Questions

These questions are designed to enrich your learning from doing. Such reflection enables you to deepen your understanding of the lessons you have just provided.

You might also consider modifying these questions to further guide your students' reflection on this thinking skill.

1. How might you prepare a collaborative assignment in which students represent their thinking in a role play or multimedia project?

2. In mathematics, what progress are you seeing with your students' ability to make mathematical representations?

6

Cognitive Transfer

This proficiency includes skills involved in cognitive transfer and the practical use of what has been transferred. These skills can be used to transfer learning from one setting to another, or to apply an idea, concept, or skill in useful and relevant ways. A simple example of transfer is learning mathematics facts early in the school curriculum. These facts, once known, can be transferred and used in computations and calculations in various school disciplines and in real-world scenarios for the rest of the students' lives.

The three skills included in this proficiency are (1) synthesize, (2) generalize, and (3) apply. Each contributes to the cognitive transfer of ideas, skills, and concepts.

Synthesizing requires the blending of component parts to create a whole, leaving one with the core essence of the reading. *Generalizing* describes how an idea travels from one context to the next. For example, formulas taught in mathematics class can later be used to determine how much paint to buy for a room. Finally, *applying* is the skill used to move ideas in the most practical ways.

This proficiency closes the book on the twenty-one selected thinking skills of the CCSS. Each is critical to the ultimate goal of the new standards, which serve to delineate the thinking skills of literacy across the disciplines and into college and career learning.

Chapter 19: Synthesize

James Joyce was a synthesizer, trying to bring in as much as he could. I am an analyzer, trying to leave out as much as I can.

—Samuel Beckett

———————————

One day, a youngster captured the synthesis of his grandfather as he sat in his lap. Touching the lines on his grandfather's face, the little one blurted out, "Gramps, your face looks like a road map." In that one sentence, the youngster encapsulated the man's entire life journey.

The skill of synthesizing, as positioned in the upper levels of Bloom's taxonomy, often requires a conscious and deliberate mindfulness. Synthesizing is not merely summarizing. It is not retelling, and it is not creating a synopsis of disparate parts. Synthesizing raises the thinking bar to get to the core of the matter. A multinational corporation with positive brand recognition in every corner of the earth is synthesized in three words: "Just do it." The monumental effort to communicate the role each citizen plays in the worldwide environmental movement while at the same time empowering everyone everywhere to join the effort is synthesized as "Think global, act local."

Synthesizing is the thinking skill most necessary for creating and building new ideas, products, and performances. Synthesizing encompasses imagination, invention, innovation, and risk taking, which are essential to the creative process. Companies are always searching for a synthesizing term or phrase that will encapsulate the essence of their product or line.

7

Table 19.1 provides examples of what synthesizing looks and sounds like in the classroom.

Table 19.1: Synthesize Look-Fors and Sound Bites

Looks Like	Sounds Like
Students coming up with five words to summarize a story	"My take on the essence of this is . . ."
Students creating a symbol to represent a character	"A creative blending . . ."
Students drawing a four-panel cartoon depicting a key concept	"My idea is a synthesis of . . ."
	"Combining the ideas . . ."
Students displaying specific artifacts for a field-trip report	"We need a blending, not a mosaic of . . ."

All problem solving and decision making—the macroskills of intelligent behavior—depend on a synthesis of the data, facts, and information. Without the ability to synthesize factors, to blend elements and fuse random thoughts, creativity shuts down.

Examples From the State Standards: Synthesize

Integration of Knowledge and Ideas: RST.11–12.9. Synthesize information from a range of sources (e.g., texts, experiments, simulations) into a coherent understanding of a process, phenomenon, or concept, resolving conflicting information when possible.

Research to Build and Present Knowledge: W.11–12.7. Conduct short as well as more sustained research projects to answer a question (including a self-generated question) or solve a problem; narrow or broaden the inquiry when appropriate; synthesize multiple sources on the subject, demonstrating understanding of the subject under investigation.

Source for standards: Wisconsin Department of Public Instruction, 2011.

Explicit Teaching Lesson

In the Talk-Through, phase I, the educator teaches the thinking skill explicitly. There are several elements to aid the teacher in this phase: motivational mindset, order of operations, instructional strategy, assessment, and metacognitive reflection.

To *synthesize* is to combine elements into a single entity. Related terms include *blend, amalgamate, combine,* and *mix.*

Motivational Mindset

Spark interest and curiosity in the higher-order thinking skill of synthesizing by using pudding cups. Set a pudding cup on each student's desk, alternating chocolate and vanilla. At the beginning of the class, allow the students to hypothesize about the purpose of the pudding. When they have exhausted their ideas, tell them that the pudding represents a type of thinking that they must learn to do with skill and effectiveness.

Form student pairs, with each pair having one cup of vanilla and one of chocolate. Instruct the pairs to synthesize both flavors into one new creation. Offer a supply of containers, utensils, and condiments such as sprinkles, candy, and raisins. Advise students that they must be creative in their synthesis and name their final creation. Of course, they can then eat the synthesized creation.

Order of Operations

The acronym BLEND delineates the general steps of the synthesizing process. While the actual process may vary, requiring a longer or shorter version, these steps work well for explicit instruction on how to synthesize ideas in reading, writing, speaking, or listening across all disciplines.

Begin with the big picture.

Look at the elements.

Extract the essence.

Name the nuggets.

Design a seamless image.

For example, student groups are asked to choose a famous slogan and use the BLEND order of operations to create a possible thought process for coming up with the particular slogan. One group's members choose Nike's slogan of "Just do it." They start with the big picture; Nike sports equipment is what it is all about. Then they look for defining elements and extract the key words that matter. The words that come to mind from past campaigns with Michael Jordan and Tiger Woods, among others, are *elite athlete*. Now they name the nuggets, or the ideas Jordan and Woods project: actions that get the job done, or just doing the work. This leads to designing a memorable synthesizing slogan around that idea of just doing the work needed to be great, the golden nugget: "Just do it."

7

Instructional Strategy

In a specifically designed strategy called *synectics* (Osborn, 1963), synthesis is the key thinking skill used to create what is called a *forced relationship*. Synectics is a technique to foster creative combinations that yield unusual or extraordinary results.

Use synectics to introduce students to the skill of synthesizing. Provide each table team with a die and a story grid, such as the one in figure 19.1. A blank story grid can be found in appendix A (page 220). Have students roll the die for each column to determine their selected elements. For example, if the team rolls a 5 for the Hero column, its hero will be a dentist. Then ask the teams to create a story that blends all the designated elements. Finally, have the teams write a *TV Guide* synthesis (two to three lines) of the story as if it were a television show.

	Hero	Heroine	Villain	Setting	Plot	Resolution
1	Lawyer	Doctor	Sibling	Shop	Kidnapping	Punishment
2	Salesman	Professor	Merchant	Street	Murder	Escape
3	Teacher	Electrician	Broker	Backyard	Argument	Cliff-hanger
4	Webmaster	Editor	Accountant	Lakefront	Death	Happy ending
5	Dentist	Blogger	Author	High-rise	Surprise	Tragic ending
6	Musician	Life coach	Banker	House	Fight	Unresolved ending

Figure 19.1: Story grid example.

*Visit **go.SolutionTree.com/instruction** for a free reproducible version of this figure.*

Assessment

Ask students to dialogue in an alternating partner-talk activity about the BLEND process and whether it is a valuable skill that students need to know. Student A talks about the B in BLEND, then student B talks about the L, and so on, alternating back and forth between the partners.

Metacognitive Reflection

Have students respond to these questions: Are there certain subjects and topics that you find easier to synthesize? If so, what does that tell you about you and your familiarity with those subjects or topics?

Classroom Content Lesson

In the Walk-Through, phase II, teachers practice the thinking skill within content-based lessons, providing guidance to ensure the proper application of the skill. ELA standard 10 recommends literature and instructional texts that are available for coupling with grade-level lessons (available at www.corestandards.org/ELA-Literacy/standard-10-range-quality-complexity/).

▶ Elementary Level

Ask students to roll their die five times to generate five random numbers. They find the corresponding numbers in a completed mathematics grid, such as the one in figure 19.2, so that each roll of the die corresponds to one of the columns under the five mathematical operations. Have the students then use the operations from the grid to create their equation. They then solve the equation.

For example, a student rolls the following five numbers: 3, 4, 5, 4, 1. After selecting the numbers in the grid that correspond to these rolls, the equation is $98 + 333 - 9 \times 5 \div 36$.

A blank mathematics grid can be found in appendix A on page 221.

	+	−	×	÷	=
1	694	235	7	4	36
2	2	34	9	3	10
3	98	59	12	2	25
4	1,000	333	3	5	78
5	329	326	9	6	99
6	76	48	5	7	100

Figure 19.2: Mathematics grid example.

*Visit **go.SolutionTree.com/instruction** for a free reproducible version of this figure.*

▶▶ Middle Level

The object of this lesson is to learn different parts of speech and how they are applied in sentences. Ask student teams of three to find examples of adverbs, verbs, adjectives, nouns, prepositions, and conjunctions from material they have been reading. Have them fill in their grid with six examples of each part of speech (see figure

19.3 for an example). Once finished, have the teams trade grids with another team, so that they are working with a collection of words they have not seen before. Then they roll the die six times to generate six random numbers, select the words in the columns that correspond to those rolled numbers, learn the words they have to work with, and create a sentence using those words.

For example, a team rolls the numbers 4, 3, 2, 6, 5, and 2, resulting in the following words: *hurriedly* (adverb), *sorted* (verb), *pretty* (adjective), *lamp* (noun), *on* (preposition), and *but* (conjunction). The team members create the following sentence using those words: "*Hurriedly*, Sue *sorted* the *pretty* shells *on* the table by the *lamp*, *but* in her rush to finish, she knocked some on the floor."

A blank parts-of-speech grid can be found in appendix A on page 222.

	Adverb	Verb	Adjective	Noun	Preposition	Conjunction
1	Gingerly	Carried	Colorful	Jar	Over	Yet
2	Spritely	Lifted	Pretty	Suitcase	Under	But
3	Lazily	Sorted	Worn	Chest	Above	However
4	Hurriedly	Walked	Old	Bike	Into	Therefore
5	Lovingly	Shifted	Ugly	Mirror	On	Without
6	Sloppily	Moved	New	Lamp	Beyond	While

Figure 19.3: Parts-of-speech grid example.

*Visit **go.SolutionTree.com/instruction** for a free reproducible version of this figure.*

▶▶▶ Secondary Level

Have each student roll a single die six times to generate six random numbers and then match these numbers with the appropriate cell in a book-blurb grid (see figure 19.4 for an example). A blank book-blurb grid can be found in appendix A on page 223. Instruct the students to take the elements from the grid, make up a book, and write a one-paragraph description of the book suitable for the book's dust jacket. They should include a title for the book. Inform the students that their objective is persuasive writing.

	Hero	Heroine	Plot	Setting	Genre	Theme
1	Gentleman	Queen	Failing marriage	Battleground	Romance	Nationalism
2	Salesman	Blogger	Botched kidnapping	Courtroom	Mythology	Fate
3	Boxer	Gentlewoman	Overcoming depression	Hospital	Fable	Isolation
4	Millionaire	Baroness	Pursuit of treasure	Racetrack	Tall tale	Pride
5	General	Dancer	Stormy romance	Ship at sea	Fantasy	Suffering
6	Statesman	Singer	Revenge planning	Country home	Mystery	Ambition

Figure 19.4: Book-blurb grid example.

*Visit **go.SolutionTree.com/instruction** for a free reproducible version of this figure.*

For example, a student who rolls the numbers 2, 5, 2, 1, 5, and 4 must use a salesman for the hero, a dancer for the heroine, a botched kidnapping for the plot, a battleground for the setting, fantasy for the genre, and pride for the theme. Following is an example of the assignment.

Book title: Love Is a Cosmic Battlefield

Jacket copy: The epic battle between the cyborgs and the humans has raged on for centuries, leaving both worlds exhausted, impoverished, and without hope; but with humans and cyborgs alike too proud to admit defeat, there is no end in sight. Tired of selling cheap laser guns and shoddy used hover tanks just to make a quick buck, smooth-talking salesman Danny Steele devises a scheme to kidnap the cyborg king and bring certain victory to the humans—and to make him a very, very rich man. But when the kidnapping goes awry, he ends up with Sue Ann, the cyborgs' beautiful and haughty ballerina princess, as his hostage. Still, perhaps this mix-up is better than he could have hoped for; that is, if he can keep himself from falling in love with her. And is it his imagination, or behind that pompous façade, does she seem to be falling for him too? Can this unlikely pair bring peace to the cosmic battlefield, or will pride destroy the universe?

7

CCR Performance Task Lesson

During the Drive-Through, phase III, the thinking skill is transferred to authentic applications using selected performance tasks from the state CCR standards, allowing educators to make a direct connection between the selected thinking skill and the new version of the standards. While Wisconsin's state standard is presented as the example in this chapter (see "Examples From the State Standards: Synthesize," page 186), the Common Core State Standards' *Appendix B: Text Exemplars and Sample Performance Tasks* (NGA & CCSSO, 2010b) is applied as a resource to the performance tasks in this section. There are almost always similarities among the state standards, and readers can consider the teaching of thinking skills within this example as they would their own state standards. The key is that the task requires a performance that demonstrates evidence of learning in concrete, meaningful, and real-world applications.

To deepen students' confidence with this skill, the teacher facilitates the student work, moving the students closer and closer to independent practice. Once the students are able to employ the skill independently, they are ready to transfer it across the curriculum. (For additional performance tasks, browse the state standards that appear in the References and Resources section, page 241.)

▶ Elementary Level

The following sample performance task illustrates the application of the ELA standard RL.1.4 (Reading: Literature, grade 1, standard 4):

> Students identify words and phrases within Molly Bang's *The Paper Crane* that appeal to the senses and suggest the feelings of happiness experienced by the owner of the restaurant (e.g., *clapped, played, loved, overjoyed*). (NGA & CCSSO, 2010b, p. 28)

▶▶ Middle Level

The following sample performance task illustrates the application of the ELA standard RST.6–8.9 (Science and Technical Subjects, grades 6–8, standard 9):

> Students construct a holistic picture of the history of Manhattan by comparing and contrasting the information gained from Donald Mackay's *The Building of Manhattan* with the multimedia sources available on the "Manhattan on the Web" portal hosted by the New York Public Library. (NGA & CCSSO, 2010b, p. 100)

▶▶▶ Secondary Level

The following sample performance task illustrates the application of the ELA standard RH.11–12.7 (History/Social Studies, grades 11–12, standard 7):

> Students integrate the information provided by Mary C. Daly, vice president at the Federal Reserve Bank of San Francisco, with the data presented visually in the *FedViews* report. In their analysis of these sources of information presented in diverse formats, students frame and address a question or solve a problem raised by their evaluation of the evidence. (NGA & CCSSO, 2010b, p. 183)

Reflection Questions

These questions are designed to enrich your learning from doing. Such reflection enables you to deepen your understanding of the lessons you have just provided. You might also consider modifying these questions to further guide your students' reflection on this thinking skill.

1. How does the grid concept simulate the thinking skill of synthesizing?

2. Determine the relationship between synthesizing information in the world of learning and synthesizing sounds in the world of music. How are they alike and different?

3. How might you use a grid in your classroom to reinforce the process of synthesizing?

4. Complete the following sentence: What has surprised me most about this skill is . . .

Chapter 20: Generalize

An idea is always a generalization, and generalization is a property of thinking. To generalize means to think.

—Georg Wilhelm Friedrich Hegel

A bunch of rowdy kids were playing street hockey on the corner when they were interrupted by an old man yelling at them. He was yelling about everything. "You kids are ruining the neighborhood with all this racket. You are too loud! You are making too much noise! Your game is right in the middle of the street, on all four corners. How is anyone supposed to cross the street? It's not safe! I feel like I am taking my life in my hands when I get near this intersection. Do your mothers know where you are? I doubt they would approve of you playing in the streets like this. Why don't you take your game to the park or to the schoolyard?"

It seemed like they were doing nothing right. Finally, one kid turned to the others and said, "He's just in a bad mood. But he's generally in a bad mood. It's his MO. Don't worry about it. Let's play!"

A generalization is an abstraction of a big idea gleaned from a life situation or from a text. For example, a generalization of the people of Greece is "The Greeks are great thinkers." Sometimes a qualifying detail is supplied to support the generalization: "After all, they gave us Plato, Aristotle, and Socrates." A generalization is an umbrella-like statement that encompasses the facts, data, and information provided. The idea of the Greeks as great thinkers, because there are great thinkers in Greek history, is an extrapolation of the facts as the speaker knows them.

7

It is important to know that not all generalizations are true. However, heeding the cautionary note to be careful with generalizing, it still is a critical skill supporting the cognitive transfer of ideas into practical, relevant, and rich applications.

Table 20.1 provides examples of what generalizing looks and sounds like in the classroom.

Table 20.1: Generalize Look-Fors and Sound Bites

Looks Like	Sounds Like
Students creating an umbrella phrase	"This says it all."
Students determining the big idea of a text	"The big idea . . ."
Students giving historical figures one-word descriptions	"An umbrella theme is . . ."
	"To generalize . . ."
Students making assumptions about an author's collection of works	"My takeaway is . . ."

Generalizing is a higher-order thinking skill that definitely warrants explicit teaching as part of student preparation in the CCSS. It is a skill that allows the learner to take a new idea or emerging understanding and transfer it to other situations. For example, when learning the communication skill of conflict resolution, a student may realize that in negotiating with others during a disagreement, it always helps to start the rebuttal with an affirming statement: "You are absolutely right. This is where we agree. My only concern is how we might find the best alternative for all." In essence, the student has learned to generalize a behavior that works.

Another example involves homework. After missing an important deadline on his report and getting a poor grade, a student makes a generalization about procrastinating. He tells his buddy, "I learned my lesson. I know I can't put off doing my homework because I just don't get back to it. I have a new general policy: do it now!" He may apply this generalization to all future instances of possible procrastination.

Generalizations are patterns that people form based on the big idea that they extrapolate from specific instances. It is a skill of life that helps learners mature in their thinking.

Explicit Teaching Lesson

In the Talk-Through, phase I, the educator teaches the thinking skill explicitly. There are several elements to aid the teacher in this phase: motivational mindset, order of operations, instructional strategy, assessment, and metacognitive reflection.

To *generalize* is to make an assumption, to draw inferences, and to form a conclusion based on generalities. Related terms include *assume, universalize, conclude, judge,* and *determine.*

Examples From the State Standards: Generalize

Conventions of Standard English: L.2.2. Demonstrate command of the conventions of standard English capitalization, punctuation, and spelling when writing.

   d. Generalize learned spelling patterns when writing words (e.g., *cage* → *badge; boy* → *boil*).

Vocabulary Acquisition and Use: L.9–10.4c. Consult general and specialized reference materials (e.g., dictionaries, glossaries, thesauruses), both print and digital, to find the pronunciation of a word or determine or clarify its precise meaning, its part of speech, or its etymology.

Source for standards: Alabama State Department of Education, 2016.

Motivational Mindset

To introduce the skill of generalizing, ask your students to spot overgeneralizations, or *wild-and-woolly claims,* that people make. Get them started by asking them to spot the overgeneralizations from the following list and signal with thumbs-up or thumbs-down. If they spot a wild-and-woolly claim, ask them to tone it down to a more reasonable generalization.

- Everyone is going to the party.
- No other kid has chores.
- All politicians are crooks.
- Nobody else has this early a bedtime.
- Old people forget.
- I never get to do fun things.
- People on TV have better lives than we do.
- Everyone is going on vacation but us.
- This is the worst day of my life.

End with a homework assignment to collect wild-and-woolly claims for a week and turn in the completed list for a class webpage.

7

Order of Operations

The acronym THEME will help students understand the process of generalizing.

Take it all in with the first reading.

Home in on the key ideas of the piece.

Extrapolate one big (prevailing) idea.

Make a motto or slogan about the big idea.

Express the theme statement.

For example, students read a brief piece about what both Karl Marx and Pope Leo XIII said about child labor. First, they take it all in during the first reading. The piece is about the issue of child labor and how this issue brought Marx and the pope into agreement. After that, the students try to home in on the key points or details that matter: economic pressure turns fathers into slave traders and jeopardizes our future as a society. Next, they skim the piece and try to extrapolate the big idea of all that is presented. The big idea is the impact poverty and market economies have on the family structure. The students then generalize the message and come up with a motto or slogan: "Child labor hurts." Finally, they create a theme statement to express the big idea in the form of a tagline or refrain: "Child labor will cost society its future!"

Instructional Strategy

To teach the skill of generalizing, use the activity *themes, big idea, tagline*. In this activity, students apply the THEME process to determine the central theme of a text or topic. Following this, they use the skill of generalization to make a statement of the big idea presented in the text or topic.

Choose a topic. Following are some examples based on school level.

- **Elementary:** Plants, space, community, dinosaurs, shapes, words, machines, technology

- **Middle:** Environment, democracy, geometry, social networking, wellness, government, algebra, poetry

- **Secondary:** 19th century English literature, world history, careers, physics, novel study, geography, athletics

Lead table teams through the activity with the following steps.

1. Read about, take in, or explore each topic or concept through a brief discussion using TAG (toss around the group) interaction so you include responses from all members. Use a piece of paper crunched into a small ball to indicate whose turn it is to speak. For example, start the discussion off with the topic of cycles. Then have the students toss around the paper

ball. Each time a student catches the ball, he or she must add to the discussion of cycles. You may hear such words as *beginning, end, circle, unending path, recurring, repeating, circular,* and *pattern.*

2. Home in on the key details from the conversation, and jot them down. For example, students may jot down, "Circular pattern, no ending, no beginning."

3. Extrapolate or pull out the big idea or prevailing message from the ongoing discussion. For example, students may write, "The big idea is that a cycle is a circular repeating pattern."

4. Make a motto or a slogan that captures the essence of the topic or concept. For example, students may come up with, "The end is the beginning! The beginning is the end!"

5. Express a theme statement that includes the big idea as a tagline. For example, a team may decide on "Cycles: No end in sight."

Assessment

Ask the students to rank the difficulty of the instructional strategy task with a *fist to five* activity. Have them hold up the appropriate number of fingers according to the following and explain why they voted the way they did.

- **Five fingers:** I loved the challenge.
- **Four fingers:** I felt successful.
- **Three fingers:** I was able to do it.
- **Two fingers:** It was hard.
- **One finger:** I struggled.
- **Fist:** I felt total frustration.

Metacognitive Reflection

Ask students to complete the following analogy: Generalizing is like _____ because both _____.

Classroom Content Lesson

In the Walk-Through, phase II, teachers practice the thinking skill within content-based lessons, providing guidance to ensure the proper application of the skill. ELA standard 10 recommends literature and instructional texts that are available for coupling with grade-level lessons (available at www.corestandards.org/ELA-Literacy/standard-10-range-quality-complexity/).

► Elementary Level

At this level, teach the thinking skill of generalizing as a whole-group activity. Walk the students through the use of THEME with a news article from the local paper. Have them work through the steps guided by your prompts.

►► Middle Level

Ask students to view a film that is scheduled to be on television, explaining that they will be working with the ideas from the film in class, or watch the film as a class. Then, guide them through the THEME process of generalizing. Debrief the class once the students have completed the process.

►►► Secondary Level

Ask students to work with a partner, and assign the task of reading a political blog of their choosing for an entire week. Then have them work through the THEME process for that particular blog, explaining how they would represent this blog to others.

CCR Performance Task Lesson

During the Drive-Through, phase III, the thinking skill is transferred to authentic applications using selected performance tasks from the state CCR standards, allowing educators to make a direct connection between the selected thinking skill and the new version of the standards. While Alabama's state standard is presented as the example in this chapter (see "Examples From the State Standards: Generalize," page 197), the Common Core State Standards' *Appendix B: Text Exemplars and Sample Performance Tasks* (NGA & CCSSO, 2010b) is applied as a resource to the performance tasks in this section. There are almost always similarities among the state standards, and readers can consider the teaching of thinking skills within this example as they would their own state standards. The key is that the task requires a performance that demonstrates evidence of learning in concrete, meaningful, and real-world applications.

To deepen students' confidence with this skill, the teacher facilitates the student work, moving the students closer and closer to independent practice. Once the students are able to employ the skill independently, they are ready to transfer it across the curriculum. (For additional performance tasks, browse the state standards that appear in the References and Resources section, page 241.)

► Elementary Level

The following sample performance task illustrates the application of the ELA standard RI.K.2 (Reading: Informational Text, kindergarten, standard 2):

Students (with prompting and support from the teacher) read "Garden Helpers" in *National Geographic Young Explorers* and demonstrate their understanding of the main idea of the text—not all bugs are bad—by retelling key details. (NGA & CCSSO, 2010b, p. 36)

▶▶ Middle Level

The following sample performance task illustrates the application of the ELA standard RL.6.7 (Reading: Literature, grade 6, standard 7):

Students compare and contrast the effect Henry Wadsworth Longfellow's poem "Paul Revere's Ride" has on them to the effect they experience from a multimedia dramatization of the event presented in an interactive digital map (www.paulreverehouse .org/ride), analyzing the impact of different techniques employed that are unique to each medium. (NGA & CCSSO, 2010b, p. 89)

▶▶▶ Secondary Level

The following sample performance task illustrates the application of the ELA standard RL.11–12.4 (Reading: Literature, grades 11–12, standard 4):

Students compare and contrast the figurative and connotative meanings as well as specific word choices in John Donne's "Valediction Forbidding Mourning" and Emily Dickinson's "Because I Would Not Stop for Death" in order to determine how the metaphors of the carriage and the compass shape the meaning and tone of each poem. Students analyze the ways both poets use language that is particularly fresh, engaging, or beautiful to convey the multiple meanings regarding death contained in each poem. (NGA & CCSSO, 2010b, p. 164)

 Technology Integration

> **Featured technology:** SMART Board, Google Share, SmartTools (https://smarttools.com) interview organizer, Google Docs (https://docs.google.com), LinkedIn (www.linkedin.com), voice-over internet protocol (VoIP; for example, Skype or FaceTime), YouTube games, Google Slides (https://docs.google .com/presentation), digital storytelling resources

7

The following tasks provide guidance on incorporating technology into lessons using this chapter's instructional strategy.

Digital Integration Task

To add technology to big-idea strategies for *generalizing,* use an online and age-appropriate STEM instructional article that relates to STEM careers (for example, careers in electrical engineering). Invite students to search and open the online article at www.indeed.com/career-advice/interviewing/top-interview-questions-and-answers to identify a list of top job interview questions. Display the article on your SMART Board or share it to student devices. Divide students into trios, and assign each member a collaboration role: interviewer, interviewee, and observer (to give feedback on specific answers). Trios will then role-play an interview for a job at a fast food store, rotating roles so each team member gets the chance to play each role. Then, have each trio research how to write an effective résumé on Indeed.com (available at www.indeed.com/career-advice/resumes-cover-letters?from=careeradvice-US) and prepare their own résumés for a STEM position.

Open and watch Interview Success Formula's video on a successful interview (available at www.interviewsuccessformula.com/job-interview/vsl1472019/). As they watch the video, instruct students to take notes on what will help them perform a good interview. Using the interview questions found on Indeed.com, trios will then conduct a new set of interviews, again providing feedback to each other.

In a final lesson, have the students post an open invitation on LinkedIn that seeks a professional in that field (for example, an engineer) willing to complete a voice-over internet protocol (VoIP) interview on the VoIP tool of their choice (for example, Skype or FaceTime). Instruct teams to use their questions to interview the guest and then prepare a summary of what generalizations they could make based on the professional's responses. Provide the following guiding questions:

- In what way is this candidate good for a job in this field?
- What would prevent the hiring of this candidate?

Be sure students give examples to support their responses.

Grade-Level Digital Variations

The following sections provide grade-level variations for incorporating technology into lessons.

▶ Elementary Level

Following the Instructional Strategy (page 198), prepare to show the video game *Kid Eats Raw Onion Like It Was An Apple* (available at www.youtube.com

/watch?v=FnC8xGGEPRM) to your class. Before sharing the video, explain that the child in the video believes she is eating an apple and has told her mother she is eating an apple. Despite the bitter taste, her running nose, and the tears from the uncomfortable sharp flavor, she continues to eat the onion.

After watching the video have the students, in groups of three, discuss what they see in the video and make generalizations about what they think the video is showing.

Emphasizing the acronym THEME will help students understand the process of generalizing.

Take it all in with the first viewing. *(The child is eating an onion like an apple.)*

Home in on the key ideas of the piece. *(She continues to think it's an apple, and keeps eating.)*

Extrapolate one Big (prevailing) Idea. *(She is being stubborn, and won't change her mind)*

Make a motto or slogan about the Big Idea. *(Never Give Up!)*

Express the theme statement. *(Believe in yourself!)*

Scaffold the assignment by asking the groups of students to come up with three main words that explain what they think is the theme or Big Idea of the video. Collect the three-word summaries and post them on the SMART Board. Then, have the groups create a motto or slogan that captures the theme of the video.

Upload the video to the class website and post the mottos created by the students underneath. Have the students view the video with their parents at home and vote on the best motto.

▶▶ Middle Level and Secondary Levels

In following the instructions for this skill's Instructional Strategy (page 198), replace step 4 by asking student trios to create a digital story about a Big Idea that interests them. (You do not have to be an English teacher to engage students in digital storytelling; any subject area's curriculum can provide Big Ideas from which students can build a story.) To prime the students for a shareware story, let the class brainstorm big ideas on the SMART Board, making a list from which each team can select. If you have never facilitated a digital story with a class, see the Creative Educator (n.d.; https://bit.ly/2Hxl3qF) and Tech4Learning (n.d.; www.tech4learning.com /kits/digital-storytelling) websites for more information, or contact MindQuest21 (https://ilc21.org) for a how-to workshop.

Have teams create storyboards with the Big Ideas and the story details before writing text and sketching or downloading images to Google Slides or the selected

7

shareware. The text and image should illustrate or describe the Big Ideas and their details to tell the story. If telling a fictional story, the Big Idea slide statement will describe what type of story it is (for example, "A story of tragic love" or "A tale of modern adventure"). If telling a nonfictional story, the Big Idea slide statement will identify the purpose. The remaining slides will tell or show the story or explain the Big Idea. Add a presentation rubric reproducible from this book so teams can decide to whom they will present their story and how they will assess their work (see figure 20.1 for an example).

Reflection Questions

These questions are designed to enrich your learning from doing. Such reflection enables you to deepen your understanding of the lessons you have just provided. You might also consider modifying these questions to further guide your students' reflection on this thinking skill.

1. How does the skill of generalizing impact student understanding and transfer of learning in your subject area? Across other subject areas?

2. What topics might you use for lessons on generalizing to pique your students' interest?

3. Complete the following sentence: The most fascinating idea from this chapter is . . .

Assessing Our Presentation

Team Names: _____

Project Title: _____

Site: _____

Teacher Name: _____   Date: _____

This is the team's feedback _____   This is the teacher's feedback _____

This is my assessment _____

Rank each statement

0 = not at all, 1 = not much, 2 = sometimes, 3 = almost always, 4 = always, DNA = did not apply

To what degree did we/you:

1. ____ Make a written plan for our presentation with a ____ high interest start ____ summary conclusions?

2. ____ Include all in the planning and presenting?

3. ____ Dress for the occasion?

4. ____ Support with visual aids or other special effects?

5. ____ Practice and revise the presentation as needed?

6. ____ Explain or show how the project was connected with STEAM?

7. ____ Meet our schedule for presenting, including allowance of a Q&A about STEAM connections?

8. ____ Allow each team member to respond during the Q&A?

9. ____ Speak loudly, firmly, and clearly to our audience?

10. ____ Capture and engage our audience in creative ways?

Total = ____

What was best about our presentation? What could we improve? (Use back)

Source: © James Bellanca, 2017.

Figure 20.1: Assessing a presentation template.

*Visit **go.SolutionTree.com/instruction** for a free reproducible version of this figure.*

7

Chapter 21: Apply

I have been impressed with the urgency of doing. Knowing is not enough; we must apply. Being willing is not enough; we must do.

—Leonardo da Vinci

A boy was helping his grandma learn how to send email. She was very excited about her success with Skype and was now motivated to know more about her computer. He showed her how to compose and send an email and even tested it by sending an email back to her computer. He could see she was really interested, so he also showed her how to send multiple emails at once and even how to send photos. Finally, completely exasperated at the show-and-tell session, she took the mouse from her grandson and said, "Let me have the mouse. I want to do it myself. Until I use it, I won't really know it."

To make use of learning is to apply the learning, the last step of cognitive transfer. This assumes that the understanding is clear and the learning is deep enough to be used in practical, relevant, and meaningful ways. When ideas, skills, or lessons are applied in purposeful ways, they take on a deeper level of meaning and become solidified. Once a person applies a skill or concept, the learning is anchored in a lasting way; the person remembers and retains it for future use.

For example, sixth graders learn about the Pythagorean theorem. They can then apply this learning by building a model to see how the theory relates to real-life problems. Eighth graders learn about the Bill of Rights. To apply this learning, they can create simulations and role plays about what happens when those personal rights are infringed upon. That is what applied learning is all about; it is about the experience, the actual realization of the abstract concepts and complex skills.

7

Renate Nummela Caine, Geoffrey Caine, Carol McClintic, and Karl Klimek (2009) write about curriculum and the brain and learning. They state that school extracurricular activities need to be center stage in the school curriculum. The school newspaper, the yearbook, the daily announcements, the gym demonstration, the science fair, the social studies exhibition, and the school play—these are the applied learning experiences that showcase student learning in authentic ways. These are the examples of purposeful learning that require mastery in the skills of reading, writing, speaking, and listening. Project-based learning should assume an important role in today's classrooms.

Table 21.1 provides examples of what this thinking skill looks and sounds like in the classroom.

Table 21.1: Apply Look-Fors and Sound Bites

Looks Like	Sounds Like
Students carrying out an experiment	"This is not exactly the right way to use this, but . . ."
Students using tools they built	"It's such a practical idea."
Students conversing in a foreign language	"I didn't know it would be this easy."
Students engaging in a community project	"Now, I see how it works."
Students constructing a model	"This really cements it for me."

The skill of applying is, beyond a doubt, one of the most neglected skills in the school curriculum, yet the rationale is overwhelmingly simple: all learning is for transfer!

Teachers frequently hear students complain that they don't see how they will ever use the information or skills they are learning. Their concern has merit, to some extent. If all learning is for transfer, then teachers need to provide students with the answer to that very legitimate question: "When am I going to use this?" When students understand how the lessons they learn in school apply to real-world situations, the lessons become more valuable to them.

Examples From the State Standards: Apply

Phonics and Word Recognition: RF.K.3. Know and apply grade-level phonics and word analysis skills in decoding words.

Geometric Measurement and Dimension: G-GMD.6. Verify experimentally that in a triangle, angles opposite longer sides are larger, sides opposite larger angles are longer, and the sum of any two side lengths is greater than the remaining side length; apply these relationships to solve real-world and mathematical problems.

Source for standards: California Department of Education, 2013a, 2013b.

Explicit Teaching Lesson

In the Talk-Through, phase I, the educator teaches the thinking skill explicitly. There are several elements to aid the teacher in this phase: motivational mindset, order of operations, instructional strategy, assessment, and metacognitive reflection.

To *apply* is to put something to use, to put it into action. Related terms include *utilize, employ, practice, assign, address, use, transfer*, and *implement*.

Motivational Mindset

Have a special guest who is an expert in sign language teach the whole class how to say, "I would prefer to not do my homework this week," in sign language. Then tell the class that the first five people who can accurately communicate this message in sign language will be excused from homework.

Order of Operations

The acronym USE delineates the steps of applying skills or concepts to an authentic problem or challenging situation.

Use it in a talk-through.

Simulate it in a guided walk-through.

Extend and employ the learning independently.

For example, learner drivers rarely learn to drive by just getting behind the wheel. They first learn driving skills in a classroom setting and then use a driving simulator, with a guide talking them through the various procedures. The students then apply the learning in a somewhat contrived and sterile environment for safety purposes—driving in empty parking lots and along quiet neighborhood streets with little traffic. When it is deemed that their skill level is such that they can use their skills safely, they do so in a real, on-road situation with moving traffic, road signs, stoplights, exit ramps, and parallel parking spots.

Instructional Strategy

It is important to come up with possible authentic experiences that students can have in the classroom. It's one thing to learn about fractions; it's quite another task to apply one's understanding of fractions in, for example, designing a scale drawing of the classroom. This kind of hands-on performance task takes a fair amount of time to plan, schedule, organize the materials for, and actually execute with fidelity and assessments. An easy way to approach this is to employ the *talk-through, walk-through, drive-through* strategy, which allows for the gradual release of responsibility to the students.

7

Start students on the path to writing a five-paragraph essay. Read the following prompts, with appropriate pauses between the steps, as each student responds on paper.

1. Name a good thinker—a fictional character, a historical figure, or a personal acquaintance.

2. Tell two traits of or details about your good thinker.

3. Describe someone who is not a good thinker.

4. Compare and contrast the two.

5. Write a closing statement.

6. Give your piece a telling title.

7. Edit and fix any mistakes and, when ready, share your writing with a partner.

This talk-through stage does not result in a five-paragraph essay, but it does model the traditional structure of a comprehensive piece of writing.

Now, choose a different topic, and post the prompts on the board or screen. Instruct the students to follow along with the prompts on their own. Tell them that you are providing ten minutes for the exercise. This walk-through stage still does not produce a five-paragraph essay, but the process is becoming clear.

Finally, for the drive-through, the students are assigned a five-paragraph essay on a specific topic but are given no prompts. They are expected to devise their own prompts to guide themselves through the essay.

Assessment

Have the students, in pairs, use prompts to guide their partner to complete a task other than writing. Ask them to provide two examples of where this process could apply.

Metacognitive Reflection

Have the students answer the following question: What have you learned in school that you apply in your everyday life?

Classroom Content Lesson

In the Walk-Through, phase II, teachers practice the thinking skill within content-based lessons, providing guidance to ensure the proper application of the skill. ELA standard 10 recommends literature and instructional texts that are available for coupling with grade-level lessons (available at www.corestandards.org/ELA-Literacy/standard-10-range-quality-complexity/).

▶ Elementary and Middle Levels

Instruct students to draw for one minute on a topic. Then ask them to draw again on the same topic for another minute to revise and refine the first drawing. Repeat the instructions five times so the students can fine-tune the product and apply their skill of rendering with accuracy and precision.

▶▶▶ Secondary Level

Instruct students to write for one minute on an informational text topic. Then ask them to write again on the same topic for another minute to revise and refine the first writing. Ask the students to exchange their paper with another student, who will then revise and refine the paper. The students then retrieve their original paper to apply a final minute of editing.

CCR Performance Task Lesson

During the Drive-Through, phase III, the thinking skill is transferred to authentic applications using selected performance tasks from the state CCR standards, allowing educators to make a direct connection between the selected thinking skill and the new version of the standards. While California's state standard is presented as the example in this chapter (see "Examples From the State Standards: Apply," page 208), the Common Core State Standards' *Appendix B: Text Exemplars and Sample Performance Tasks* (NGA & CCSSO, 2010b) is applied as a resource to the performance tasks in this section. There are almost always similarities among the state standards, and readers can consider the teaching of thinking skills within this example as they would their own state standards. The key is that the task requires a performance that demonstrates evidence of learning in concrete, meaningful, and real-world applications.

To deepen students' confidence with this skill, the teacher facilitates the student work, moving the students closer and closer to independent practice. Once the students are able to employ the skill independently, they are ready to transfer it across the curriculum. (For additional performance tasks, browse the state standards that appear in the References and Resources section, page 241.)

▶ Elementary Level

The following sample performance task illustrates the application of the ELA standard RI.3.3 (Reading: Informational Text, grade 3, standard 3):

> Students read Robert Coles's retelling of a series of historical
> events in *The Story of Ruby Bridges*. Using their knowledge of
> how cause and effect gives order to events, they use specific

7

language to describe the sequence of events that leads to Ruby desegregating her school. (NGA & CCSSO, 2010b, p. 62)

▶▶ Middle Level

The following sample performance task illustrates the application of the ELA standard RST.6–8.3 (Science and Technical Subjects, grades 6–8, standard 3):

> Students learn about fractal geometry by reading Ivars Peterson and Nancy Henderson's *Math Trek: Adventures in the Math Zone* and then generate their own fractal geometric structure by following the multistep procedure for creating a Koch's curve. (NGA & CCSSO, 2010b, p. 100)

▶▶▶ Secondary Level

The following sample performance task illustrates the application of the ELA standard RST.11–12.4 (Science and Technical Subjects, grades 11–12, standard 4):

> Students determine the meaning of key terms such as *hydraulic*, *trajectory*, and *torque* as well as other domain-specific words and phrases such as *actuators*, *antilock brakes*, and *traction control* used in Mark Fischetti's "Working Knowledge: Electronic Stability Control." (NGA & CCSSO, 2010b, p. 183)

Reflection Questions

These questions are designed to enrich your learning from doing. Such reflection enables you to deepen your understanding of the lessons you have just provided. You might also consider modifying these questions to further guide your students' reflection on this thinking skill.

1. List specific examples of performance tasks that you use successfully to illustrate the application and transfer of skills to real-world situations.

2. How might you address the application of learning in a more explicit way?

3. What skills do you teach your students that they will apply in their daily lives five years after they leave your classroom?

Appendix A: Reproducibles

Fishbone Diagram

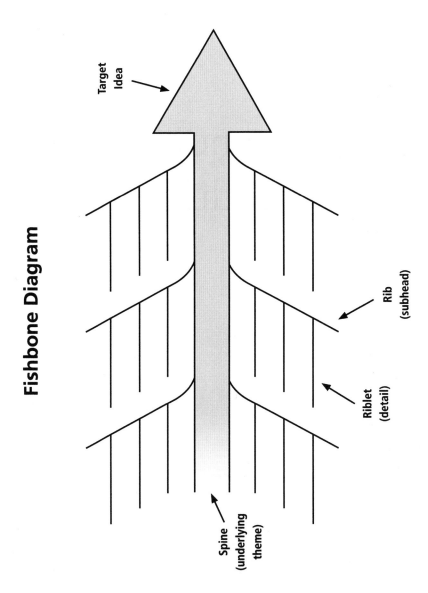

Target Idea

Rib (subhead)

Riblet (detail)

Spine (underlying theme)

Ranking Ladder

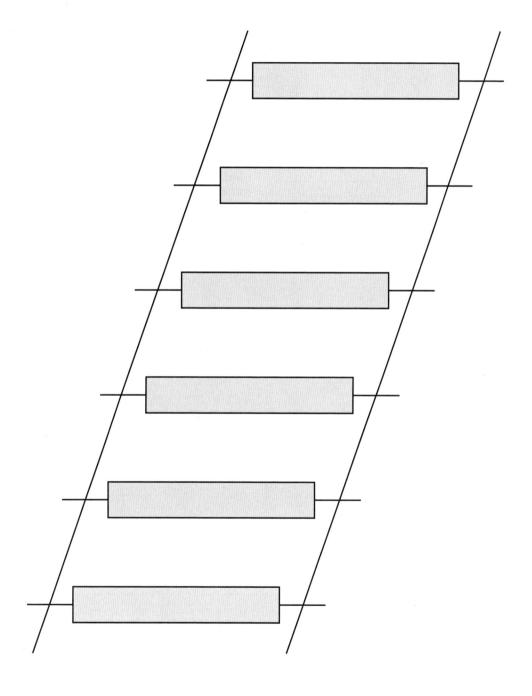

Four-Fold Concept Development

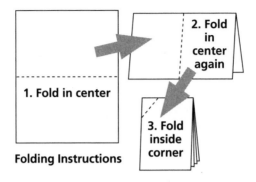

Folding Instructions

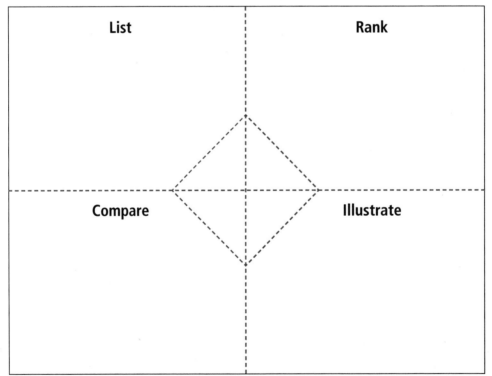

ABC Graffiti

Topic:

A	N
B	O
C	P
D	Q
E	R
F	S
G	T
H	U
I	V
J	W
K	X
L	Y
M	Z

Comic Strip Template

Draw the opening scene.	Draw the characters described.	Draw the plot or setup.	Draw the actual event.	Draw people reacting.	Draw the punch line.

KWL Chart

K What I Know	W What I Want to Know	L What I Learned

Story Grid

	Hero	Heroine	Villain	Setting	Plot	Resolution
1						
2						
3						
4						
5						
6						

Mathematics Grid

	+	−	×	÷	=
1					
2					
3					
4					
5					
6					

Parts-of-Speech Grid

	Adverb	Verb	Adjective	Noun	Preposition	Conjunction
1						
2						
3						
4						
5						
6						

Book-Blurb Grid

	Hero	Heroine	Plot	Setting	Genre	Theme
1						
2						
3						
4						
5						
6						

Appendix B:
Additional Resources

Books and Articles

Barrows, H. S. (1985). *How to design a problem-based curriculum for preclinical years.* New York: Springer.

Bellanca, J. A. (2010). *Enriched learning projects: A practical pathway to 21st century skills.* Bloomington, IN: Solution Tree Press.

Bellanca, J. A., & Brandt, R. (Eds.). (2010). *21st century skills: Rethinking how students learn.* Bloomington, IN: Solution Tree Press.

Bellanca, J. A., & Stirling, T. (2011). *Classrooms without borders: Using internet projects to teach communication and collaboration.* New York: Teachers College Press.

Bloom, B. S. (Ed.). (1956). *Taxonomy of educational objectives: The classification of educational goals—Handbook I: Cognitive domain.* New York: McKay.

Brookhart, S. M. (2010). *How to assess higher-order thinking skills in your classroom.* Alexandria, VA: Association for Supervision and Curriculum Development.

Burke, K. (2006). *From standards to rubrics in six steps: Tools for assessing student learning, K–8.* Thousand Oaks, CA: Corwin Press.

Burke, K. (2010). *Balanced assessment: From formative to summative.* Bloomington, IN: Solution Tree Press.

Costa, A. L., & Liebmann, R. M. (Eds.). (1997). *Supporting the spirit of learning: When process is content.* Thousand Oaks, CA: Corwin Press.

Coyle, D. (2009). *The talent code: Greatness isn't born. It's grown. Here's how.* New York: Bantam Books.

Darling-Hammond, L. (2010). *The flat world and education: How America's commitment to equity will determine our future.* New York: Teachers College Press.

de Bono, E. (1973). *CoRT thinking.* Blandford, Dorset, England: Direct Education Services.

de Bono, E. (1993). *Teach your child how to think.* London: Penguin.

Dede, C. (2010). Comparing frameworks for 21st century skills. In J. A. Bellanca & R. Brandt (Eds.), *21st century skills: Rethinking how students learn* (pp. 51–76). Bloomington, IN: Solution Tree Press.

Drucker, P. F. (1959). Long-range planning: Challenge to management science. *Management Science, 5*(3), 238–249.

DuFour, R., & DuFour, R. (2010). The role of professional learning communities in advancing 21st century skills. In J. A. Bellanca & R. Brandt (Eds.), *21st century skills: Rethinking how students learn* (pp. 77–96). Bloomington, IN: Solution Tree Press.

Dweck, C. S. (2007). *Mindset: The new psychology of success.* New York: Random House.

Fogarty, R. J. (1997). *Problem-based learning and other curriculum models for the multiple intelligences classroom.* Arlington Heights, IL: IRI/Skylight Training.

Fogarty, R. J., & Bellanca, J. A. (1993). *Patterns for thinking, patterns for transfer: A cooperative team approach for critical and creative thinking in the classroom* (4th ed.). Palatine, IL: IRI/Skylight.

Fogarty, R. J., & Pete, B. M. (2010). *Supporting differentiated instruction: A professional learning communities approach.* Bloomington, IN: Solution Tree Press.

Fogarty, R. J., & Pete, B. M. (2017). *From staff room to classroom: A guide for planning and coaching professional development* (2nd ed.). Thousand Oaks, CA: Corwin Press.

Frost, R. (2011). *The span of life.* Accessed at www.americanpoems.com/poets /robertfrost/5540 on February 15, 2019.

Gardner, H. (2007). *Five minds for the future.* Boston: Harvard Business School Press.

Goleman, D. (1996). *Emotional intelligence: Why it can matter more than IQ.* New York: Bantam Dell.

Hargreaves, A., & Fullan, M. (Eds.). (2009). *Change wars.* Bloomington, IN: Solution Tree Press.

Hattie, J. (2009). *Visible learning: A synthesis of over 800 meta-analyses relating to achievement.* New York: Routledge.

Joyce, B. R., & Showers, B. (1983). *Power in staff development through research on training.* Alexandria, VA: Association for Supervision and Curriculum Development.

Joyce, B. R., & Showers, B. (2002). *Student achievement through staff development* (3rd ed.). Alexandria, VA: Association for Supervision and Curriculum Development.

Kao, J. J. (2007). *Innovation nation: How America is losing its innovation edge, why it matters, and what we can do to get it back.* New York: Free Press.

Kolderie, T., & McDonald, T. (2009, July). *How information technology can enable 21st century schools.* Washington, DC: Information Technology and Innovation Foundation.

McGregor, D. (2007). *Developing thinking, developing learning: A guide to thinking skills in education.* Maidenhead, Berkshire, England: Open University Press.

McTighe, J., & Seif, E. (2010). An implementation framework to support 21st century skills. In J. A. Bellanca & R. Brandt (Eds.), *21st century skills: Rethinking how students learn* (pp. 149–174). Bloomington, IN: Solution Tree Press.

Parnes, S. J. (1975). *Aha! Insights into creative behavior.* New York: D.O.K.

Partnership for 21st Century Learning. (2019). *Framework for 21st century learning.* Accessed at www.battelleforkids.org/networks/p21/frameworks-resources on February 20, 2019.

Perkins, D. N., & Salomon, G. (1988). Teaching for transfer. *Educational Leadership, 46*(1), 22–32.

Pink, D. H. (2009). *Drive: The surprising truth about what motivates us.* New York: Riverhead Books.

Ravitch, D. (2010). *Stop the madness.* Washington, DC: National Education Association.

Resnick, L. B. (1987). *Education and learning to think.* Washington, DC: National Academies Press.

Schlechty, P. C. (2009). *Leading for learning: How to transform schools into learning organizations.* San Francisco: Jossey-Bass.

Simon, S. (2006). *Volcanoes.* New York: HarperCollins.

Strunk, W., Jr., & White, E. B. (1979). *The elements of style* (3rd ed.). New York: Macmillan.

Toffler, A. (1970). *Future shock.* New York: Bantam Books.

Trilling, B., & Fadel, C. (2009). *21st century skills: Learning for life in our times.* San Francisco: Jossey-Bass.

Tucker, M. S. (2009). Industrial benchmarking: A research method for education. In A. Hargreaves & M. Fullan (Eds.), *Change wars* (pp. 117–134). Bloomington, IN: Solution Tree Press.

Wagner, T. (2008). *The global achievement gap: Why even our best schools don't teach the new survival skills our children need—and what we can do about it.* New York: Basic Books.

Wiggins, G., & McTighe, J. (2005). *Understanding by design* (expanded 2nd ed.). Alexandria, VA: Association for Supervision and Curriculum Development.

Willis, J. (2006). *Research-based strategies to ignite student learning: Insights from a neurologist and classroom teacher.* Alexandria, VA: Association for Supervision and Curriculum Development.

Willis, J. (2008a). *How your child learns best: Brain-friendly strategies you can use to ignite your child's learning and increase school success.* Naperville, IL: Sourcebooks.

Willis, J. (2008b). *Teaching the brain to read: Strategies for improving fluency, vocabulary, and comprehension.* Alexandria, VA: Association for Supervision and Curriculum Development.

Willis, J. (2010a). The current impact of neuroscience on teaching and learning. In D. A. Sousa (Ed.), *Mind, brain, and education: Neuroscience implications for the classroom* (pp. 45–68). Bloomington, IN: Solution Tree Press.

Willis, J. (2010b). *Learning to love math: Teaching strategies that change student attitudes and get results.* Alexandria, VA: Association for Supervision and Curriculum Development.

Technology Tools

The wide and deep use of technology to manage, operate, govern, and instruct is a key indicator of a 21st century school. This list identifies specific sites that school administrators, teachers, and students who are prolific users of technology employ in their schoolwork life. (Visit **go.SolutionTree.com/instruction** to access links to the websites in this book.)

- Audacity (https://sourceforge.net/projects/audacity): A tool that offers a sound editor and recording software

- Classroom 2.0 (www.classroom20.com): A social media site and a collaborative network for educators that offers multiple tools

- ClassTools (www.classtools.net): A site that allows educators to create a variety of tools for classroom use

- CmapTools (https://cmap.ihmc.us): A site that offers tools for creating concept maps

- Creaza (https://web.creaza.com/en/): A site that offers a suite of online tools that students can use to create, publish, and share digital stories, in and out of school (The premium version has a fee.)

- ePals (www.epals.com): An international K–12 social networking site with school mail, projects, and collaborations

- FreeMind (https://sourceforge.net/projects/freemind): An open-source tool that offers mind-mapping software

- Goodreads (www.goodreads.com): A social network for people who love books

- Google Docs (https://docs.google.com): A collaborative site where students and teachers can create and share work online and access documents (spreadsheets, presentations, surveys, and more) from anywhere

- Intel Education (www.intel.com/content/www/us/en/education/intel -education.html): Online courses that teachers can use to develop 21st century skills

- JumpStart (www.jumpstart.com): A site that offers 3-D virtual-world games

- Mind42 (https://mind42.com): An online mind-mapping collaboration tool

- Moodle (https://moodle.org): A content management tool and community site for online learning

- Ning (www.ning.com): An online service to create, customize, and share a social network

- Partnership for 21st Century Learning (www.battelleforkids.org/networks /p21): A site that offers multiple resources to help schools transfer to a 21st century agenda

- Podbean (www.podbean.com): A podcast publishing and social subscribing site, which students can use to publish their own podcasts

- Poll Everywhere (www.polleverywhere.com): A student response system

- ReadWriteThink (www.readwritethink.org): A site that offers online tools, tactics, and strategies to develop students' CCSS-aligned language arts skills

- Second Life (https://secondlife.com): A virtual world that offers avatars, chat, and online meetings

- SimCEO (www.simceo.org): A simulation site that students can use to create and operate their own companies while advancing financial literacy

- SurveyMonkey (www.surveymonkey.com): Software for conducting online questionnaires and surveys, which can show results numerically or graphically

- Wordle (www.wordle.net): A tool for generating word clouds from text

Websites

Educators may find the following websites useful as informational sources or for planning and executing lessons.

- Common Core State Standards Initiative (www.corestandards.org)

- Cooperative Learning Institute (www.co-operation.org)

- Education World, "National Standards" (www.educationworld.com /standards)

- Educational Testing Service (www.ets.org)

- Edutopia (www.edutopia.org)

- International Renewal Institute (https://issuu.com/iriinc)

- International Society for Technology in Education Standards (www.iste.org/ standards)

- Khan Academy (www.khanacademy.org)

- Learning Forward (https://learningforward.org; formerly National Staff Development Council)

- Massachusetts Curriculum Frameworks (www.doe.mass.edu/frameworks /current.html)

- National Education Technology Plan 2010 (www.ed.gov/sites/default/files /netp2010.pdf)

- New Tech Network (https://newtechnetwork.org)

- PBLWorks (www.pblworks.org)

- ReadWriteThink (www.readwritethink.org)

Appendix C: Technology Applications by Chapter

Thinking Skill 1: Analyze

- ClassTools (www.classtools.net)
- Diamond 9 model education game (www.classtools.net/education -games-php/diamond9)
- Digital portfolio (https://sites.google.com/site/resourcecentereportfolio /how-to-use-google-sites)

Thinking Skill 4: Generate

- Word cloud generators (www.smashingapps.com/2011/12/15/nine -excellent-yet-free-online-word-cloud-generators.html)
- Public sculpture example (www.youtube.com/watch?v=WW0vmgQEb78)

Thinking Skill 7: Clarify

- RubiStar (http://rubistar.4teachers.org)

Thinking Skill 10: Understand

- Bio Cube tool for writing an autobiography (www.readwritethink.org /classroom-resources/student-interactives/cube-30057.html)
- Master sequence chart graphic organizer (www.eduplace.com /graphicorganizer/pdf/sequence.pdf)
- Character epitaphs (www.readwritethink.org/classroom-resources/student -interactives/cube-30057.html)
- Drama maps (www.readwritethink.org/files/resources/interactives /dramamap)

Thinking Skill 13: Explain

- Digital tree charts (www.edrawsoft.com/template-blank-tree-chart.php)
- Example portmanteaus (www.vappingo.com/word-blog/86-great -examples-of-portmanteau)
- Wordle (www.wordle.net)
- Teacher Toolkit gallery walk (www.theteachertoolkit.com/index.php/tool /gallery-walk)
- Random word generator (https://randomwordgenerator.com)

Thinking Skill 18: Represent

- Place value chart (www.sampletemplates.com/business-templates /place-value-chart.html)

- Place value games (www.math-play.com/place-value-games.html)

Thinking Skill 20: Generalize

- YouTube video (www.youtube.com/watch?v=FnC8xGGEPRM)

- Digital storytelling lessons (https://creativeeducator.tech4learning.com /lessons/digital-storytelling)

- Digital storytelling kits (www.tech4learning.com/kits/digital-storytelling)

- MindQuest21 (https://ilc21.org)

Glossary

anchor standards. A framework for the Common Core ELA standards that guides the standards' generic elements at the various grade levels (for example, Key Ideas and Details, Craft and Structure, Integration of Knowledge and Ideas, and Range of Reading and Level of Complexity).

application. The act of putting a basic skill or mental operation into practice.

balanced assessment. An approach that assesses both the cognitive skill that processes the content of a standard and one's knowledge of the actual subject-matter content.

cognitive function. A mental ability that prepares the learner to put thinking and problem solving into action.

cognitive transfer. The mental act of moving learned concepts or skills from the mind to real-world practice; the student proficiency that includes the skills of synthesize, generalize, and apply.

collaborative thinking. The student proficiency that includes the skills of explain, develop, and decide.

Common Core State Standards (CCSS). The Common Core State Standards for English Language Arts and Literacy in History/Social Studies, Science, and Technical Subjects and for Mathematics are broad-based K–12 standards intended to guide schools in making students college and career ready.

communicative thinking. The student proficiency that includes the skills of reason, connect, and represent.

complex thinking. The student proficiency that includes the skills of clarify, interpret, and determine.

comprehensive thinking. The student proficiency that includes the skills of understand, infer, and compare and contrast.

concept development. The intentional development of abstract ideas from specific instances or concrete actions.

connotation. A variety of meanings suggested or implied by a word.

content. The concepts, skills, facts, or ideas that compose a subject matter within an academic discipline.

cooperative learning. A highly effective instructional strategy defined by five key attributes (positive interdependence, individual accountability, group reflection, explicit social skills, face-to-face discussion with a shared goal) and most commonly used to strengthen collaboration skills in the classroom.

creative thinking. The student proficiency that includes the skills of generate, associate, and hypothesize.

critical thinking. The student proficiency that includes the skills of analyze, evaluate, and problem solve.

deep understanding. The result of students' making sense of ideas and finding the underlying meaning in data or texts they are examining.

denotation. The literal definition of a word.

direct instruction. A model of instruction that uses teacher-directed lessons with specific procedures detailed in a recommended sequential order.

Drive-Through. The third phase of the explicit teaching model; it requires students to work independently on a CCSS performance task to show evidence of learning.

explicit teaching. An approach to teaching that identifies and targets a specific behavior or skill in the standards and uses formal, teacher-directed instruction and assessment.

formative assessment. A range of formal and informal assessment procedures that teachers employ during the learning process in order to modify teaching and learning strategies with a goal to increase student achievement or the development of 21st century skills.

high-frequency words. The thinking skills that appear most frequently within the state standards.

innovation. The result of a thinking process that uses both critical and creative thinking skills to produce an invention or a new process or method for making a new product.

inquiry. A process that requires investigation, experimentation, or exploration to answer a question or to solve a problem. In project-based learning scenarios, the investigation will proceed through three phases: (1) gathering information, (2) making sense of that information, and (3) communicating the findings.

instructional strategy. The method a teacher may use to achieve a learning objective.

look-for. Observable, specific behavior that a teacher can see or hear as students work in the classroom.

mental operation. An operation, or way of thinking, that helps form ideas.

metacognitive reflection. A mental process of intentionally thinking about one's thinking to assess the development of a thinking function or cognitive operation; awareness of and control over one's thinking.

performance task. A task given to students in phase III, the Drive-Through, with decreasing scaffolding so that students can show increasing competence in their ability to apply a stated thinking skill to a standard's stated content.

PISA. The Programme for International Student Assessment is an international test taken by members of the Organisation for Economic Co-operation and Development. The United States is one of thirty members. The computer-based test is presented every three years to countries choosing to participate in all or one of the frameworks offered (literacy, mathematical problem solving, cross-curricular problem solving, science literacy, and financial literacy).

problem-based learning. An inquiry model of standards-aligned instruction that starts with a loosely structured, authentic problem and ends with a solution to that problem. Students complete activities that allow them to find and apply the information needed to proceed throughout the problem-solving endeavor.

problem scenario. A statement of an open-ended problem that includes a stakeholder role.

problem solving. A comprehensive cognitive act that combines the use of several thinking skills to move from the definition of the problem to its solution.

project-based learning. A model of standards-aligned instruction that starts with an essential question of authentic interest to students. Students systematically gather information, make sense of the information, and then decide how to communicate their new understandings. Project-based learning typically concludes with a product that shows the rigor of their study via a presentation to an invited audience.

sound bite. A term used to describe a quick description of what a thinking behavior sounds like.

stakeholder role. Stakeholders are those who have an interest in an outcome, who affect or can be affected by an action. Parents, teachers, and other caregivers are significant stakeholders in students' education.

Talk-Through. The first phase of the explicit teaching model; it requires a direct instruction lesson or an inquiry lesson with step-by-step scaffolding to teach a cognitive process for a thinking skill.

technology tool. Hardware, software, and internet sites and applications that teachers can include in lessons and projects to enrich student learning.

transfer of learning. What occurs when learning in one context enhances (positive transfer) or undermines (negative transfer) a related performance in another context.

Walk-Through. The second phase of the explicit teaching model; it requires a teacher-guided classroom lesson that provides the needed support and scaffolding—guided practice that precedes independent practice.

well-defined problem. Also called a clean or tight problem, the elements of the problem statement are specific and clearly defined within one teaching and learning discipline or real-world situation. The most well-defined problems are found in mathematics.

References and Resources

Achieve.org. (2017). *Strong standards: A review of changes to state standards since the Common Core*. Accessed at www.achieve.org/files/StrongStandards_032919 .pdf on June 29, 2019.

Alabama State Department of Education. (2016). *2016 Revised Alabama course of study, English language arts: English language literacy for college and career readiness*. Accessed at https://www.alsde.edu/sec/ari/Tier%20II%20Support /K-5%20Standards%20for%20Print.pdf#search=standards on June 29, 2019.

Allard, H., & Marshall, J. (1977). *Miss Nelson is missing*. Boston: Houghton Mifflin.

American Management Association. (2010). *AMA 2010 critical skills survey*. Accessed at http://onondagacitizensleague.org/wp-content/uploads/2014/02/Critical -Skills-Survey-Executive-Summary-1.pdf on February 15, 2019.

Anderson, R. C., Hiebert, E. H., Scott, J. A., & Wilkinson, I. A. G. (1984). *Becoming a nation of readers: The report of the Commission on Reading*. Pittsburgh: National Academy of Education.

Arizona Department of Education. (n.d.). *Arizona's English language arts standards: 9–10th grade*. Accessed at https://cms.azed.gov/home/GetDocumentFile?id =585aab01aadebe12481b8455 on June 29, 2019.

Arizona Department of Education. (2018). *Arizona mathematics standards: Quantitative reasoning*. Accessed at https://cms.azed.gov/home/GetDocumentFile?id =5b92d80a1dcb250c0c77fd90 on June 29, 2019.

Arizona Department of Education. (2019). *Academic standards*. Accessed at www .azed.gov/standards-practices/ on June 29, 2019.

Atkin, J., Barratt, R., Dutton, S., Foster, M., Green, C., Leaker, J., Parker, J., Sawley, L., Stratfold, J., & Thompson, L. (2010). *South Australian teaching for effective learning framework guide: A resource for developing quality teaching and learning in South Australia*. Adelaide, South Australia: Department of Education and Children's Services.

Atkin, J., & Foster, M. (2011). *South Australian teaching for effective learning review tools handbook: A resource for reflecting on teaching and learning in South Australia*. Adelaide, South Australia: Department of Education and Children's Services.

Ausubel, D. P. (1960). The use of advance organizers in the learning and retention of meaningful verbal material. *Journal of Educational Psychology, 51*(5), 267–272.

Bach, R. (2002). *Writer ferrets: Chasing the muse (Ferret chronicles #3)*. New York: Scribner.

Bacon, F. (1625). *Of studies*. Accessed at www.authorama.com/essays-of-francis -bacon-50.html on February 15, 2019.

Barell, J. (2007). *Problem-based learning: An inquiry approach* (2nd ed.). Thousand Oaks, CA: Corwin Press.

Bellanca, J. A., & Fogarty, R. J. (2003). *Blueprints for thinking in the cooperative classroom* (3rd ed.). Glenview, IL: Pearson Education.

Bellanca, J. A., Fogarty, R. J., & Pete, B. M. (2012). *How to teach thinking skills within the Common Core: Seven key student proficiencies of the new national standards*. Bloomington, IN: Solution Tree Press.

Browne, J. (1972). *Jackson Browne* [Album]. New York: Asylum Records.

Caine, R. N., Caine, G., McClintic, C., & Klimek, K. J. (2009). *12 brain/mind learning principles in action: Developing executive functions of the human brain* (2nd ed.). Thousand Oaks, CA: Corwin Press.

California Department of Education. (2013a). California Common Core State Standards: English language arts & literacy in history/social studies, science, and technical subjects. Accessed at https://www.cde.ca.gov/be/st/ss /documents/finalelaccssstandards.pdf on June 29, 2019.

California Department of Education. (2013b). California Common Core State Standards: Mathematics. Accessed at https://www.cde.ca.gov/be/st/ss /documents/finalelaccssstandards.pdf on June 29, 2019.

California State Board of Education. (n.d.). *Content standards*. Accessed at www.cde .ca.gov/be/st/ss/ on June 29, 2019.

ClassTools. (n.d.). *Diamond 9*. Accessed at www.classtools.net/education-games-php /diamond9 on April 24, 2019.

Colorado Department of Education. (n.d.). *Colorado standards—academic standards*. Accessed at www.cde.state.co.us/standardsandinstruction/coloradostandards -academicstandards on June 29, 2019.

Costa, A. L. (1991). *The school as a home for the mind: A collection of articles.* Thousand Oaks, CA: Corwin Press.

Costa, A. L., & Kallick, B. (Eds.). (2000). *Discovering and exploring habits of mind.* Alexandria, VA: Association for Supervision and Curriculum Development.

Costa, A. L., & Kallick, B. (2009). *Habits of mind across the curriculum: Practical and creative strategies for teachers.* Alexandria, VA: Association for Supervision and Curriculum Development.

Coyle, D. (2009). *The talent code: Greatness isn't born. It's grown. Here's how.* New York, NY: Bantam Books.

Creative Educator. (n.d.). *Digital storytelling lessons.* Accessed at https://creativeeducator .tech4learning.com/lessons/digital-storytelling on April 24, 2019.

Dean, C. B., Hubbell, E. R., Pitler, H., & Stone, B. (2012). *Classroom instruction that works: Research-based strategies for increasing student achievement* (2nd ed.). Alexandria, VA: Association for Supervision and Curriculum Development.

de Bono, E. (1985). *Six thinking hats: The power of focused thinking: Six proven ways to effectively focus your creative thinking.* Mamaroneck, NY: International Center for Creative Thinking.

Delaware Department of Education. (n.d.). *Delaware standards and instruction: English language arts.* Accessed at www.doe.k12.de.us/domain/374 on June 29, 2019.

Deming, W. E. (1982). *Out of the crisis.* Cambridge, MA: Massachusetts Institute of Technology Press.

Duckworth, E. (1964). Piaget rediscovered. *The Arithmetic Teacher, 11*(4), 496–499.

DuFour, R., & Eaker, R. (1998). *Professional learning communities at work: Best practices for enhancing student achievement.* Bloomington, IN: Solution Tree Press.

EdrawSoft. (n.d.). *Blank tree chart template.* Accessed at https://www.edrawsoft.com /template-blank-tree-chart.php on April 24, 2019.

Edutopia. (2010, April 7). *Anatomy of a project: Kinetic conundrum* [Video file]. Accessed at www.youtube.com/watch?v=WW0vmgQEb78 on April 24, 2019.

Eportfolio Resource Center. (n.d.). *Using Google Sites for creating an eportfolio.* Accessed at https://sites.google.com/site/resourcecentereportfolio/how-to -use-google-sites on April 24, 2019.

Ericsson, A., & Pool, R. (2017). *Peak: Secrets from the new science of expertise.* Boston: Houghton Mifflin.

Feuerstein, R., Feuerstein, R. S., & Falik, L. H. (2010). *Beyond smarter: Mediated learning and the brain's capacity for change.* New York: Teachers College Press.

Feuerstein, R., Rand, Y., Hoffman, M. B., & Miller, R. (1980). *Instrumental enrichment: An intervention program for cognitive modifiability.* Baltimore: University Park Press.

Feuerstein, R., Rand, Y., & Rynders, E. J. (1988). *Don't accept me as I am: Helping "retarded" people to excel.* U.S.: Plenum.

Fischer, M. H. (n.d.). *BrainyQuote: Martin H. Fischer quotes.* Accessed at www .brainyquote.com/quotes/quotes/m/martinhfi402160.html on February 20, 2019.

Fisher, D., & Frey, N. (2008). *Better learning through structured teaching: A framework for the gradual release of responsibility.* Alexandria, VA: Association for Supervision and Curriculum Development.

Fogarty, R., & Bellanca, J. A. (1993). *Patterns for thinking, patterns for transfer: A cooperative team approach for critical and creative thinking in the classroom* (4th ed.). Palatine, IL: IRI/Skylight Publishing.

Fogarty, R. J., & Pete, B. (2004). *A look at transfer: Seven strategies that work.* Thousand Oaks, CA: Corwin Press.

Gardner, H. (1984). *Frames of mind: The theory of multiple intelligences.* New York: Basic Books.

Georgia Department of Education. (n.d.). *Georgia standards.* Accessed at www.georgia standards.org/Pages/default.aspx on June 29, 2019.

Gokhale, A. A. (1995). Collaborative learning enhances critical thinking. *Journal of Technology Education, 7*(1), 22–30.

H. Jackson Brown, Jr. Quotes. (n.d.). BrainyQuote.com. Accessed at www.brainy quote.com/quotes/h_jackson_brown_jr_119648 on August 29, 2019.

Hall, G. E. (1979). The concerns-based approach to facilitating change. *Educational Horizons, 57*(4), 202–208.

Hirsch, E. D., Jr. (2017). *Why knowledge matters: Rescuing our children from failed educational theories.* Cambridge, MA: Harvard Education Press.

Hunter, M. C. (1971). *Teach for transfer.* Thousand Oaks, CA: Corwin Press.

Idaho State Department of Education. (n.d.). *Idaho content standards.* Accessed at www.sde.idaho.gov/academic/standards/ on June 29, 2019.

IdeaMerge. (n.d.). *European road signs and traffic signals.* Accessed at www.ideamerge .com/motoeuropa/roadsigns on April 24, 2019.

Indiana Department of Education. (2011). *Indiana academic standards*. Accessed at www.doe.in.gov/standards on June 29, 2019.

Iowa Department of Education. (n.d.). *Iowa core*. Accessed at iowacore.gov/iowa-core on June 29, 2019.

Iowa Department of Education. (2010). *Iowa core: Mathematics*. Accessed at https://iowacore.gov/sites/default/files/k-12_mathematics_0.pdf on June 29, 2019.

Jay, A. (2011, December 15). *Nine excellent (yet free) online word cloud generators*. Accessed at www.smashingapps.com/2011/12/15/nine-excellent-yet-free -online-word-cloud-generators.html on April 24, 2019.

Jervis, K., & Tobier, A. (Eds.). (1988). *Education for democracy: Proceedings from the Cambridge School Conference on Progressive Education, October 1987*. Weston, MA: Cambridge School.

Johnson, D. W., & Johnson, R. T. (1975). *Learning together and alone: Cooperation, competition, and individualization*. Englewood Cliffs, NJ: Prentice Hall.

Johnson, D. W., & Johnson, R. T. (1981). Effects of cooperative and individualistic learning experiences on interethnic interaction. *Journal of Educational Psychology, 73*(3), 444–449.

Johnson, D. W., & Johnson, R. T. (1989). *Cooperation and competition: Theory and research*. Edina, MN: Interaction Book Company.

Johnson, D. W., & Johnson, R. T. (2005). New developments in social interdependence theory. *Psychological Monographs, 131*(4), 285–358.

Johnson, D. W., & Johnson, R. T. (2010). Cooperative learning and conflict resolution: Essential 21st century skills. In J. A. Bellanca & R. Brandt (Eds.), *21st century skills: Rethinking how students learn* (pp. 201–220). Bloomington, IN: Solution Tree Press.

Johnson, D. W., & Johnson, R. T. (2014). *Using technology to revolutionize cooperative learning: An opinion. Frontiers in Psychology, 5*. Accessed at https://www.ncbi .nlm.nih.gov/pmc/articles/PMC4195269/ on June 29, 2019.

Joyce, B., & Weil, M. (1996). *Models of teaching* (5th ed.). New York: Allyn & Bacon.

Kagan, S. (1994). *Cooperative learning*. San Clemente, CA: Kagan.

Kao, J. J. (2007). *Innovation nation: How America is losing its innovation edge, why it matters, and what we can do to get it back*. New York: Free Press.

Lemov, D. (2012). *Practice perfect: 42 rules for getting better at getting better*. San Francisco, CA: Jossey-Bass.

Louisiana Department of Education. (n.d.a). *Academic standards.* Accessed at www
.louisianabelieves.com/academics/academic-standards on June 29, 2019.

Louisiana Department of Education. (n.d.b). *Louisiana student standards for English
language arts & literacy.* Accessed at http://www.louisianabelieves.com/docs
/default-source/academic-standards/louisiana-state-standards-(ela-math)
.pdf?sfvrsn=6 on June 29, 2019.

Maryland State Department of Education. (2014a). Maryland college and career
ready curriculum framework: Reading informational text, grades 9 and
10, grades 11 and 12. Accessed at http://mdk12.msde.maryland.gov/share
/frameworks/CCSC_Reading_Informational_Text_gr9-12.pdf on June 29,
2019.

Maryland State Department of Education. (2014b). Maryland college and career
ready curriculum framework: Speaking and listening, grades 3 through 5.
Accessed at http://mdk12.msde.maryland.gov/share/frameworks/CCSC
_Speaking_Listening_gr3-5.pdf on June 29, 2019.

Marzano, R. J. (1991). Fostering thinking across the curriculum through knowledge
restructuring. *Journal of Reading, 34*(7), 518–525.

Marzano, R. J. (1998). Cognitive, metacognitive, and conative considerations in
classroom assessment. In N. M. Lambert & B. L. McCombs (Eds.), *How
students learn: Reforming schools through learner-centered education* (pp. 241–
266). Washington, DC: American Psychological Association.

Marzano, R. J., Pickering, D. J., & Pollock, J. E. (2001). *Classroom instruction that
works: Research-based strategies for increasing student achievement.* Alexandria,
VA: Association for Supervision and Curriculum Development.

Massachusetts Department of Elementary and Secondary Education. (n.d.). *Current
frameworks.* Accessed at www.doe.mass.edu/frameworks/current.html on
June 29, 2019.

Math Play. (n.d.). *Place value games.* Accessed at www.math-play.com/place-value
-games.html on April 24, 2019.

McGee, K. (2014, April 24). *Are Common Core and Texas teaching standards really
that different?* Accessed at www.kut.org/post/are-common-core-and-texas
-teaching-standards-really-different on January 20, 2019.

McTighe, J., & Wiggins, G. (2013). *Essential questions: Opening doors to student
understanding.* Alexandria, VA: Association for Supervision and Curriculum
Development.

Michigan Department of Education. (n.d.a). *Michigan academic standards.* Accessed at www.michigan.gov/mde/0,4615,7-140-28753_64839_65510---,00.html on June 29, 2019.

Michigan Department of Education. (n.d.b). *Michigan K–12 standards: English language arts.* Accessed at https://www.michigan.gov/documents/mde /MDE_ELA_Standards_599599_7.pdf on June 29, 2019.

Minnesota Department of Education. (n.d.a). *English language arts.* Accessed at https://education.mn.gov/MDE/dse/stds/ela/ on June 29, 2019.

Minnesota Department of Education. (n.d.b). *Mathematics.* Accessed at https:// education.mn.gov/MDE/dse/stds/Math/ on June 29, 2019.

Minnesota Department of Education. (2016). *Academic standards (K–12).* Accessed at https://education.mn.gov/MDE/dse/stds/ on June 29, 2019.

Missouri Department of Elementary and Secondary Education. (n.d.). *Missouri learning standards.* Accessed at dese.mo.gov/college-career-readiness/curriculum /missouri-learning-standards on June 29, 2019.

Missouri Department of Elementary and Secondary Education. (2016a). *6–12 English language arts grade-level expectations.* Accessed at https://dese.mo.gov /sites/default/files/curr-mls-standards-ela-6-12-sboa-2016.docx on June 29, 2019.

Missouri Department of Elementary and Secondary Education. (2016b). *6–12 mathematics grade-level expectations.* Accessed at https://dese.mo.gov/sites/default /files/curr-mls-standards-math-6-12-sboe-2016.pdf on June 29, 2019.

National Council for the Social Studies. (2013). *The College, Career, and Civic Life (C3) Framework for Social Studies State Standards: Guidance for enhancing the rigor of K–12 civics, economics, geography, and history.* Silver Spring, MD: Author.

National Governors Association Center for Best Practices & Council of Chief State School Officers. (2010a). *Common Core State Standards for English language arts and literacy in history/social studies, science, and technical subjects.* Washington, DC: Authors. Accessed at www.corestandards.org/assets /CCSSI_ELA%20Standards.pdf on February 20, 2019.

National Governors Association Center for Best Practices & Council of Chief State School Officers. (2010b). *Common Core State Standards for English language arts and literacy in history/social studies, science, and technical subjects: Appendix B—Text exemplars and sample performance tasks.* Washington, DC: Authors. Accessed at www.corestandards.org/assets/Appendix_B.pdf on February 20, 2019.

National Governors Association Center for Best Practices & Council of Chief State School Officers. (2010c). *Common Core State Standards for mathematics*. Washington, DC: Authors. Accessed at www.corestandards.org/assets/CCSSI_Math%20Standards.pdf on February 20, 2019.

New Hampshire Department of Education. (n.d.). *NH college and career ready standards*. Accessed at www.education.nh.gov/instruction/curriculum/ on June 29, 2019.

New York State Education Department. (2015). *Curriculum and instruction*. Accessed at www.nysed.gov/curriculum-instruction on June 29, 2019.

NGSS Lead States. (2013). *Next Generation Science Standards: For states, by states*. Washington, DC: The National Academies Press.

North Carolina Department of Public Instruction. (2017). *Extended content standards: Sixth grade*. Accessed at http://www.dpi.state.nc.us/docs/curriculum/mathematics/scos/extended-6-8.pdf on June 29, 2019.

North Dakota Department of Public Instruction. (n.d.). *Content standards*. Accessed at https://www.nd.gov/dpi/SchoolStaff/Standards/ on June 29, 2019.

North Dakota Department of Public Instruction. (2017a). *North Dakota English language arts & literacy content standards, grades K–12*. Accessed at https://www.nd.gov/dpi/uploads/87/ELALiteracyCS2017.pdf on June 29, 2019.

North Dakota Department of Public Instruction. (2017b). *North Dakota mathematics content standards, grades K–12*. Accessed at https://www.nd.gov/dpi/uploads/87/2017MathematicsStandards.pdf on June 29, 2019.

Ogle, D. M. (1986). K-W-L: A teaching model that develops action reading of expository text. *Reading Teacher, 39*(6), 564–570.

Ohio Department of Education. (2016). *Ohio's learning standards*. Accessed at education.ohio.gov/Topics/Learning-in-Ohio/OLS-Graphic-Sections/Learning-Standards on June 29, 2019.

Ohio Department of Education. (2017a). *Ohio's learning standards: English language arts*. Accessed at http://education.ohio.gov/getattachment/Topics/Learning-in-Ohio/English-Language-Art/English-Language-Arts-Standards/ELA-Learning-Standards-2017.pdf.aspx?lang=en-US on June 29, 2019.

Ohio Department of Education. (2017b). *Ohio's learning standards: Mathematics*. Accessed at http://education.ohio.gov/getattachment/Topics/Learning-in-Ohio/Mathematics/Ohio-s-Learning-Standards-in-Mathematics/MATH-Standards-2017.pdf.aspx?lang=en-US on June 29, 2019.

Oklahoma State Department of Education. (n.d.). *Oklahoma academic standards.* Accessed at sde.ok.gov/oklahoma-academic-standards on June 29, 2019.

Oklahoma State Department of Education. (2016a). *Oklahoma academic standards for English language arts.* Accessed at https://sde.ok.gov/sites/ok.gov.sde/files /documents/files/OAS-ELA-Final%20Version_0.pdf on June 29, 2019.

Oklahoma State Department of Education. (2016b). *Oklahoma academic standards for mathematics.* Accessed at https://sde.ok.gov/sites/ok.gov.sde/files/documents /files/OAS-Math-Final%20Version_3.pdf on June 29, 2019.

Oregon Department of Education. (n.d.). *Academic content standards.* Accessed at www.oregon.gov/ode/educator-resources/standards/Pages/default.aspx on June 11, 2019.

Oregon Department of Education. (2010). *Common Core State Standards for mathematics (CCSSM).* Accessed at https://www.oregon.gov/ode/educator -resources/standards/mathematics/Documents/ccssm6.pdf on June 29, 2019.

Osborn, A. F. (1963). *Applied imagination: Principles and procedures of creative problem solving.* New York: Scribner.

Partnership for 21st Century Learning. (2019). *Framework for 21st century learning.* Accessed at www.battelleforkids.org/networks/p21/frameworks-resources on February 20, 2019.

Pennsylvania Department of Education. (n.d.). *Standards.* Accessed at www.pdesas .org/Standard on June 29, 2019.

Perkins, D. (2010). *Making learning whole: How seven principles of teaching can transform education.* San Francisco, CA: Jossey-Bass.

Perkins, D. N., & Salomon, G. (1988). Teaching for transfer. *Educational Leadership, 46*(1), 22–32.

Pete, B. M., & Fogarty, R. J. (2010). *From staff room to classroom II: The one-minute professional development planner.* Thousand Oaks, CA: Corwin Press.

Programme for International Student Assessment. (2009). *PISA 2009 technical report.* Accessed at www.oecd.org/document/19/0,3746,en_2649_35845621 _48577747_1_1_1_1,00.html on February 20, 2019.

Programme for International Student Assessment. (2012). *PISA 2012 problem-solving framework.* Paris: Organisation for Economic Co-operation and Development.

Public Schools of North Carolina. (n.d.a). *English language arts: An overview (grade 4).* Accessed at http://www.ncpublicschools.org/curriculum/languagearts /elementary/elagrade4 on June 29, 2019.

Public Schools of North Carolina. (n.d.b). *K–12 standards, curriculum, and instruction*. Accessed at www.dpi.state.nc.us/curriculum/ on June 29, 2019.

ReadWriteThink. (n.d.a). *Bio Cube*. Accessed at www.readwritethink.org/classroom -resources/student-interactives/cube-30057.html on April 24, 2019.

ReadWriteThink. (n.d.b). *Drama mapping*. Accessed at www.readwritethink.org/files /resources/interactives/dramamap on April 24, 2019.

Ritchhart, R., & Perkins, D. (2008). Making thinking visible. *Educational Leadership*, *65*(5), 57–61.

Sample Templates. (n.d.). *9 sample place value chart templates to download*. Accessed at www.sampletemplates.com/business-templates/place-value-chart.html on April 24, 2019.

Schmoker, M. J. (1999). *Results: The key to continuous school improvement* (2nd ed.). Alexandria, VA: Association for Supervision and Curriculum Development.

Schmoker, M. J. (2018). *Focus: Elevating the essentials to radically improve student learning* (2nd ed.). Alexandria, VA: Association for Supervision and Curriculum Development.

School Improvement in Maryland. (n.d.). *MD college and career-ready standards*. Accessed at mdk12.msde.maryland.gov/instruction/commoncore/ on June 29, 2019.

Science Buddies. (n.d.). *Steps of the scientific method*. Accessed at www.sciencebuddies .org/science-fair-projects/project_scientific_method.shtml on February 20, 2019.

Sharan, S. (Ed.). (1990). *Cooperative learning: Theory and research*. New York: Praeger.

Shumate, L. (2017, March 24). *Teaching place value is important* [Blog post]. Accessed at https://demmelearning.com/learning-blog/place-value on April 22, 2019.

Slavin, R. E. (1996). *Education for all*. New York: Swets & Zeitlinger.

South Carolina Department of Education. (n.d.). *Standards & learning*. Accessed at ed.sc.gov/instruction/standards-learning/ on June 29, 2019.

South Carolina Department of Education. (2015a). South Carolina college and career-ready standards for English language arts. Accessed at https:// ed.sc.gov/scdoe/assets/file/programs-services/59/documents/ELA2015S CCCRStandards.pdf on June 29, 2019.

South Carolina Department of Education. (2015b). South Carolina college and career-ready standards for mathematics. Accessed at https://ed.sc.gov/instruction /standards-learning/mathematics/standards/scccr-standards-for-mathematics -final-print-on-one-side/ on June 29, 2019.

State of Idaho Department of Education. (n.d.a). *Idaho content standards: English language arts/literacy.* Accessed at http://www.sde.idaho.gov/academic/shared /ela-literacy/booklets/ELA-Literacy-Standards.pdf on June 29, 2019.

State of Idaho Department of Education. (n.d.b). *Idaho content standards: Mathematics.* Accessed at http://www.sde.idaho.gov/academic/shared/math /ICS-Mathematics.pdf on June 29, 2019.

State of New Jersey Department of Education. (n.d.). *New Jersey student learning standards.* Accessed at www.nj.gov/education/cccs/ on June 29, 2019.

State of New Jersey Department of Education. (2016a). *New Jersey student learning standards for English language arts.* Accessed at https://www.nj.gov/education /cccs/2016/ela/g07.pdf on June 29, 2019.

State of New Jersey Department of Education. (2016b). *New Jersey student learning standards for mathematics.* Accessed at https://www.nj.gov/education/cccs /2016/math/standards.pdf on June 29, 2019.

Teacher Toolkit. (n.d.). *Gallery walk.* Accessed at www.theteachertoolkit.com/index .php/tool/gallery-walk on April 24, 2019.

Tech4Learning. (n.d.). *Get started with digital storytelling in your classroom.* Accessed at www.tech4learning.com/kits/digital-storytelling on April 24, 2019.

Texas A&M University. (2013). *Developing and assessing students' collaboration in the IB Programme.* Accessed at https://www.ibo.org/globalassets/publications /ib-research/developingandassessingstudentcollaborationfinalreport.pdf on June 29, 2019.

Texas Education Agency. (n.d.a). *Texas essential knowledge and skills.* Accessed at https://tea.texas.gov/curriculum/teks on April 15, 2019.

Texas Education Agency. (n.d.b). *Texas essential knowledge and skills for English language arts and reading: Subchapter A. Elementary.* Accessed at http://ritter.tea .state.tx.us/rules/tac/chapter110/ch110a.html on June 29, 2019.

Torrance, E. P. (1974). *Torrance test of creative thinking.* New York: Scholastic Testing Service.

Tuckman, B. W. (1965). Developmental sequence in small groups. *Psychological Bulletin, 63*(6), 384–399.

Tyson, M. (n.d.). *BrainyQuote: Mike Tyson quotes.* Accessed at www.brainyquote.com /quotes/authors/m/mike_tyson_3.html on February 20, 2019.

Vappingo. (n.d.). *86 great examples of portmanteau.* Accessed at www.vappingo.com /word-blog/86-great-examples-of-portmanteau on April 24, 2019.

Virginia Department of Education. (2011). *The standards and SOL-based instructional resources.* Accessed at www.doe.virginia.gov/testing/sol/standards_docs/ on June 29, 2019.

Vygotsky, L. S. (1978). *Mind in society: The development of higher psychological processes.* Cambridge, MA: Harvard University Press.

Washington Office of Superintendent of Public Instruction. (n.d.). *Learning standards & instructional materials.* Accessed at http://www.k12.wa.us/student-success /learning-standards-instructional-materials on June 29, 2019.

Wayman, J. (1980). *The other side of reading.* New York: Good Apple.

Webb, A. (2011, January 11). *The power of words* [Blog post]. Accessed at www .thoughtfulparent.com/2011/01/power-of-words.html on January 20, 2019.

Wiggins, Grant P., and Jay McTighe. *Understanding by Design.* Association for Supervision and Curriculum Development, 2008.

Willingham, Daniel T. (2017). *The reading mind: A cognitive approach to understanding how the mind reads.* San Francisco, CA: Jossey-Bass.

Willis, J. (2008). *How your child learns best: Brain-friendly strategies you can use to ignite your child's learning and increase school success.* Naperville, IL: Sourcebooks.

Wisconsin Department of Public Instruction. (n.d.) *Academic standards.* Accessed at dpi.wi.gov/standards on June 11, 2019.

Wisconsin Department of Public Instruction. (2011). *Wisconsin standards for English language arts.* Accessed at https://dpi.wi.gov/sites/default/files/imce/standards /pdf/ela-stds-app-a-revision.pdf on June 29, 2019.

Index

Growing Tomorrow's Citizens in Today's Classrooms
Assessing Seven Critical Competencies
Cassandra Erkens, Tom Schimmer, and Nicole Dimich Vagle
For students to succeed in today's ever-changing world, they must acquire unique knowledge and skills. Practical and research-based, this resource will help educators design assessment and instruction to ensure students master critical competencies, including collaboration, critical thinking, creative thinking, communication, digital citizenship, and more.
BKF765

Connecting the Dots
Edited by James A. Bellanca
Confront the issues that profoundly affect student success. Discover the shift in day-to-day practice that must occur to prepare students for college and careers, and look forward to what exemplary professional practices will be crucial in deepening student learning as the 21st century progresses.
BKF659

Deeper Learning
Edited by James A. Bellanca
Education authorities from around the globe draw on research as well as their own experience to explore deeper learning, a process that promotes higher-order thinking, reasoning, and problem solving to better educate students and prepare them for college and careers.
BKF622

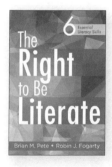

The Right to Be Literate
Brian M. Pete and Robin J. Fogarty
Explore the six comprehensive skill areas essential to 21st century literacy—reading, writing, listening, speaking, viewing, and representing. Learn practical strategies for teaching students the skills they need to think critically and communicate collaboratively in the digital age.
BKF643

Solution Tree | Press a division of Solution Tree

Visit SolutionTree.com or call 800.733.6786 to order.

Wait! Your professional development journey doesn't have to end with the last pages of this book.

We realize improving student learning doesn't happen overnight. And your school or district shouldn't be left to puzzle out all the details of this process alone.

No matter where you are on the journey, we're committed to helping you get to the next stage.

Take advantage of everything from **custom workshops** to **keynote presentations** and **interactive web and video conferencing**. We can even help you develop an action plan tailored to fit your specific needs.

Let's get the conversation started.

Call 888.763.9045 today.

solution-tree.com